Cases in Entrepreneurship

and

Small Business Management

Cases in Entrepreneurship

and

Small Business Management

Editor

Kirk C. Heriot, Ph.D.
Associate Professor of Management and Entrepreneurship
Department of Management
Western Kentucky University
Bowling Green, Kentucky 42101

Contents

Preface

The field of entrepreneurship has grown very rapidly over the past twenty five years in response to exciting developments throughout the world. In response to this phenomena, many colleges and universities in the U.S. and Europe have begun teaching courses in entrepreneurship and small business management. Dr. Jim Fiet points out that in 1971 only sixteen colleges and universities taught entrepreneurship in the U.S. "Today, there are over 800 colleges and universities with entrepreneurship classes, programs, and initiatives."

One of the challenges to educators is to identify pedagogies that will help students learn the material in the most effective manner. This case book was created after my participation in an exciting seminar at Syracuse University about entrepreneurship education. The seminar, entitled "The Experiential Classroom IV", the fourth in an annual series, emphasized pedagogies and tools for teaching entrepreneurship. Among the pedagogies that were emphasized by the facilitators was the case method. I was rather impressed with the enthusiasm that the case method received from the participants, many of whom were new to both teaching entrepreneurship and to the use of the case method. This experience reinforced my belief that the case method was a valuable pedagogy and that cases in entrepreneurship and small business would be valued by instructors and students.

Thus, twelve cases in entrepreneurship and small business management were selected from a variety of sources. The cases in this casebook cover a broad range of topics that reflect the depth and breadth of issues that small business owners and entrepreneurs may face when creating a new business venture or leading an active business. I hope you enjoy this edition of *Cases in Entrepreneurship and Small Business Management*.

Acknowledgements

I thank the people at Prentice Hall who helped make this casebook possible. I am especially grateful to David Parker and Richard Gomes who assisted a novice editor with the process of taking an idea and making it a reality.

I would also like to thank Kay Guess and David Rosenthal of the North American Case Research Association (NACRA). They were very helpful in suggesting cases from NACRA that could be adopted for use in this casebook.

In addition, I would like to thank my friends and colleagues at Western Kentucky University for their patience and support as I worked on preparing the casebook. I especially appreciate the support of my department chairperson, Zubair Mohamed, and my friend and mentor, Leo Simpson, the Mattie Newman Ford Professor of Entrepreneurship at Western Kentucky University.

Lastly, I would like to express appreciation to the faculty and students that are interested in entrepreneurship and small business management in its many forms. This casebook is especially for you.

K.C.H.
Bowling Green, Kentucky

About the Editor

Dr. Kirk C. Heriot joined the faculty at Western Kentucky University as an Associate Professor of Entrepreneurship in July 2003. Kirk has worked extensively with small firms as a researcher and a consultant since 1987. He served as a consultant at the Clemson University Small Business Development Center from 1987 – 1995 where he assisted over 200 companies. He completed an SBA-sponsored research grant entitled, "Subcontracting: A Case Study" with Dr. Caron St. John in 1991. Kirk is also the President of Palmetto Consulting, Inc., a Georgia-based corporation. His company is currently completing a competitive SBA Research Contract to study the export costs of small U.S. firms.

Dr. Heriot has served as the director of three different Small Business Institute® programs, supervising student teams to complete consulting projects for small businesses. As a graduate student, he served as the SBI Director at Clemson University from 1989 – 1992. He founded and directed the Small Business Center at North Georgia College & State University (1998 – 2002). Later, he renewed the dormant SBI program at Francis Marion University, a small, public university in SC, in 2002-2003. Overall, he has supervised over 100 student-consulting projects on behalf of small businesses.

Dr. Heriot has also conducted academic research that has been published in peer-reviewed journals and conference proceedings. He serves on the editorial review board of the Case Research Journal, Journal of Small Business Strategy and the New England Journal of Entrepreneurship. He has extensive experience teaching entrepreneurship, small business management, and new venture creation, as well as developing entrepreneurship programs. His teaching experience includes service on the faculties of Kutztown University in Pennsylvania, North Georgia College & State University and Francis Marion University.

Kirk completed his Ph.D. in Industrial Management with a concentration in Strategic Management at Clemson University in 1996. He completed his MBA at the University of South Carolina in 1984 and his Bachelor of Science degree in Industrial Management at Clemson University in 1980. Prior to entering academics, Kirk was an officer in the U.S. Army and a shift manager for a privately held textile firm. He is married to the former Jan Marie Funchess. They have five children, three dogs, and a fish named "Bob."

CASE STUDY 1

Sonoma County Crushers: Baseball or Business?

A few months after the 2002 Sonoma County Crushers baseball season had ended, team owner and president, Bob Fletcher went about business as usual trying to improve the financial situation of his independent minor league team. Over the past few seasons the possibility had emerged of having a couple franchises in such deep financial trouble that they would not be able to field a team. After eight years of playing a vital role in keeping the Western Baseball League (WBL) alive, Fletcher had heard every rumor about the league's possible demise. The Crushers had become an integral part of the Sonoma County community. Its mascot, Crusher the Abominable Sonoman, had become more embraced and recognized than any other local dignitary or politician.

As Fletcher thumbed through financial reports (Exhibits 1 & 2), his phone rang. It was the owner of the Chico Heat franchise and he told Fletcher the Heat had pulled out of the league and would not field a team for the 2003 season. The Heat, in their seven-year history, had consistently proven itself to be the most stable and financially successful team in the league. Fletcher was surprised to learn that, effective immediately, the Heat franchise would cease operations. Although the prospect of a team folding before the season started was always present, Fletcher was still optimistic that he had done enough to at least help keep the league operational. After learning of this development Fletcher was left questioning his options for the future of the Crushers.

Club history

Several investors based in Portland, Oregon founded the WBL in 1994. The league first secured sites and then owners were able to purchase territorial rights to a franchise. This provided a viable opportunity for the recently retired Fletcher. After leaving IBM in 1994, he and his wife decided to explore owning their own business (Exhibit 3). Fletcher first researched owning a tennis club based on personal interest. After considerable research he concluded a tennis club would not be a profitable business opportunity.

It was early one morning, while reading the *Wall Street Journal*, that Fletcher was first introduced to owning a minor league baseball team as he came across a team in Helena, Montana for sale. Although, he did not invest in that team, his ensuing research lead him to the new independent start-up WBL.

This being Fletcher's first solo business venture, he felt more comfortable having a few partners with whom to share the risk. Through mutual friends, he joined forces with a pair of San Francisco based attorneys, who helped front the initial start up fees, including the $50,000 franchise fee. Other expenses included extensive stadium renovations, improvements, computers, infrastructure, offices, staff and insurance. With

Prepared by Professor Armand Gilinsky , Jr., Professor Douglas Jordan, and Jarrod J. Dillon, MBA student at Sonoma State University as a basis for class discussion rather than to illustrate either effective or ineffective handling of an administrative situation. The host organization depicted in this case asked for certain financial data to be disguised. All events and characters depicted are real. Copyright 2004 by Armand Gilinsky, Jr., Douglas Jordan, and Jarrod J. Dillon.

the finances taken care of, Fletcher was asked to select one of the locations the league had secured. He considered several locations, but after much research and debate, chose Rohnert Park. Fletcher chose this location based on the inexpensive ballpark lease the city of Rohnert Park was willing to sign, the relatively high county per capita income and the wine country setting. Most importantly, Fletcher found surveys and research concluded community support for a minor league team in Sonoma County was high.

Name selection was also a very important in tying the team to Sonoma County. Fletcher chose the "Crushers," a name synonymous with the wine industry, the number one economic force in the area. Using a wine theme would not only tie in community interest, but also attract sponsorship dollars from local wineries.

The Crushers also researched the Redwood Pioneers, a once affiliated team for the Anaheim Angels, who had failed in Rohnert Park during the eighties. Kevin Wolski, the Crushers Director of Sales, Marketing & Promotions, described some of the due diligence that the Crushers' management went through in selecting Rohnert Park:

> We didn't just go and start up a team…before we started the Crushers we talked to people in the community. We wanted to try and find out why the [Redwood] Pioneers failed so we wouldn't make the same mistakes. We researched the location, we researched other teams, and we visited 3 or 4 other successful teams and found out what they charged for their inventory and adjusted it to our market. We had to gauge: do we have a stronger economy than this team? Do we anticipate drawing more fans than this team does? Take all those types of things into consideration and then change them to fit into your own marketplace. Over time you adjust and change your prices to fit the need of your area and its economy. We traded for as much of our media advertising as possible. If you have a venue where you are drawing people then people want to have a presence with you at the ballpark.

Everything seemed to be working out well for the Crushers, when Fletcher was thrown a curve ball. Before the first pitch was ever thrown, Fletcher's partners withdrew and he had no choice but to allow his first manager, Paul Deese, to double as a partial owner.

Deese served as the "baseball guy" and made the calls on all baseball-related decisions; Fletcher handled the business matters. Deese had good baseball contacts and college coaching experience. The relationship flourished, but after the 1996 season, Deese sold his stake to Fletcher and left the organization for personal reasons. Fletcher then became highly involved in the baseball decisions with whoever the field manager was at the time.

In the first eight years of the WBL's existence (1995-2002), the Sonoma County Crushers' were the only franchise to remain in the same city and operate under the same ownership group. To contrast, the other original seven franchises had roughly twenty-five location and/or ownership changes. The Crushers' were truly unique, and in the unstable industry of minor league baseball, a model of success.

Affiliation

As the owner of a minor league team, one of the most difficult questions Fletcher faced was whether to operate the team with major league affiliation or as an independent minor league team. Early on while Fletcher researched buying and operating a minor league team, he admittedly saw the benefits of running an affiliated minor league team. Affiliation offered several financial savings: the major league parent club would pay all the minor league team's salaries for players, scouts and coaches. The parent club also would pay for all insurance, workers compensation, travel, housing expenses and the majority of all team equipment. Being an affiliate of a major league club would also bring a sense of stability, confidence and a certain degree of prestige. Jeremy Shelly, San Francisco Giants baseball operations assistant remarked, "I don't see why anybody would want to own an independent team, rather than an affiliated team. Affiliated teams just have less to worry about, players, scouts, coaches are all handled for them and they can put all their efforts towards other parts of running the business."

Fletcher, being the savvy businessman he was, recognized these benefits and thoroughly explored the possibility of owning an affiliated team when he started. However, all of the benefits of being an affiliated team also carried a hefty franchise fee, anywhere from the mid-hundred thousands to several million-dollars. The combination of the relatively low price of an independent team, market trends rising in independent baseball and the freedom of non-affiliation prompted Fletcher to keep the franchise independent. Originally, Fletcher purchased the franchise with the hope of not only running his own team, but also making a lot of money. It quickly became evident that getting rich in minor league baseball would be very hard to do. Some years the Crushers made money, while others they lost. In eight years, the Crushers were able to break even and always kept a positive cash flow, allowing the Fletchers to live comfortably, but by no means get rich.

When Fletcher decided to purchase an independent franchise he invested heavily into the ball club and its facilities. He quickly learned that although the overall market demand had risen for minor league baseball, the independent franchise market was relatively untapped with possible growth and profit potential. Lastly, and perhaps most importantly, was the freedom and creativity associated with being an independent team. All business and baseball decisions were kept in house and decided upon by three or four people who had the hands on experience to determine the best direction for the team.

The freedom that was given to the sales force when selling sponsorship deals, or in ownership to take a chance on signing an aging ex-major leaguer, proved to be one of the best assets that came with being an independent baseball club. At times Fletcher considered leaving the instability of the WBL for the stability and benefits of an established affiliated league like the California (CAL) League. The CAL League was interested in the location, but not necessarily the Crushers' team, unless Fletcher bought another club's rights or purchased an expansion team. They would not allow the Crushers to join without major money being paid to the league. It was rumored that the CAL League showed interest in trying to undercut the Crushers and establish a franchise on its own in Santa Rosa.

Political landscape

Perhaps the most important question regarding the future of the franchise was whether the city of Rohnert Park wanted to keep the Crushers. This question arose as early as 2000, but became even more urgent after the 2002 season came to a close. Despite the fun, entertainment and sense of community the organization brought Rohnert Park and Sonoma County, the answer was not so simple.

Rohnert Park, one of the first planned cities in California, had been growing at an incredible rate, leaving land for commercial and residential development very scarce. As a planned city, the leadership of Rohnert Park placed growth rate limits on commercial, residential and industrial zoning. Consequently, land became increasingly scarce and highly sought-after commodity by the city leaders.

Although the ballpark lease required the Crushers to make about $75,000 worth of renovations to the facility per year, they still only paid $1 rent annually to the city for the stadium lease. In 2002, the original ten-year stadium contract only had two years before it would expire and need to be renegotiated. No major league affiliate or independent ownership group wanted to take over a lease in Rohnert Park that would expire in two years. Further, negotiations with the city council did not look promising in regards to renewing the stadium lease agreement. The city had publicly announced that although the Crushers were a local icon that provided a substantial amount of community relations, the city could sell the land to a commercial developer in order to mitigate a severe fiscal crisis.

Confidential preliminary talks had begun between the city of Santa Rosa and the Crushers regarding building a new ballpark and moving the Crushers' franchise ten miles north on Highway 101. Fletcher, however, saw in these preliminary meetings years of political red tape, loan financing and due diligence before a new ballpark could become a reality.

Dynamics of minor league baseball

Despite extensive research, market testing and due diligence, Fletcher realized that minor league baseball was an unpredictable industry. Even though he had worked his way up the corporate ladder for one of the most well-known and prominent companies in the world, Fletcher at times found himself overwhelmed with the Crushers.

There were a number of unexpected problems. From injured players regularly filing for workman's compensation to filing applications with the United States government to secure international visas for foreign players. Even with extensive business knowledge and years of real world experience, Fletcher was not fully prepared for the uncertain world of minor league baseball. Only dealing with each issue on a day-to-day basis could Fletcher gain the knowledge necessary to correctly navigate the choppy waters of minor league baseball.

Many of the unforeseen problems were directly related to Fletcher's inexperience in dealing with the community. Large, private companies such as IBM, are often in the public spotlight, but never deal with the emotions that professional sports teams encounter. Tickets and merchandise were sold out of the same small building that player negotiation and trades were taking place, putting constant pressure on the Crushers' front office to interact with customers on a daily basis. Fans were free to openly agree or disagree with the play of the team, the character or quality of players, and even the price

4

of tickets. These constant distractions were not only difficult to manage professionally but became a nuisance.

Fletcher found the best way to maintain control over these situations, was to make himself available to customers to hear their suggestions. He was also proactive in bringing people into the organization with the skills and attitude to interact with the fans. Customer service became key to the Crushers organization and the fan base grew to embrace the Crushers as their hometown team.

Several times the league seemed on the verge of collapse, and had even considered playing a season with as few as four teams (league averaged 6-8 teams). Fielding a team in 2003 could risk losing thousands of dollars that would need to be paid back to sponsors and ticket holders. Hundreds of thousands more could be lost on salaries, insurance and travel expenses.

Selling entertainment

Despite owning a professional sports team, Fletcher always considered himself a businessman first and a baseball man second. He compensated for this by surrounding himself with those most knowledgeable about baseball. Fletcher described running the Crushers:

> Owning and managing the Crushers was unlike any business I could have imagined; in fact it was more like overseeing a set of businesses: one in public relations, others in advertising, marketing, customer service, sales, merchandising, venue management and food service. No two days were ever the same, and that's what made it so fun and appealing.

The Crushers were in the entertainment business. They competed, to a degree, with the San Francisco Giants, the Oakland A's in major league baseball and other minor league baseball teams within a seventy-five mile radius. Their primary competitors were other family oriented organizations during the summer. State and national parks, outdoor recreational sports, indoor sports, Marriot's Great America, Marine World Africa-USA, the Sonoma County Fair, bowling, movies, golf, and water slides were all major competitors. As for the other teams in the league, Fletcher never worried about them from a competition angle, but he knew that in selling entertainment and specifically minor league baseball one was always dependent on his/her competition. This did not bode well for the Crushers considering how poorly some of the other organizations were run. Fletcher felt very strongly about how teams were run in the WBL:

> The majority of the organizations in the league were run improperly. They were run as hobbies, not as legitimate businesses. Business ethics were almost non-existent and certain ownership groups severely hurt the league image, and ruined site locations permanently by either destroying the fan base or driving up large debt.

Mission and values

Most of the Crushers' executive staff had shared missions and values, despite never posting these publicly or privately. The unwritten Crusher mission statement could best be described as "being Sonoma County's home team, while providing a safe, fun and inexpensive family entertainment." Kevin Wolski, the first Crusher employee and Director of Sales, Marketing and Promotions, stated: "Naming the team, tying it into the community and providing an around excellent ballpark experience was the key to our success. We took pride in representing and selling the Crusher ideology. That was what made us the organization we were." Having a pragmatic and honest professional relationship with customers, operating under the Golden Rule and most importantly, conducting a legitimate business while still having fun were all points that Fletcher stressed to his staff.

Chris Corda, Assistant General Manger, added that:

Being professional and giving off the image of professionalism was quite important for the organization. For the community to take us seriously, in terms of spending sponsorship dollars and deciding we were a worthwhile entertainment option, we had to be proactive in the public-perception of our organization, our ballpark and our employees. The organization was run as a business first and a baseball team second.

As the years went by, Fletcher became increasingly aware that the rest of the league did not have good business leadership. Many were opportunists who thought it would be fun to own a baseball team. But the allure of owning a team wore off once they had to get their hands dirty in the business side. Others saw owning a team as more of a hobby rather than a legitimate business. Thus, the professionalism and customer service of their organizations greatly suffered.

Human resources

Fletcher signed high profile players and managers, who carried high publicity value. For a minor league team, the Crushers made major waves by signing former major league players such as Jeffrey Leonard and Kevin Mitchell, the 1989 National League MVP, both former stars for the San Francisco Giants. In 2001, the team signed three Cuban All-Stars that had defected from Cuba, two of which came to the U.S. in rowboats. These players were not only great for the team's play, but also were also public relations and marketing tools. Ticket sales spiked and recognition soared, locally and nationally. ESPN, Sports Illustrated, Fox Sports and other media outlets ran stories about the Crushers. In 2001, the organization received its most prestigious honor when it was named by *Forbes FYI* Magazine as "The Best Afternoon of Baseball in America." Much of the credit from this award was due to Fletcher's commitment to hiring quality people:

With the players you try to bring in guys of that caliber so we were not too surprised by their successes. The same can be said of our front office people, we always tried to hire the best, but it was still an honor when the people we brought aboard were thought highly enough to be taken to higher levels within professional sports. All of those people helped us become the respected organization that we were.

The Crushers quickly became known around minor league baseball as a legitimate stepping stone to the next level. Three players, Chad Zerbe, James Lofton and Kevin Pickford all played for Sonoma County within three seasons of making their MLB debut. Lofton actually went from the Crushers to the Boston Red Sox in the same season. Over ten other players advanced to AA or AAA affiliated minor-league baseball teams. Such successes were not limited to players. Four announcers, Steve Bitker, Roxy Bernstein, Dave Raymond and Steve Wendt all announced at least one season on radio for the Crushers before moving to affiliated baseball organizations. Three front office executives, Jarrod Dillon, Chris Corda and Brian Sherrill, all began with the Crushers before moving on to other organizations in the sports business industry (Exhibit 4).

Marketing, promotion and sponsorship

As Director of Sales, Marketing and Promotions, Kevin Wolski, was responsible for creating "value" for Crushers' corporate sponsors and fans alike. Wolski was the primary and often the only salesperson for the Crushers. It was his job to make the Crushers so well known in the community that sponsors and fans alike would line up to invest or spend their money on the organization.

Wolski best described the Crushers original marketing plan as "an evolving process." Despite weekly sales meetings and annual planning sessions, there was never an established or written marketing plan while Wolski worked for the Crushers. With a small sales force and little resources available to him, Wolski was forced to rely on extensive personal research and professional relationships. Although tickets and sponsorship packages were completely different in price and purpose, the basic idea was to increase the perceived value for sponsors and fans as much as possible. The median age in Sonoma and Marin counties, according to the year 2000 census, was 37-41 and the median family income was between $60,000-$90,000 per year. That meant there were a lot of younger families with potentially disposable income (Exhibit 6). Wolski attributed a large part of the success of the organization's sales and marketing to its savvy use of media partnerships and playing up the "family fun" and "Sonoma County's team" ideologies.

Wolski pointed out, "We tried to do what McDonald's did, be as wholesome as possible, try to market to the kids…try to be fun and not take ourselves too seriously." Official team demographics pinned the highest percentage of the Crushers' fan base to be married couples with two or more children. This fact became an important marketing tool for Wolski.

> I tried to discover what companies spent money advertising, which of those had a good community support record and see which companies would want to advertise to the family demographic. We kept the kids and families coming back by having wacky and wild promotional give-aways and theme days.

Part of the Crushers' marketing philosophy called for trading away extra inventory, radio time, program ads and some tickets, but never trading for in-park signage. Signage was the organization's biggest moneymaker and always sold out.

A second part of Wolski's marketing strategy was to make every sponsorship package make sense. He sought to make the connection between the sponsor's product and how that tied to the ballpark, the team, family and baseball as a whole. Long-term contracts were always encouraged for revenue and to discourage turnover.

Promotions, theme days and give-aways were what minor league baseball was most known. Wolski attempted to have the Crushers follow suit:

> Do something new, have promotional items that people care about and will keep especially if you're putting a sponsor's logo on. Create that 'buzz,' did you hear what the Crushers did? What are they doing this weekend? Get the word out. We went to the El Paso promotional seminars and learned that we shouldn't try to reinvent the wheel. Some theme days don't work for every market, so you need to play on your area and your fan demographics.

Wolski's marketing plan was a success. The Crushers consistently drew crowds of about 1,700-2,000 per game, between 77,000 and 93,000 per season. The proof of success in Wolski's marketing strategy was that there was no apparent correlation between how well the team played and the number of people at the games (Exhibit 6). The team sometimes drew more fans in years the team played poorly and fewer fans in years the team played well. It became clear that the Crushers were not necessarily attracting people to the ballpark because of their team, but rather other reasons. The atmosphere, desire to support the "home team," monetary value and family entertainment were why people came to see the Crushers.

Community and public relations

The Crushers' strategy to become a valued community asset was dependent on being the "home team." Community involvement was the responsibility of Assistant General Manager Chris Corda. He attempted to make the fans feel like they were a part of the games by having in between inning games, talking with players, allowing kids run the bases, and even having local "host" families allow players to live with them over the course of the season. Corda described in depth some of the public relations strategy he was influential in implementing:

> The ballplayers, and the fan accessibility to them, played a huge role in our public image. Although most people would look at our roster and think, 'I don't know any of these guys,' our fans developed strong feelings toward the players because they could easily get an autograph, shake a hand or spend time talking to them. These guys weren't the most recognizable players, so we made them as accessible as possible. My belief was that 50% of the people who attended games were there for baseball, and the other 50% were there other reasons like entertainment value, or family value. Away from the ballpark, we tried to make the largest possible impression while spending as little money as possible to achieve that goal. The Crushers developed a reading program, ticket donation programs, and school rallies, as many events as we could to interact with the community. Visibility, in a positive light, was essential to the success of our organization.

The single most visible figure in the organization quickly became the mascot, Crusher the Abominable Sonoman. Standing seven feet tall, with size thirty purple wine stained feet he was the most recognizable part of the organization. With players constantly changing it was essential to develop a mascot that would be a consistent figurehead for the organization. The Crushers took him to as many fairs, parades and other public events as possible. Everyone recognized him and associated him with the team.

The future

Fletcher's exit strategy had always been to sell, as he had no intention to pass the business on to his sons. However, after the 2002 season, he reflected, "I kept hanging on, working hard and hoping the league will turn around enough that we can sell out, but in the end it seems just too risky for any potential investors. I have no regrets except I wish we could have had a stronger league from top to bottom."

Fletcher now had several options. He could liquidate the remaining team's assets. He could sell to a new owner, leaving the location of the team an issue. He could try to keep the WBL going with fewer teams. He could sit out a season and move the team to a new location or join a new league entirely. He could also buy a new affiliated franchise and try to have them play in Sonoma County or elsewhere.

The league had survived so many close calls that Fletcher never really believed it would come to this. Now, with the 2003 season only eight months away, the loss of one of its few prosperous franchisees (the Chico Heat) magnified the possibility of the entire league going under. Fletcher reflected on all the hard work he and his wife, Susan, had put into the organization and wondered how to proceed.

Exhibit 1
Sonoma County Crushers -- Comparative Income Statements, 1997-2001*

Fiscal Year Ending	12/31/97	12/31/98	12/31/99	12/31/00	12/31/01
Sales	422,175	472,619	456,372	490,113	$457,188
Cost of Sales	9,212	15,175	16,917	19,014	16,192
Gross Profit	412,963	457,445	439,455	471,099	440,996
Expenses:					
Salaries	175,697	202,923	204,010	203,322	213,076
Equipment	14,962	18,147	14,189	15,720	15,436
Utilities	15,313	12,078	11,379	13,082	11,728
Travel	25,447	35,479	37,889	42,415	38,093
Umpires	0	548	180	300	218
Insurance	22,421	25,437	22,840	20,945	18,164
Advert/Promo	8,607	6,087	15,658	14,463	11,557
Amortization	2,970	2,960	2,740	1,667	1,667
Dues/Subscriptions	12,906	25,813	16,734	15,279	13,889
Contributions	313	405	658	800	1,083
Legal	2,232	968	1,182	2,479	4,231
Employee Meals	12,359	12,230	13,931	12,612	13,117
Medical	306	83	236	3,201	1,576
Office/Supplies	18,211	22,392	25,999	23,277	24,169
Taxes/licenses	18,630	20,729	21,663	20,801	22,671
Repair/maintenance	18,051	12,590	15,332	17,551	18,412
Depreciation	11,379	17,062	12,870	9,830	8,548
Bank services	1,834	1,702	3,611	3,344	2,255
Recruiting/housing	9,307	7,984	5,964	11,776	13,295
Interest	3,811	5,806	5,653	1,859	1,902
Game day	1,984	3,821	1,720	1,716	1,446
League fines	175	75	188	400	613
Equipment rentals	3,771	4,987	5,116	3,505	1,917
Misc.	1,544	2,241	3,359	4,458	3,619
Total Expenses	$382,224	438,287	440,431	445,282	442,674
Net Expenses Over Revenues	30,739	19,158	(976)	25,817	(1,678)
Interest Inc.	19	80	52		
Net Ex/Rev.	30,758	19,238	(950)		
Retained Earnings 12/31/96	(79,557)	RE 12/31/97 (48,799)	RE 12/31/98 (29,561)	RE 12/31/99 (30,511)	RE 12/31/00 (30,511)
Retained Earnings 12/31/97	(48,799)	RE 12/31/98 (29,561)	RE 12/31/99 (30,511)	RE 12/31/00 (4,694)	RE 12/31/01 (4,694)
					(6,372)

*NOTE: All figures have been disguised by using a consistent multiplier

EXHIBIT 2

Sonoma County Crushers – Comparative Balance Sheets, 1997-2001*

	1997	1998	1999	2000	2001
ASSETS					
Current Assets:					
Cash	8,270	8,004	8,337	9,842	8,574
Loans receivable	0	0	150	150	575
Deposits	500	500	500	500	500
	8,770	8,504	8,987	10,492	9,649
Property & Equip:					
Leasehold improvements	140,134	140,134	140,134	148,894	148,894
Furniture & fixtures	4,535	7,406	7,723	8,456	8,502
Equip.	16,030	31,658	36,022	29,398	32,068
	160,698	179,197	183,878	186,747	189,463
Less accumulated amortization	(28,030)	(45,091)	(57,961)	(67,791)	(76,339)
	132,669	134,106	125,918	118,956	113,125
Intangible Assets:					
Software	205	205	205	205	205
Franchise fee	25,000	25,000	25,000	25,000	25,000
Organization costs	6,447	6,447	6,447	6,447	6,447
	31,652	31,652	31,652	31,652	31,652
Less accumulated amortization	(9,498)	(12,458)	(15,198)	(16,864)	(18,531)
	22,154	19,194	16,454	14,788	13,121
TOTAL ASSETS	$ 163,593	161,804	151,359	144,235	135,894
LIABILITIES & STOCKHOLDERS' EQUITY					
Current Liab:					
Deposits	83,882	79,848	69,024	64,113	66,217
Notes payable	16,283	21,699	39,232	10,004	12,504
	100,165	101,546	108,256	74,117	78,721
Long-Term Liab:					
Notes Payable-stockholders	74,727	52,319	36,114	36,112	26,046
Stockholders' Equity:					
Common stock, $1 par value					
500,000 shares authorized					
& 37,500 shares issued	37,500	37,500	37,500	37,500	37,500
Retained Earnings	(48,799)	(29,561)	(30,511)	(4,694)	(6,372)
	(11,299)	7,939	6,989	32,806	31,128
Total Liab. & SH Equity	$ 163,593	161,804	151,359	144,235	135,894

*NOTE: All figures have been disguised by using a consistent multiplier

Exhibit 3
Robert Fletcher's Biography

Robert Fletcher was born in 1940. He grew up in a small town in upstate New York and eventually attended college at Syracuse University. Graduating in 1963 with a bachelor of the arts in Mathematics from Syracuse, Fletcher went to earn his masters of the arts in System Information Sciences.

Upon graduating from college he went to work for IBM from 1966 to 1994. With IBM he was originally based in Washington DC as a systems engineer. After a few years, he moved into technology sales, where he met his future wife Susan, also an IBM employee.

In 1976, the couple moved to the Bay Area in order for Bob to take a management position inside IBM. He was the Chief Information Officer of the Western Area until his retirement in 1994. Upon his retirement he and Susan decided to pursue owning their own company, which would eventually lead to the purchase of the Sonoma County Crushers.

Bob and Susan have two sons, Mark 32 and Brian 30. They currently reside in Santa Rosa, California with their three cats: Ally, Bo, Homer and their dog Murphy.

Exhibit 4
Player/Front Office Advancement

Player	Position	Year(s) w/ Crushers	Professional Organization
Chad Zerbe	Player	1997	San Francisco Giants
James Lofton	Player	2001	Boston Red Sox
Kevin Pickford	Player	2001	San Diego Padres
Steve Bitker	Announcer	1996-2002	Oakland A's & KCBS Sports Radio
Dave Raymond	Announcer	1997-1999	AAA* Iowa Cubs & San Francisco Giants
Roxy Bernstein	Announcer	2000	UC Berkley, San Jose Sharks & San Francisco Giants
Steve Wendt	Announcer	2001	A* Stockton Ports
Chris Corda	Front Office	1997-2002	Oakland A's
Jarrod Dillon	Front Office	2001	San Francisco Giants
Brian Sherril	Front Office	2002	A* Tri-City Dirt Devils

*Letter A denotes the level of minor league club, AAA representing the highest level.

Exhibit 5
Demographics of Sonoma & Marin Counties – 2000 census

Sonoma County

Population	458,614
Median Age	37.5
Income Per Capita	$25,724
Median Family Income	$61,921

Marin County

Population	247,289
Median Age	41.3
Income Per Capita	$44,962
Median Family Income	$88,934

*Source: U.S. Census Bureau http://www.census.gov/main/www/cen2000.html

Exhibit 6
Crushers Attendance & Team Won-Lost Record 1995-2002*

Year	2002	2001	2000	1999	1998	1997	1996	1995
Attendance Total	78,218	77,200	86,151	85,362	92,598	91,692	92,020	84,173
Per Game Average	1,738	1,716	1,914	1,897	2,058	2,038	2,045	1,871
Won/Lost Record	49-41	48-42	38-52	41-49	49-41	56-34	34-56	44-46

* Sources: Robert Fletcher & Western Baseball League

CASE STUDY 2

MetalBenders Industries, Inc.: The Accidental Entrepreneur

"Darn it all! I never wanted to be a CEO," muttered Maria Brouwer, CEO of MetalBenders Industries, Inc. of Grand Rapids, Michigan, to herself as she maneuvered her Lincoln Town Car into the garage of her contemporary home. "I've been doing my best to run this company for the past six years... here it is May of 2002 and I haven't even started weeding my perennials garden! Not only do I dislike going into the office before 11:00 in the morning, but I detest coming home this late at night. I wish we hadn't scheduled that strategic planning meeting this week. But I know with José leaving on vacation in June, we just can't wait any longer... things have to get resolved!"

She unlocked the back door, walked in the kitchen, and poured herself a glass of wine. Here she was, arriving home from the office after 8:00 p.m., exhausted again. She recalled the advertising slogan "You've come a long way baby!" and thought how true that was for her. She really *had* come a long way over the last sixty years. Born in Mexico, Maria and her family had immigrated to the United States to seek a better life. As a teenager, she had met and subsequently married William, a handsome and ambitious young man of Dutch heritage. Together, they had built a successful metal fabricating company.[1]

As Maria's diary had revealed,

> *I was born in Tubutama, a small town that is not far from Nogales, Mexico. When I was six years old, my cousins from Tucson came to visit us. They told us that they*
> came back to Mexico to see us because nobody in America made tortillas that were as good as las tortillas de mi madre [my mother's tortillas]. They said that the American tortillas tasted like cardboard! But they said that life was good in Estados Unidos [United States]... my uncle worked as a carpenter and helped to build tall buildings. My cousin, Amarita, went to a school that had something called a "merry-go-round." She said that she liked to play on it. She also said that she had a bedroom of her own to sleep in at night... she didn't have to share a bed with her sister, like I did. It seemed to me that the United States must be like el vivir en cielo [living in heaven].

By Nancy M. Levenburg, Thomas D. Wolterink, and Ram Subramanian of Grand Valley State University. This case was prepared as the basis for class discussion and is not intended to illustrate either effective or ineffective handling of administrative situations. Reprinted by Permission from the Case Research Journal. Copyright 2003 by Nancy M. Levenburg, Thomas D. Wolterink, and Ram Subrammanian and the North American Case Research Association. All rights reserved.
[1] The case (disguised) was prepared based on discussions with Maria Brouwer and information obtained during the winter of 2002 by students enrolled in an undergraduate Small Business Management course at Grand Valley State University.

When I was twelve years old, my family moved to Tucson. We took a bus from Nogales. I remember the border crossing very clearly. There were many government officials: Border Police, Immigration Officers, Customs Inspectors, and even dogs! I was scared. They made us stand in a line to inspect our papers. I hid behind my mother. It seemed like it took days before we finally got to Tucson. We stayed with my uncle until we moved into our own apartment. It had three bedrooms!

On my first day of school in the United States, I met a girl named Margaret. She told me that the lunch her mother had packed for her was way too big, and that she would be happy to share with me. I knew immediately that I had a friend! Margaret gave me the long, yellow fruit from her lunch bag. I had never seen one before, and I didn't know how to eat it. But I didn't want her to think that I was stupid, so I took a bite of it. It was awful! I wish she had told me that you're not supposed to eat the peel on a banana! Margaret was my best friend when we lived in Tucson. She helped me with learning English. We used to laugh about my first banana. But I don't think I ever ate another one.

My uncle, Fernando, lived in Grand Rapids, Michigan. He told my father that there were many good jobs in Grand Rapids because of the auto industry. He said he would help my father to find a job there and that we could live with his family until we found an apartment. My mother didn't want to leave Tucson since it was only a few hours from our old home in Mexico. My mother said we would all freeze to death if we moved to Michigan. But I knew that if my father made the decision to go, we would go. Still, my mother cried and cried when my father said that we were leaving. It took over two weeks for my mother and me to pack everything. My job was to watch my brother, Juan, who was two years old because all he wanted to do was play hide-and-seek in the boxes. I was fourteen years old at the time.

I met William when I was a junior in high school. We were in the same World History class. William literally swept me off my feet! He was tall and blond... he said I had the most beautiful brown eyes he had ever seen. William played on the high school's football team, too. And he was the senior class president. Can you imagine that!?! When William gave me his letter sweater to wear, you can't believe how I felt... a short little girl from Mexico in an American boy's letter sweater! I absolutely swam in it, but I felt so proud! There was never anyone like William. We graduated from high school and got married two months later, in August.

The years together absolutely flew by! William wanted me to pursue an education, so I enrolled in the community college and, because I helped William at the office during the day, I took classes at night. It took over five years to do it, but eventually I earned my Associate's degree in Secretarial Science. Although my father never did understand all the "fuss" about getting an education, my mother was so proud of me that she cried! Not only was I the first in my family to graduate from high school, I was also the first to have a college degree!

William described Maria as "the best secretary a boss could ever have." She loved all those years they had spent together... sharing the drive into the office (they only had one automobile) and happily assisting William throughout the day, making coffee for meetings, answering the telephone, and aiding with the bookkeeping. They had no

17

children. As Maria had said, "I was trained to be a secretary, and that's what I'm happiest doing."

Life was good... until the car accident in 1995. William and Maria were traveling southbound along a divided highway en-route to meet with a prospective customer when a northbound car strayed across the median and struck the rear of their van. Eye-witnesses had said that the vehicle rolled over five or six times. William died instantaneously, leaving Maria with a closed-head injury, grief-stricken, and very alone. While she recovered from injuries that meant she was only able to work two hours per day, she decided to sell the business and listed it with a business broker. However, after six months of being unable to find a buyer, she reluctantly decided to run the business herself. As she readily admitted, it was a role and responsibility that she never wanted.

In 1996, Maria sought assistance from the local Small Business Development Center (SBDC) office. With their help, she found a "try-and-buy" purchaser who ran the business with her for a year. At the end of the year, he declined to purchase the company so he and Maria parted ways. Maria then decided to run the business on her own. As she put it,

> It was my only choice. William had always taken care of me; he was – and always will be – my "knight in shining armor." But when he died, my brothers, sisters, and their children were the only family I had. Although one of my brothers moved back to Mexico and two sisters moved to Texas, William and I took trips to visit them every year. Mexican families are very close, you know. Unfortunately, I figured out pretty quickly that I wouldn't be able to afford many trips to Mexico on a secretary's wage. So if I couldn't find a buyer, I'd just have to run the business myself!

That was six years ago. Still unable to work more than a few hours each day (and never earlier than 11:00 a.m.), she was frustrated. She often wondered if she had done the right thing when she decided to continue running the business on her own. "As I look back, I can see that we're still only doing two-thirds in sales of what we did when William was alive. Yet José, my sales manager, is convinced that if the company achieved ISO 9000 certification and we expanded our operations, our sales would double. Should I listen to him?"

Company Overview

Lakeside Sheet Metal was a family-owned business established in 1969 by George and Virginia Brouwer, Maria's in-laws, after they acquired the assets of A.V. Levinson Company, a metal fabricating job shop. In January of 1970, William, George's oldest son, began working for his father as a shop foreman. In 1972, he married Maria, and by 1976, William had assumed responsibility for many managerial duties. In 1984, George decided to retire and sold the company to his two sons, William and Steven, while staying on as a consultant. William was made the majority stockholder while Steven, who lived in Texas, retained a minority position.[2] In June of 1984, William

---

[2] George also assisted Steven in starting a metal fabricating business in Texas which, on occasion, competed directly with Lakeside. As a part-owner of Lakeside (and later MetalBenders), he contributed cash into the business over the years, eventually accounting for 3/8 of the total net worth of the business. Maria did not divulge whether these cash infusions were loans, equity, or some form of loan with an equity

decided to acquire RoofRITE, Inc., one of Lakeside's major customers. The two companies operated independently until November of 1988 when they merged to form MetalBenders Industries, Inc. Metalfab was purchased in 1994 as a complement to the earlier two divisions. Maria took over operations of the MetalBenders Industries in 1995, as shown in Exhibit 1. It was located in Grand Rapids (Kent County), which was one of the fastest growth regions in the country.[3]

MetalBenders Industries manufactured customized metal products and provided expert installation to contractors, architects, and manufacturer. It prided itself on its thirty-two years of experience in the sheet metal industry, high quality craftsmanship, and on-time delivery. Over the previous four years, however, the business had been marginal – one quarter it was often profitable while the next two quarters it might operate in the red. For the year ending October 31, 2001, the company reported sales of $1.7 million with a gross profit of $419,635, or 24.41 % of sales. Within the industry, the gross profit margin was 37%.

Dismayed by the company's continuing lackluster performance, Maria again sought the assistance of the Small Business Development Center in January of 2002. The business counselor with whom she met advised her to enroll in a business planning workshop, which she did. In it, she learned about the importance of engaging in strategic planning and promptly decided to convene MetalBenders's management team to develop a mission statement and corporate objectives. The mission statement that emerged was as follows:

> *We strive to foster a working environment where employees are mutually respected and to cultivate a genuine MetalBenders Industries team that is successful in both profitability and enjoyment, as well as to create long-term career opportunities through growth. Our two divisions, RoofRITE, Inc., an architectural sheet metal contractor, and MetalBenders, Inc., a metal fabrication shop, build valuable customer relationships through our commitment to providing the highest quality, price conscious products available worldwide that are installed in a timely manner.*

Exhibit 2 contains the corporate objectives identified by MetalBenders's management team.

Industry Overview

MetalBenders Industries was classified as SIC code 3444, Sheet Metal Work or NAICS code 332322 (Sheet Metal Work Manufacturing) or 332439 (Other Metal

---

conversion feature; however, she was very assertive about the fact that she had controlling interest in the company.

[3] Grand Rapids was Michigan's second largest city with more than a half million residents and was the home for a number of office furniture and industrial machinery manufacturers, as well as metal, food, paper, plastics, printing products and information technology companies. In <u>Entrepreneur</u> magazine and Dun & Bradstreet's 8th Annual "Best Cities for Entrepreneurs" survey conducted in 2001, the Grand Rapids area ranked #2 among the top cities in the Midwest. Criteria included number of businesses that are five years old or younger, small-business growth amongst businesses with 20 or fewer employees, economic growth over a three year period, and risk (cities with the lowest business failure rates).

Container Manufacturing). The category included "establishments primarily engaged in manufacturing sheet metal work for buildings (not including fabrication work done by construction contractors at the place of construction), and manufacturing stovepipes, light tanks, and other products of sheet metal" (SIC Description, 2002). In recent years, the structure of the metal industry had undergone significant changes, particularly consolidations resulting in large cost savings due to integrating various stages of production (Today's metals, 2002). As an example, Alcoa controlled every stage of production from mining ore (bauxite) to fabricating finished metal into sheets for aerospace manufacturers. This trend was predicted to continue for the next few years.

During 2001, per-unit metal prices declined – 17.4% for stainless steel sheet and strip, 8.1% for carbon sheet steel and strip, and 3.5% for aluminum sheet and plate.[4] Industry analysts forecasted that during 2002, metal producers would pass along only a small portion of the savings to buyers, thereby increasing fabricated metal margins. It was predicted that despite the price decreases, average sheet metal work prices would rise just 0.5% in 2002 (Cost trends, 2002). Service sheet metal was also a growing and important segment of the automotive industry.

Locally, there had been a "dramatic decline" in the level of business confidence in the region, according to local experts. Based on survey results from 110 businesses in the area, the confidence index declined from 77 percent in December 2000 to 63 percent in December 2001.[5] According to one article,

The downward shift of Grand Rapids respondents' expectations is a microcosm of what is happening at the national level. In December 2000, West Michigan respondents were 75 percent confident about the performance of the regional economy in 2001. The current confidence index of 63 percent is significantly lower than the 75 percent projected in December 2000. Given the somber mood of the nation and all the intervening factors that occurred in 2001, the current confidence of 63 percent reflects economic expectations at the trough of a recession. The respondents' confidence for 2002 of 69 percent indicates guarded optimism. In summary, the West Michigan economy is going through a significant downturn – but there are latent signs of an upturn next year. (Singh and Boese, 2002).

One bright spot in the community was the construction of a new convention center. Scheduled for completion in 2004, the $220 million complex would include more than one million square feet along a thirteen-acre site on the Grand River, a 160,000-square-foot "Class A" exhibition hall, and a 40,000-square-foot flexible-use ballroom with theater seating capacity of 5,600 people. Bids were currently being accepted for the facia (trim) on the building. José believed that the job might go for $3 million or more.

According to information provided by the Michigan Small Business Development Center, approximately forty competitors existed in the region. Total sales revenue for the category within the region was $148 million. On average, these competitors had 35

---

[4] Like oil prices, metals prices were generally cyclical. For an extended discussion, see "Today's metals, tomorrow's prices" in Supply Management, 7 (6), 34-36.

[5] Each year, the study was conducted to measure and track the overall business confidence of the Grand Rapids metropolitan area. The confidence index was scaled from zero (no confidence at all) to one hundred percent (complete confidence).

employees and annual sales of $4.4 million. Among these firms, MetalBenders's three major local competitors were Trusty Sheet Metal, Better Sheet Metal Company, and Spartan Sheet Metal. (Their specialties and other demographics is shown in Exhibit 3.) All three were small companies with similarly sized facilities and number of employees, although MetalBenders was the only firm that possessed CAD equipment. Trusty Sheet Metal and Better Sheet Metal Company competed directly with MetalBenders in the roofing market.

Additionally, Quick-Line, Inc. and T&S Metals were larger competitors, though neither was currently involved in the roofing business. Quick-Line had eighty full-time employees, 46,000 square feet of manufacturing space, a complete line of metal fabrication services, and carried both OS-9000 and ISO-9001 certification. The firm was known as a high quality, full-service metal fabricator. T&S Metals had fifty-five full-time employees, 45,000 square feet of manufacturing space, and specialized in small batch products made out of aluminum. T&S Metals was known for offering quick shipments (on-time delivery) and fast response times. It was in the process of seeking OS-9000 certification. Both firms offered CAD options and had Web sites.

Within the region, most firms' only form of advertising was a Yellow Pages listing. As José said, "In the sheet metal industry, word-of-mouth is the primary way to get new business." Quick-Line, however, placed display ads in MichBiz West, a local business publication and also had a Web site.

Management

MetalBenders's organizational chart appears in Exhibit 4. As Maria described her leadership style,

> We just developed our first organizational chart. If it looks confusing, it's because we're still working on formalizing reporting relationships. Mark says he doesn't want any more of those comments like the one he got a few months ago in the suggestion box; "we have no clear chain of command... I never know who I'm supposed to report to." I'm really concerned about that because my management style is built on having good relationships with employees who are like family to me. Sometimes they even kid me about that... they call me "Mother Maria." When we have meetings, I want it to be like a family sitting around the dining room table. In fact, the table in our conference room really is a dining room table... it's the one William and I used to have in our dining room.
>
> We usually begin our meetings with sharing events of the day. We're all extremely close. For example, when Mark [MetalBenders's Production Manager] needed money to pay for his child's medical expenses, I was there to help him. Not only did I loan him the money, but gave him generous amounts of time off so he could be with his son. It's very important to me that MetalBenders survives so that I can provide income for my "family."
>
> Mark has been with us for eight years. He's like my middle child. While he tries very hard to get along with and please everyone, he and José haven't hit

21

it off very well. Mark makes things happen here...scheduling the jobs and people. He's a real plodder... he makes do with everything we have.

But our General Manager and my #2 man is Ted. In fact, in many ways, Ted is like an oldest son. He's been with us for over twenty years! He can and has done everything in the organization over the years, so he's extremely valuable to me. If only he was interested in taking over the business... then all my worries would be over and I could happily retire. But it seems the older he gets, the more he has the "call of the wild" – hunting and fishing. We might as well shut down when deer season starts in the fall. It's all that's on his mind. Ted sometimes chides me, though, for taking him for granted. Can you believe that I actually forget to invite him to meetings from time to time?

And José, our sales manager, is really a charmer! And he's had quite a long history in sales... he used to call on us with stationary and paper products. Before that, he was managed a shoe store. After William died, I stayed at home a lot. I just didn't feel comfortable going out as a "single woman." José invited me to have dinner with him one night... now we often attend social events in the community together. He has really helped me to overcome my fears and feel confident being out in public again. So even though he's only been with MetalBenders for two years (we hired him away from the paper company), because he's Hispanic, we have so much in common! I've gotten to know him quite well in a very short time.

Sometimes Ted or Mark discuss an idea with me but I don't buy into it. So even if I've heard about it before from one of them, when José presents it, he has such a way of expressing things that I can't help but agree with him. Naturally, of course, I try to please him. He's such a wonderful addition to our company!.

The Market

MetalBenders Industries targeted manufacturers (particularly in the automobile

and office furniture industries), contractors, and architects. As a

subcontractor for the

latter two, MetalBenders work often went into their "trophy buildings" (high

profile).

The area was home to several office furniture manufacturers, such as

Steelcase, Herman

Miller, and Trendway. The <u>Grand Rapids Business Journal</u>'s "Book of

Lists" database

listed twenty-nine general contractors in the area generating $6 million to $297 million in

2001 revenues, twenty-nine engineering firms ($550,000 to $77 million in 2001

revenues), and thirty-seven architectural firms ($800,000 to $34 million in 2001

revenues).[6] To date, the company had not been awarded any government contracts; however, José believed that the firm's newly-achieved minority certification could be the key to entering this market. The company provided metal components involving cutting, bending, notching, welding, and punching or drilling. Additionally, the firm manufactured OEM components such as angles, brackets, channels, dividers, enclosures, and fixtures. MetalBenders also made specialty material handling components such as: custom hoppers, stands, boxes, and shelves. They custom fabricated fascia trim, beam covers, gravel stop, wall coping, valley flashing, and any other specialty item contractors required. MetalBenders had a nationwide market in the production of storefront metal column covers. They were currently capable of producing a column up to 40 inches in diameter and 12 feet in length.

As Ted described things, "We are basically at the whim of our customers. We really don't have a product of our own. Heck! We don't even have a sign of our own on the building! We make what our customers ask us to make, often one-of-a-kind items… frequently trim pieces. We stay away from making anything that might be risky or built to a standard, such as an over-the-road trailer. People have suggested that we make trailers for many years, but honestly, we are scared to death to take the risk. Trailers have to be tested, and we would have to carry insurance in case one would fail in use. So it's just too risky. We want to keep things simple."

---

[6] The Book of Lists database contained hundreds of companies, identifying decision-makers and providing key facts about company services, employment and revenue by industry. Many business leaders relied on the Book of Lists as their first source for information about potential customers and for information about their competitors.

"Likewise, people have also suggested we manufacture our own line of metal roofs. We understand there is a big and growing market for this, especially in the West where wooden roofs have been especially popular and are now being eliminated as a fire hazard. But then again, a roof would have to be tested, and we would have to carry insurance for roof failures."

José thinks we should bid on the convention center project; however, I think it's just too big for us. He says it's supposed to have 10 to 12 percent minority contractors and that's why we should go after it. He forgets about the fact that it's hard enough for us to get out the jobs we have right now. I even had to skip the last Management Team meeting so we could get a job out the door on time. And while we depend heavily on what our production workers do by hand, we don't seem to pay them much more than the average manufacturing wage in the area... no bonuses or anything. So what I really prefer is the $10,000 to $15,000 jobs like we have with the greenhouses. They need racks to hold plants. They're easy for us to produce because all that we really need to do is cut and weld the metal.

So... all in all, even though consultants have said that we need to improve the "value added" part of our product line, it is just too risky to make roofs... or trailers. And the convention center project is just too big. To me, the consultants just seem to complicate things.

Maria believed that MetalBenders served their customers well. However, when she had met with the SBDC business counselor in January, he had also recommended that MetalBenders conduct a customer satisfaction study to gain feedback on their performance. Subsequently, during the winter semester of 2002, a group of students enrolled in a Small Business Management class at a nearby university were commissioned to conduct a customer satisfaction study for MetalBenders. The company furnished the names and contact information to the students; telephone interviews were conducted with thirty current customers during March of 2002. The purpose of the study was to collect information pertaining to customers' perceptions about quality, timeliness of installations, customer service, and so on.

Based on the interviews, the students found that over half of surveyed customers had been doing business with MetalBenders for more than five years. Most had initially become aware of the company through referrals or word-of-mouth. Nearly two-thirds of respondents stated that they were not aware that MetalBenders Industries was a certified minority-owned business. Research findings are shown in Exhibit 5.

Responses to open-ended questions revealed the following:

- *MetalBenders is always willing to take on our spur-of-the-moment jobs.*
- *We had to wait for MetalBenders to finish the job, they went past their deadline*
- *We would fax MetalBenders bids and never hear from them.*
- *MetalBenders is a good company… they do good work, but they're always late! I wish they could learn to deliver products on time.*
- *We've been very pleased with MetalBenders's products over the years. If José returned phone calls a little quicker, I'd be even happier.*
- *Communication is below average.*
- *MetalBenders is so anxious to please the customer that they don't say no to any job. Nothing's too small, or too inconvenient. We appreciate that!*
- *There may be a breakdown between the inside and outside staff.*

Manufacturing

MetalBenders Industries was organized into four divisions: Building Production, Store Fronts, Custom Production and Greenhouse (previously MetalFab). The Building Production encompassed fairly standardized products used architecturally, including items such as exterior trims, angles and similar products. However, the firm did not maintain finished goods inventory on them. Often the products varied in color, dimension, and/or thickness of material to fit the specific situation. The products were typically installed by roofers and carpenters. The Store Fronts division produced columns and window frames that were largely used as store fronts in shopping malls. Custom Production included a miscellany of products: frames for office modules, metal containers, storage boxes, shelving, and virtually everything that fell within MetalBenders's cutting, bending and welding capacity. The Greenhouse division produced large racks that were used by greenhouses to hold flats and pots for shipping, display, growing, and so on.

The physical layout of MetalBenders Industries' 16,000 square foot facility appears in Exhibit 6. Based on the process flow diagram, shipments of raw material were received in the rear of the manufacturing facility. They were then stored in inventory, with the more frequently used materials being stored closest to the respective machines.[7] When raw materials were needed, they passed through shears and brake presses until they were finished. As shown on the process flow chart, inventory required more space than production. Ted had suggested to Maria that perhaps MetalBinders should reduce the amount of inventory in storage. He also thought the company could order in smaller quantities to increase inventory turnover, free up production space, and help the plant become more organized. Labeling raw materials in inventory, he felt, would also be helpful in achieving a better process flow and overall organization.

In terms of quality, Ted believed that customers rated MetalBenders's quality highly, despite the fact that the company maintained no set standards for quality control and quality inspections were done only sporadically. Quality measurement was done by

---

[7] Less frequently used materials were stored high or in the back of the plant where convenient access was not as critical.

hand or using a tape measure, a far cry from the standard he knew was required for ISO 9000/9001 certification. Consequently, Ted believed that achieving ISO 9000/9001 certification (one of José's goals) was a "pie in the sky" idea… trying to improve quality control processes at MetalBenders, he thought, would be too expensive at present based on both feasibility and cost.

As Ted put it,

> The only value that we really add to projects is following the specs for architectural firms. Anybody could build greenhouse racks if they had the time, including the greenhouses themselves… which they often do!

> MetalBenders doesn't really have a "balanced scorecard" of production equipment. As an example, some of the bending and shearing equipment is very precise. It could easily perform standard operations and produce products to ISO 9000 standards. No problem. But the welding and hole drilling/punching equipment is another story. Our welders have to connect the pieces together without having jigs, holders, or other equipment that would be needed to insure consistency and accuracy. We also drill holes using hand presses. In fact, the dimensions are measured by hand, which means that we really don't have a good way to insure accuracy. So what it all boils down to is that quality control is a real hit-or-miss kind of thing. That's why I think ISO 9000 certification is not going to happen.

According to Mark,

> As far as I'm concerned, ISO 9000 is just another one of José's wild ideas. I wish he would open up his eyes and see what we're really capable of… when he goes out and sells jobs, he really doesn't have any idea what our capabilities are. Maria says he's valuable to us because he's great with ideas, but I just wish his head was screwed on a little better so he'd think about the follow-through before he opened his mouth. He could get us into a heap of trouble!

> Regarding ISO, I agree with what Ted says. So I sure hope that Maria doesn't forget to invite Ted to our next planning meeting, especially if José wants to talk about ISO again. Trying to get into ISO, a worldwide organization, when we cannot even serve our local customers is ridiculous! Ted knows our cost system is so crude, often nonexistent, that we have to ask our customers what they paid for the product last time in order to come up with a price for the item they're currently buying.

> Only Ted knows how to quote – based on his twenty years of past experience and some old data. When Ted is gone, nothing gets quoted. But even more embarrassing is when we do not meet the shipment dates and hold up an entire large construction project. This used to happen on occasion, but it seems it is becoming more frequent each year.

Financial Performance

During the last few years, MetalBenders Industries' sales ranged from $1.4 million to $1.7 million, meaning that the company teetered on the breakeven point of $1.5 million.[8] Within a given year, cash flow fluctuated greatly as the building business

---

[8] The accounting system currently used was purchased by William Brouwer in 1985.

was both seasonal and cyclical. Exhibits 7, 8 and 9 contain industry and company financial data. The major reason for the loss in 2000 was the increase in payroll expenses from adding José without a corresponding increase in revenue.

Regarding compensation, MetalBenders employees earned wages that were comparable within the industry. Maria drew a salary of $75,000. As she stated,

> I know I am being paid $75,000 per year from MetalBenders. But that is not all. José and I have become quite a couple in the Hispanic community. We do everything together and I love being seen with him. People expect us at all the major social events, including fundraisers. Most of these events are paid for by MetalBenders as corporate sponsorships. I am sure the total of these perks adds up to close to my salary. So I'm currently spending at about a $150,000/year level... and I don't want to cut back.

The firm contracted out a major portion of its labor. For the year just ended [2001], in fact, the company contracted out more labor than it had paid out to its own employees. According to Ted, the reason for this contracted labor was to ensure an adequate supply of installation labor for the construction contracts.

Options

According to Maria, MetalBenders is not making any money, so if I tried to sell the company, maybe the most I can expect for it "as is" is the asset value of about $800,000. Subtract from this the $300,000 that I owe Steven in Texas, and I would only have about $500,000 left. My retirement planner says I should only withdraw five or six percent, at most, from my fund. This would give me about $25,000 to $30,000 a year to live on... only about twenty percent of what I am currently spending! So selling the business right now doesn't look like a viable option for me.

> Somehow, I need to make this business worth about five times what it currently is doing so that I can sell it and retire. After all these years, I'm ready for a break... and I want to devote more time to my gardening! But what are we going to do?

Maria saw four options to generate additional revenue.

- Increase value-added. Consultants had suggested that MetalBenders needed to improve the "value added" part of the business and suggested making manufacturing roofs and trailers. Another idea that José had suggested was entering the roof shingles market with metal shingles that give the appearance of wooden shakes. He said this was a huge market as more and more Planned Unit Developments (PUDs) were phasing out wood shingles as a fire hazard. Once the shingles market was in place, he said, the value of the company could be increased due to more customer options, such as the large variety of designs and colors. José said this would increase MetalBenders's margins. Maria knew, though, that entering a new market or engaging in new product development could be risky. Was MetalBenders up to the challenge? Developing a new product would require the employees to be excited about the firm and its future. Were they?

- Pursue government contracts due to Michigan Minority Business Development Council certification. Should MetalBenders go after the convention center project? According to the SBDC counselor, because MetalBenders had achieved minority certification status in 2001, it could be the company's ticket to being awarded government contracts, or being selected as a subcontractor when general contractors bid on jobs that were public projects since general contractors were required to specify on bids whether subcontractors were unionized and minority. While Ted saw this as "a lot of paperwork to get jobs that we're nowhere capable of performing," it seemed to Maria that there was little risk associated with competing as a certified minority-owned business. After all, she was not only female (and already involved in the Association for Women Entrepreneurs [AWE]), but also Hispanic and partially disabled. Should they be more aggressive in "advertising" the business this way?

- Pursue ISO 9000/9001 certification. Maria saw this option as a means to an end if MetalBenders was wanted to go after business within the auto industry. José said the business could double if MetalBenders became ISO 9000/9001 certified. On the other hand, she knew that Ted was skeptical. Maria knew that Shirley[9] was trying to use the accounting package to produce more sophisticated analyses, but was still relatively new at analyzing the options. While Maria knew that other accounting systems allowed users to generate various reports (i.e., sales outstanding, sales growth, inventory turnover, as well as quarterly standings in comparison to liquidity, activity, leverage and profit ratios), they were basically accomplished manually.

- Revise internal policies. Although the sample size was small, Maria was concerned that half of their customers had chosen another company over MetalBenders for a particular job. Why was this? Was there something more they could do to keep customers loyal... perhaps offer cumulative quantity discounts in order to sell more to current customers? Or try to increase the turnaround time on jobs?

One additional possibility that Maria contemplated was the feasibility of expanding the physical plant. The SBDC counselor had advised that there were government loans and special tax exempt status available to minority firms. In fact, the two houses next door (zoned as commercial and already a part of the tax-free "Renaissance Zone")[10] were available. Maria knew that MetalBenders was desperately short on finished goods storage space; the houses could be torn down to make room for expansion. There was also a large old manufacturing building across the street that had been subleased into many small businesses. According to its owner, any and all operations in the building qualified for tax credits and other financial aid under the Small Business Incentives programs.

Maria knew, though, that in order to expand the company, she might need to acquire additional capital, which she was reluctant to do. "In this respect, José has become so much more 'Americanized' that me and he often teases me about the fact that I don't have one single credit card in my purse. 'Everybody in America has credit cards,' he tells me. 'Not me,' I tell him. That's not how I grew up." Since 1995, she had tried to operate on a cash basis and was very apprehensive about giving up any control of the company for fear of losing the company itself.

---

[9] Shirley was an outside consultant who worked for Lakeshore Bookkeeping Services. She did the payroll and prepared monthly financial statements for MetalBenders Industries, as well as a number of other firms.
[10] While MetalBenders had initiated a Renaissance Zone application, it was later dropped because Ted felt that it was "too much paperwork."

Puzzled over MetalBenders's lack of success since William's death, Maria conceded that the company clearly needed to increase sales as well as operate more efficiently. Since 1995, MetalBenders had consistently hovered at the breakeven point. But what would help to generate sales? Should they try to find a niche in which the company could operate profitably, as José advocated? The strategic planning meeting was only two days away. Maria conceded,

I just don't know what to think... or do. But I know one thing for certain... I'm getting older and it's time for me to retire and enjoy my life!

José says our best option is to go after the convention center job. Yet Mark and Ted aren't going to like that idea one bit... should I try to get them on-board? Of course, José also wants us to be ISO certified and to go after new markets. But would that be trying to do too much too soon? Are we ready for that?

Maybe what we really need is a good CEO who has more energy than I have! Steven would be ideal since he knows the industry, but I know that he and his family would never leave Texas. Ted knows the nuts and bolts of the business, but at 58 years, I know he's not interested... in fact, he already told me that. And while José is a dear, he's still learning the business... and he doesn't like operations and dealing with all the production issues.

If our payroll wasn't already so high, we could hire a CEO from the outside... I guess one idea would be to cut payroll. Should I encourage Ted to take early retirement and use that money to hire a CEO? José has been so good with going after new jobs... and says that he thinks there's a real chance we could get the convention center job. I just couldn't fire him... and Mark's salary isn't nearly enough to pay for a CEO.

Oh dear... I don't know what to think. I just wish William was still here so he could tell me what to do...

References

Cost trends: Metal prices drop. (2002, February). Plant Engineering, 56 (2), 96-97.

Grand Rapids Business Journal 2003 Book of Lists. (2003). Gemini Publications.

SIC Descriptions. (2002). U.S. Department of Labor, Occupational Safety & Health Administration, available at: http://www.osha.gov/oshstats/sicser.html

Singh, Hari and Nancy Boese. (2002, Winter). West Michigan Economic Forecast 2002, Seidman Business Review, Vol. 8, 3-6.

Today's metals, tomorrow's prices. (2002, March 14). Supply Management, 7 (6), 34-36.

Exhibit 1

Company TimeLine
(Source: Company Records)

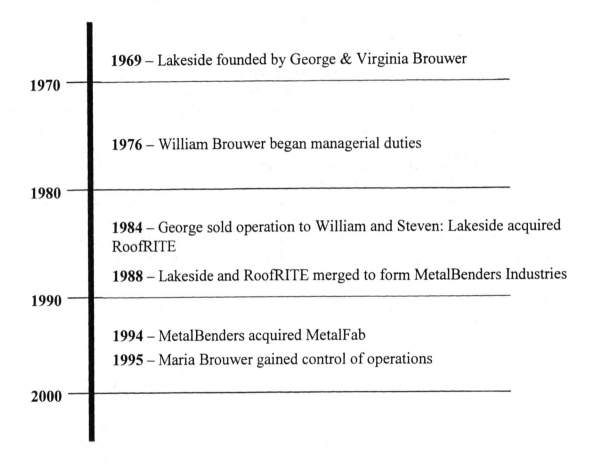

1969 – Lakeside founded by George & Virginia Brouwer

1970

1976 – William Brouwer began managerial duties

1980

1984 – George sold operation to William and Steven: Lakeside acquired RoofRITE

1988 – Lakeside and RoofRITE merged to form MetalBenders Industries

1990

1994 – MetalBenders acquired MetalFab

1995 – Maria Brouwer gained control of operations

2000

Exhibit 2

Corporate Objectives
(Source: Company Records)

- Sales growth. Expand the business while developing technology and providing employees with a future. MetalBenders's long-term goal was to double sales, add 5-6 employees, and add a second shift.

- Become ISO 9000 certified.

- Build a strong relationship with suppliers.

- Expand to new product markets.

- Use minority status as a competitive advantage in order to obtain government contracts.[11]

- Build a team-working environment between employees and management.

- Target original equipment manufacturers (OEMs) for longer-run jobs in order to stay productive year-round.

- Research the possibility of entering the medical manufacturing market.

---

[11] The SBDC business counselor advised Maria that minority certification could a competitive advantage for conducting business with government contracts since the U.S. government required five percent of all U.S. procurement spending should be awarded to women-owned businesses. Contractors needed to validate their use of minority owned businesses for the completion of the government contract. Maria was told that being minority certified, however, was not enough for developing ongoing relationships – quality products, meeting deadlines, and a strong business acumen were still necessary.

Exhibit 3
Competitive Grid
(Source: Company Records)

	Trusty Sheet Metal	Better Sheet Metal Company	Spartan Sheet Metal	MetalBenders Industries
Services:	Standard roofing, wall panels, E P Md trim	Buy products (roofing, gutters) and install for builders	Metal Fabrication/ Job Shop	Metal fabrication and roofs
Structure:		James Better	N/A	Owner Maria Brouwer
Online Quote:	No	No	No	No
Specialty:	Architectural sheet metal	None defined	Custom Fabrication	Custom Fabrication and metal roofs
Reputation:	High quality, associated with leading businesses	Member of the Better Business Bureau	Small job shop	Member of Michigan Minority Business Development Council (MMBDC)
Level of Service:	Custom building fabrication & installation	On-time delivery, Highest quality	Low	Low
Competitive Advantage:	High quality product in the fastest way possible	Member of the Better Business Bureau for over a decade	None	Minority Status
Advertising & Promotion:	Only phonebook, and word of mouth	Brochure	Only phonebook	Phonebook
Manufacturing space: (sq. ft.)	8,000	20,000	12,500	16,000
Number of Employees:	15	10	20	12
CAD options:	Not at present; tried but unsuccessful	No	No	Yes, have equipment but do not use
OS-9000 or ISO-9001:	No	No	No	Seeking
Website:	No	No	None	No
Minority Status	No	No	No	Yes
Competitors:	Better, RoofRITE	RoofRITE	Not known	All listed
Years in Business:	18	55	40	33

Exhibit 4
Organizational Chart
(Source: Company Records)

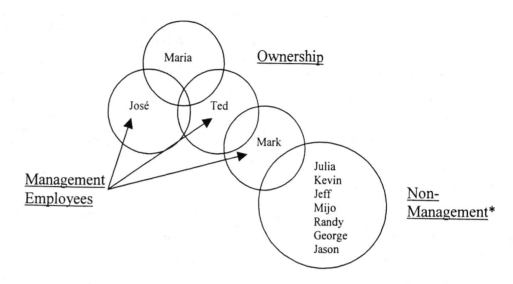

Note: All non-management employees reported directly to Mark, MetalBenders's Production Manager.

Exhibit 5
Customer Research Results
(Source: Students' Research Report)

How long has your company done business with MetalBenders?				
	Frequency	**Percent**	**Valid Percent**	**Cumulative Percent**
Less than one year	4	13.3	13.3	13.3
One to two years	5	16.7	16.7	30.0
Three to five years	4	13.3	13.3	43.3
More than five years	17	56.7	56.7	100.0
Total	30	100.0	100.0	

How did your company originally become aware of MetalBenders?				
	Frequency	**Percent**	**Valid Percent**	**Cumulative Percent**
Yellow Pages advertising	1	3.3	3.3	3.3
Referral	8	26.7	26.7	30.0
Word-of-mouth	9	30.0	30.0	60.0
Other	12	40.0	40.0	100.0
Total	30	100.0	100.0	

Are you aware that MetalBenders is a certified minority owned business and a member of the Michigan Minority Business Development Council?				
	Frequency	**Percent**	**Valid Percent**	**Cumulative Percent**
Yes	9	30.0	30.0	30.0
No	19	63.3	63.3	93.3
Was aware that MetalBenders was minority owned but not certified	2	6.7	6.7	100.0
Total	30	100.0	100.0	

How important are each of the following factors to you in making purchasing decisions? *(valid percentages shown)*						
	Price	**Quality**	**Timeliness**	**Minority-Owned**	**After Sales Service**	**Past Experiences**
Highly important	36.0	76.9	60.9		4.2	26.1
Somewhat important	24.0	11.5	17.4	5.3	33.3	26.1
Indifferent / Neutral	28.0	11.5	17.4	21.1	25.0	34.8
Somewhat unimportant	8.0			42.1	33.4	13.0
Not important at all	4.0		4.3	31.6	4.2	

How satisfied are you with MetalBenders's performance with respect to... ? *(valid percentages shown)*						
	Price	Quality	Installation	Timeliness of Installation	Customer Relations	Product Knowledge	Communications with Customers
Highly satisfied	28.6	50.0	21.4	21.4	50.0	57.1	46.2
Somewhat satisfied	39.3	35.7	42.9	35.7	20.8	21.4	23.1
Average	32.1	14.4	35.7	35.7	29.2	21.4	26.9
Somewhat dissatisfied				7.1			3.8
Highly dissatisfied							

How satisfied are you with MetalBenders's <u>competitors'</u> performance with respect to... ? *(valid percentages shown)*						
	Price	Quality	Installation	Timeliness of Installation	Customer Relations	Product Knowledge	Communications with Customers
Highly satisfied	21.4	41.7	28.6	28.6	27.3	27.3	16.7
Somewhat satisfied	50.0	41.7	57.1	42.9	45.5	45.5	50.0
Average	21.4	8.3	14.3	28.6	27.3	27.3	33.3
Somewhat dissatisfied	7.1	8.3					
Highly dissatisfied							

In general, when selecting a supplier or installer, how important are each of the following factors? *(valid percentages shown)*							
	Best Price	High Quality	On-time Delivery & Installation	Product Availability	Customer Service	Sales Staff Knowledge	Communications with Customers	Sales Presentation
Highly important	42.9	76.1	66.7	71.4	66.6	42.8	57.1	36.8
Somewhat important	27.6	19.0	33.3	23.8	23.8	47.6	28.5	31.6
Indifferent / Neutral	28.6	4.8		4.8	4.8	9.5		21.0
Somewhat unimportant							14.3	
Not important at all					4.8			10.5

Based on your company's observations, how would you rate MetalBenders's employees' internal teamworking skills?				
	Frequency	Percent	Valid Percent	Cumulative Percent
Excellent	8	26.7	50.0	50.0
Good	4	13.3	25.0	75.0
Average	3	10.0	18.8	93.7
Fair				
Poor	1	3.3	6.3	100.0
Total	16	53.3	100.0	
Missing	14	46.7		
Total	30	100.0		

Based on your company's observations, how would you rate MetalBenders's employees' internal communication skills?				
	Frequency	Percent	Valid Percent	Cumulative Percent
Excellent	9	30.0	60.0	60.0
Good	4	13.3	26.7	86.7
Average	1	3.3	6.7	93.4
Fair				
Poor	1	3.3	6.7	100.0
Total	15	50.0	100.0	
Missing	15	50.0		
Total	30	100.0		

Has your company chosen another company over MetalBenders for particular work?				
	Frequency	Percent	Valid Percent	Cumulative Percent
Yes	12	40.0	50.0	50.0
No	12	40.0	50.0	100.0
Total	24	80.0	100.0	
Missing	6	20.0		
Total	30	100.0		

Exhibit 6
Process Flow of Most Popular Products
(Source: Company Records)

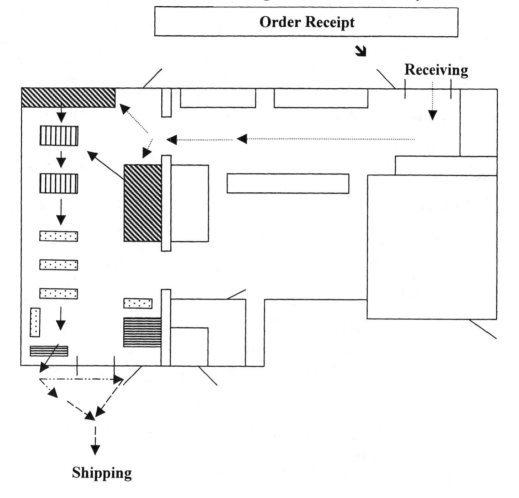

Customer Design Specifications

↓↑ *Discussion/negotiation/finalization of specs; explore using existing raw materials inventory*

Order Receipt

Receiving

Shipping

KEY:

Most Popular Raw Materials Inventory	▨	Flow From Receiving to Stock ⋯▶
Other Inventory[a] ▭		Flow Between Equipment ──▶
Shears ▥		Flow From Equipment to Stock ─·─▶
Break Presses ⬚		Flow From Stock to Shipping ──▶
Most Popular Finished Goods Inventory ▤		

[a] *This included both raw materials (75%) and finished goods (25%). The limited storage space could be a capacity bottleneck.*

Exhibit 7
Selected Industry Ratios
(Source: Robert Morris Associates)

	1999 Industry	2000 Industry	2001 Industry	2001 Industry $1-3MM
Current Ratio	1.7	1.7	1.7	1.6
Quick Ratio	1.0	1.1	1.2	1.2
Inventory Turnover	9.9	10.5	11.3	15.8
Cost of Sales/Payables	15.1	14.9	12.9	13.9
Times Covered	3.5	3.8	3.7	3.5
Sales/Total Assets	2.4	2.3	2.3	2.4
Sales/Receivables	8.2	8.0	7.7	8.6
Gross Profit Margin	29.1	29.0	29.8	37.0

Exhibit 8
MetalBenders Industries, Inc. Balance Sheet as of October 31
(in $)
(Source: Company Records)

	2001	2000	1999
Assets			
Current Assets			
Cash	99,527	89,400	76,300
Acc. Receivable	332,045	255,870	211,797
Inventory	98,128	112,730	84,903
Total Current Assets	529,700	458,000	373,000
Fixed Assets	303,300	337,000	374,000
Total Assets	**833,000**	**795,000**	**747,000**
Liabilities and Equity			
Current Liabilities	212,049	204,613	140,921
Notes Payable	515,951	622,166	605,881
Total Liabilities	728,000	826,779	746,802
<u>Equity</u>			
Stockholders' Equity	516,000	516,000	516,000
Retained Earnings	(411,000)	(547,779)	(515,802)
Total Equity	105,000	(31,779)	198
Total Liabilities & Equity[a]	**833,000**	**795,000**	**747,000**

[a] *It is unknown whether Maria owns all of this or it is shared with Steven. Maria would not divulge this information.*

Exhibit 9
Income Information – Fiscal Year Ending October 31
(Source: Company Records)

Annual Fiscal Year Profit:

	1999	2000	2001
Sales:	$1,636,079.65	$1,445,201.64	$1,718,987.45
Total Cost of Sales:	$1,276,116.88	$1,167,277.53	$1,299,352.04
Gross Profit:	$359,962.77	$277,924.11	$419,635.41
Total sales & admin. Expense:	$264,394.82	$279,129.51	$210,101.74
Income from operations:	$95,567.95	$(1,205.40)	$209,533.67
Total Other Income:	$(17,909.27)	$(34,771.63)	$(13,254.27)
Net Income before Taxes:	$77,658.68	$(35,977.03)	$196,279.40
Total Income Tax Expense:	$13,500.25	$(4,000.00)	$59,500.00
Net Income:	**$64,158.43**	**$(31,977.03)**	**$136,779.40**

Quarterly Profit for Fiscal Year 2001 ending Oct 31:

	31-Jan-01	30-Apr-01	31-Jul-01	31-Oct-01
Sales:	$321,880.45	$284,149.14	$460,226.49	$652,731.37
Total Cost of Sales:	$261,814.53	$226,860.11	$329,729.35	$480,948.05
Gross Profit:	$60,065.92	$57,289.03	$130,497.14	$171,783.32
Total sales & admin. Expense:	$50,911.80	$43,282.64	$41,723.49	$74,183.81
Income from operations:	$9,154.12	$14,006.39	$88,773.65	$97,599.51
Total Other Income:	$859.77	$(3,699.18)	$(3,589.35)	$(6,825.51)
Net Income before Taxes:	$10,013.89	$10,307.21	$85,184.30	$90,774.00
Total Income Tax Expense:	$-	$-	$-	$59,500.00
Net Income:	**$10,013.89**	**$10,307.21**	**$85,184.30**	**$31,274.00**

Exhibit 10
ISO 9000 Certification[12]

"ISO 9000 is about standardizing the approach organizations everywhere take to managing and improving the process that ultimately result in their products and services. This is different from simply conforming to a specification for a specific level of quality.

ISO is not a European organization, although it is based in Geneva, Switzerland. Nor is ISO an agent of any government or federation of governments. When ISO was established in 1947, the American National Standards Institute (ANSI) was a founding member. ANSI is one of the five permanent members of ISO's governing council, and one of four permanent members of ISO's Technical Management Board. ISO is a worldwide organization."

"The fact that we have a high degree of standardization has made life simpler in ways so basic and so obvious that we do not realize they exist. It has given us the free national market which we take so casually. To you, as end man, the American consumer, it has given lower prices and better quality, more safety, greater availability, prompter exchange and repair service, and all other material advantages of mass production. Is this something to be taken for granted?"
                    -- *W. Edwards Deming*

---

[12] Goetsch, D.L. and Davis, S.B. (2000). Understanding and Implementing ISO 9000, 2nd ed. Upper Saddle River, NJ: Prentice-Hall.

Exhibit 11
A Note on Hispanic Culture[13]

Two well-accepted and widely used measures of culture are the dimensions identified by Hostede and Trompenaars. Hofstede's cultural dimensions are: *power distance* – the extent to which less powerful members of institutions and organizations accept that power is distributed unequally; *uncertainty avoidance* – the extent to which people feel threatened by ambiguous situations and have created beliefs and institutions that avoid these; *individualism* – the tendency of people to look after themselves and their immediate family only, versus *collectivism* – the tendency of people to below to groups or collectives and to look after each other in exchange for loyalty; and *masculinity* – the degree to which motivational behavior is associated with value systems as described in masculine versus feminine terms.

Using Hofstede's framework, we can classify the Hispanic culture as follows: large power distance, strong uncertainty avoidance, collectivist, and masculine. In this culture, formal hierarchical authority is respected, and employees seldom violate a chain of command or openly question decisions by superiors. The culture also endorses group harmony, social order, and family relationships. Finally, gender roles are clearly specified: men are generally expected to hold the primary jobs and women are expected to remain at home and raise families. Male offspring are groomed for work roles, while female children are relegated to supporting roles.

The key cultural dimensions identified by Trompenaars are: *universalism* – the belief that ideas and practices can be applied everywhere in the world without modification, versus *particularism* – the belief that circumstances dictate how ideas and practices should be applied and something cannot be done the same everywhere; *communitarianism* – which refers to people regarding themselves as part of a group; *neutral* – a culture where emotions are held in check, versus *affective* – where emotions are expressed openly and naturally; *specific* – where individuals have a large public space they readily share with others and a small private space they guard closely and share only with close friends and relatives, versus *diffuse* – where both public and private space are similar in size and individuals guard their public space carefully, because entry into public space affords entry into private space as well; *achievement* – where people are accorded status based on how well they perform their functions, versus *ascription* – where status is attributed based on who or what a person is.

In contrast to Hofstede's classification of Hispanics as being collectivist, Trompenaars puts them as being more individualistic rather than communitarian. As far as other Trompenaars' dimensions go, Hispanics can be classified as: particularistic, affective, diffuse, and achievement oriented.

---

[13] While Hispanic and Mexican are not interchangeable terms, this exhibit uses cultural variables specific to Mexico since that is the culture that the key decision maker, Maria Brouwer, comes from. Sources: Holt and Wigginton, International Management, 2nd edition, Harcourt, 2002; and Hodgetts and Luthans, International Management, 5th edition, Mc-Graw Hill, 2003.

CASE STUDY 3

NEGOTIATING WITH THE CHINESE: CHINESE TIGER BARRELS IN THE CALIFORNIA WINE INDUSTRY

In a Napa Valley, California restaurant

It was May 18, 2001, and Erik Lynn, sole owner and sole salesperson of American Consolidated Barrels, an importer of wine barrels and wood products, was sitting at a Napa Valley restaurant. He had just struggled through a negotiation with his Chinese supplier, Director Wang Chan of the Forestry Division of the Kweilin Forestry Bureau, about problems with the wine barrels Lynn had received from them five months prior. Yu Wen, the Oregon-based, independent wood broker who had introduced Lynn to the Chinese almost two years before, had also been present. For the past year and a half Lynn had dealt with the Kweilin Forestry Bureau, a division of the Chinese Government, to secure a business deal to sell Chinese Tiger Barrels in the California winery market. Lynn had come to the meeting angry because he felt he had been cornered into a purchase that had stuck him with prepaid inventory of 40 faulty barrels shipped from China in December, 2000. Every new Tiger Barrel leaked from the sides and corners as it made its debut into the California market.

Less than two years ago at the first negotiation, Lynne had been on Chinese turf and had let the Chinese control the whole visit. Feeling pressured by all the attention the Chinese bestowed upon him, Lynn had signed an agreement that he later regretted. This time, Lynn turned the tables by setting the agenda and booking a table at a modest local restaurant.

The meeting with Wang and Yu had been surprisingly cordial and conciliatory. Yu, acting as interpreter, had successfully conveyed the congenial atmosphere that Wang wished to establish. Over lunch Wang had discussed the sales contract both parties had signed in China. He reminded Lynn of the second-year quantity of 300 barrels that Lynn had committed to order for shipment before the September 2001 harvest. Lynn had complained that he had not yet been able to deliver to his customers any of the forty barrels that he purchased in the first year of the contract due to their unacceptable quality. All forty barrels had major repairs to undergo, and the barrel repairman Lynn hired had not been able to fix them yet. A distressed Lynn explained with that he was stuck with paid inventory, a future repair bill and advertising expenses, yet no sales revenue.

Wang had replied, "Our two parties have committed a lot of energy and time to this project; we must both remain committed to making it work." Wang emphasized that they trusted Lynn's technical expertise and that it was unfortunate that the first attempt was not a success but that Lynn could trust them to correct the situation. Wang reminded Lynn that both parties had committed to establishing and maintaining a long-term relationship when they signed the business deal. Due to this commitment, Lynn could expect that the barrels would soon improve in quality.

Lynn had argued that American Consolidated Barrels was not a large enough company to support these setbacks. He had invested $6,000 in advertising, which included ads placed in four major wine journals. The forty barrels paid in advance had cost him $16,400 and the ongoing repairs to the shipped barrels would be about $4,000,

During the meeting Wang had repeated his conviction that once winemakers tried the Tiger Barrels there would be many return customers no matter what the price. Yet Lynn insisted that price was indeed a factor if they wanted to move any amount of barrels in the future. He couldn't justify trying any longer to sell the barrels at $450, a price too close to the current pricing of French barrels, the best quality barrels used in the U.S.which also benefited from favorable exchange rates. Lynn was covering all of his costs with gross profits of only $20 per barrel; he normally grossed between $60 and $110 per barrel.

Prior to the meeting, Lynn had concluded the chances of the project succeeding were dwindling and had almost decided not to commit more time and money to it. But before making a final decision, Lynn had wanted to see how his Chinese business associates would address both the faulty barrel quality and the mounting repair bills. In the meeting, Wang had graciously offered to pay for the barrel repairs. He was so convinced of the future success of his barrels in the U.S. market and obligated to his long-term relationship to Lynn that he had also promised to be flexible about the upcoming year's contracted order quantity so that Lynn would continue the venture.

At the end of the meeting, Lynn had delayed making commitments to buy more product until he received reimbursement for barrel repairs. Even if these problems were resolved to his satisfaction, he would still initiate more negotiation regarding more favorable terms for shipments, pricing, and payments.

After the Chinese had left the luncheon, Lynn sat back down by himself to think about his business. What had motivated him to attempt this novel project as the sole owner of a small business? Was this too big and risky a venture for his small business? Should he have attempted his first foray into the international marketplace singlehandedly? What had he done right to make it work? What had he done wrong? Could he trust the Chinese to correct the quality problems? Could he trust the contract that Yu had convinced him to sign? Could he trust the Chinese about anything? If the quality of the barrels were improved, was the deal financially viable for him to pursue? Would the Chinese truly work with him to create a deal that worked for Lynn as Yu had indicated?

The wine barrel industry in California

The California wine industry was first established in the 1700's when Spanish missionaries traveled north from Mexico. The industry continued to develop as many European explorers and gold diggers turned to winemaking. Most of the historical wineries still standing today were founded by Germans, French, and Italians. These strong European roots combine the ancient practices of winemaking with modern science. Since 1990 the U.S. has become the fourth largest producer of wine in the world, with California contributing 95% of the nation's

46

production.

Oak barrels became a very important part of the California wine industry beginning in the 1980's. The fascination of California winemakers with new barrels was based on their desire to emulate the European top growths, or top wine houses, by making wines in the old European way. In Bordeaux, where the most prestigious Cabernet Sauvignon wines come from, and in Burgundy, where arguably the best Chardonnay wines originate, the top wineries use new oak barrels. Wine not only attributes its flavor characteristics to the grape source but also to the environment in which it is stored, traditionally a 55 gallon oak barrel. Barrels offer complex flavor compounds, comparable to spices used in very complex recipes, that are extracted into the wine over time. The cost to attain these aromas and flavors, however, is only allotted to wines that can justify them, wines priced at $20 and more per bottle. This high-priced segment of the California wine market had been growing between 10% and 20% since the mid 1990's; therefore, there was a growing need for barrels.

In 1999, the wine barrel industry sold about 200,000 French barrels; 200,000 American barrels; and about 20,000 Eastern European barrels to California vintners. Total barrel sales revenue that year was about $135 million to the California wine industry, whose wine wholesale revenue was valued at $3 billion. Barrels represented a large part of a winery's budget so finding less expensive sources was important. Low pricing of American oak kept many American oak barrels in place at wineries that continued to believe that any 55 gallon oak barrel was better than none. Hungarian and Eastern European barrels offered flavors similar to French barrels, and these were sold as an upgrade to American oak. The price of the Eastern European barrels was strategically placed between the American and French barrels because the market could bear the higher cost for them, although the raw product and labor costs were largely reduced compared to French and American barrels.

In 2000, the Eastern European and American barrel prices were pushed as high as the market could bear in order to compete with French barrels. Barrels fetched as much as $600 for a French barrel, $420 for an Eastern European, and $200-300 for an American oak barrel. As the barrel price declined, the wine aged in them developed flavors considered less favorable, more one-dimensional, than wines aged in French barrels.

Interestingly, barrel production costs show a similar breakdown regardless of origin. This breakdown is approximately the following: one third raw wood, one third construction of the barrel, and one third sales costs including marketing and transportation. French forests, managed by the French government, are considerably more expensive to harvest than American private forests where clear-cutting is permitted. The labor in France is unionized, so barrel construction costs are high. Transport to California is expensive as well. Profit margins on French barrels are very high in the US compared to the other wine markets of the world because of high demand; thus they are proportionately more expensive than American barrels.

Barrels have always been hand-made at a barrel manufacturing plant, called a cooperage, by assembling pre-cut staves into a ring shape, adding the hoops or metal rings around the outside, bending the staves over a fire, and then placing the headboards into the two ends. French and Eastern European wood is split with a maul; American oak is sawn. Only two French barrels are made from one cubic yard of wood, whereas five American barrels are produced with the same amount of wood.

47

French oak barrels are accepted as the highest standard for winemaking in California. This confidence in French barrel quality persists even as economic considerations has led many producers of less expensive wines to shift toward less costly American oak barrels. With a strong attraction to create the most elegant wines in the world comes the desire to experiment with old and new techniques. Each winemaker normally tests independently the idea of a new method or material that could make a more interesting or complex flavored product.

Barrels are sold through a variety of distribution channels in the California wine industry. The largest US and French cooperages have established their own production facilities almost exclusively in Napa and Sonoma Counties, for example, to produce, market, and repair their barrels. They hire their own salespeople who are paid a salary and commission on what is sold. This is the least risky compensation arrangement for the salesperson but also the most financially limiting.

Smaller producers hire local sales people as agents who are paid on commission. Sometimes expenses and a small salary are included since barrel sales are very competitive and market development is time consuming. The salesperson is independent but carries minimal risk, and their financial cap is set by the manufacturer.

Some individuals act as "brokers" (distributors); they take title to the product and handle all the activity from the production facility to the final destinations. Handling the importation and storage is a risk, but it can double or triple the $50,000 to $80,000 yearly income that a successful agent can expect to make.

Barrels from overseas are imported in closed containers. They can be 20 or 40 foot containers, the most economical being a 40 foot container which holds around 150 barrels. A 20 foot container holds about 70 barrels. Transport costs for a 40 foot container are about $3,000 to bring in from France, compared to about $2,500 for a 20 foot container. Once product cost, shipping and insurance are accounted for, the total outlay for a 40 foot container of barrels averages about $60,000.

The fact that barrels contribute to and alter wine flavors makes liability issues a serious risk. If a barrel damages 55 gallons of wine worth $20 per gallon, and if this wine is blended into other wines, the damage claim can be astronomical. No small American-based distributor would want to be the target of a financial claim, so extensive insurance is required. To compensate for these risks, however, distributors enjoy considerably higher financial rewards than agents who work only on commission.

American Consolidated Barrels, owned by Erik Lynn, sold about 1,500 barrels in 2000. This represented about 0.3% of the total California market.

American Consolidated Barrels, LLC

Erik Lynn, born into a diplomatic family, grew up around the world. His father served as ambassador to several African countries during Lynn's childhood. Living abroad for many years, Lynn felt comfortable interacting with many cultures. He graduated from Harvard University in 1981 and then received an International Business Degree from The Fletcher School of Law and Diplomacy in Boston in 1985 where he became a skillful negotiator and communicator. Lynn applied his skills to the corporate world after graduation but dropped out in

Prepared by Erica Louise Harrop, Sarah Louise Dove, Duane Dove, and Wingham Liddell of Sonoma State University the basis for class discussion rather than to illustrate either effective or ineffective handling of an administrative situation. Reprinted with permission from Erica Louise Harrop, Sarah Louise Dove, Duane Dove, and Wingham Liddell. Copyright 2003 by Erica Louise Harrop, Sarah Louise Dove, Duane Dove, and Wingham Liddell. All rights reserved.

1992, unsatisfied with the limited opportunities that large organizations offered for exercising creativity.

Lynn moved to Sonoma and Napa Counties where he began working for wineries and their suppliers. In 1996, he joined Parrelle Barrels, a small importer of barrels from a French cooperage. This was late in the game when the marketplace was nearly saturated with barrel salespeople; Parrelle was the 25th French cooperage to enter the California wine market was rather disconcerting. Only a few wineries had ever bought Parrelle barrels in the past, so making inroads was very challenging. A record grape crop in 1997 gave Lynn his break; a shortage of barrels allowed him the opportunity to make some important sales. Due to Parrelle's poor barrel craftsmanship, however, 30% of Lynn's existing customers failed to reorder in subsequent years. Too many barrels leaked, and the winemakers would not tolerate a second bad experience even if the barrels sold to them were quickly repaired. Fighting to be added as a barrel supplier to a winery was a very tough task, especially when it was difficult to present a consistent list of satisfied references.

Lynn purchased Parrelle Barrels in 1998 for only $12,000. He renamed it American Consolidated Barrels and created an LLC because of the flexibility it offered if the company grew. The real cost to Lynn was the outlay of capital amounting to about $700,000, required each barrel delivery season, which lasts from August to December. Lynn's annual sales from 1998 to 2000 were ten to twelve containers, each valued at $60,000 and each containing about 150 barrels. Lynn was required to secure a bank line of credit for $150,000 against his personal assets, his home and property. He negotiated with the cooperage to have 90-day terms ex-works for payment. Lynn was responsible for the transport as well. He paid upfront all the transport fees, and the liability for shipment was his responsibility. Early in the grape harvest season Lynn had no problems paying the cooperage. Later, however, the wineries were busy with the grape harvest and would pay Lynn late, making it difficult for him to pay the cooperage after the third or fourth container. Lynn was one of a few American entrepreneurial salespeople who established distributorship agreements with cooperages, but this is rare as buying and reselling barrels requires a great deal of investment. Lynn could be extended $300,000 at any one time if the harvest were late.

Currency issues were a major factor for the Parrelle products during the barrel selling season, March through November as customer prices were based not only on margins but also on the currency rate. The barrels were paid for in French francs and Lynn bought forwards in order to minimize his risk. This allowed him a floating average in his currency exchange so he could move prices up or down during the selling season. During the first years he found the tendency was for the dollar to get stronger during the delivery season so delaying his full coverage seemed to benefit him. Lynn also had seen the prices drop 15% between 1999 and 2000 as the US dollar gained against the French Franc.

Following his marketing strategy to offer "the one-stop shop for all your oak aging needs", Lynn began looking for a lower-end product to sell to the larger wineries who did not use high grade French oak. He diversified his product line in 1999 by becoming sole U.S. agent for Duxon Timbers, an Australian manufacturer of oak inserts and chips. The fact that there was little competition in oak inserts made this product a valuable addition to his line. Inserts are planks put into old oak barrels or stainless tanks that impart flavors to the wines similar to what new barrels might extract. Not every winery could afford expensive oak barrels to enhance the flavors of their wine and this was a relatively new method to add wood flavors to wine. Duxon oak inserts could be sold to wineries whose wines were going to retail at $10 and less a bottle, a segment estimated at more than 80 percent of the world consumer wine market in 1999. The added cost of the oak inserts to the wine was about one fifth the cost of a real oak barrel.

Duxon inserts were an immediate success in the market. Strictly commission-based, they limited Lynn's risk, but he would not be able to base his future income on these sales because they were inexpensive products with low margins. The products were sold to customers in US dollars, and customer pricing was more elastic due to the favorable currency exchange.

Lynn continued to sell Parrelle barrels, his original product, because even though sales were static between 1997 and 2000, he could still make a very good living off this product. Duxon Timbers contributed only a small part of American Consolidated Barrells' net revenue due to the small rate of commissions Lynn could make from this product, but the sale of the products was going exceedingly well. To round out his product line Lynn began looking for a middle range product to complement his high priced French barrel and the lower priced Australian product.

The Tiger Barrel project

One day in the fall of 1999 Lynn received a letter from a wood broker, Yu Wen of FineWood Imports, a large Oregon-based producer of high quality carved furniture and other wood products which were exported around the world. Yu, the liaison between China and American-based distributors, inquired about Lynn's possible interest in selling a new line of oak barrels into the California market. She explained that the Chinese oak grown by the Chinese was the same genus as the white oak sold for American and French barrels. Lynn had once seen some Chinese oak but only a very few barrels were ever released into the American market due to their very inferior craftsmanship. No one, it seemed, knew about the flavors the wood might offer. Lynn's interest was piqued because this unique and enticing product would complete his product line.

Lynn accepted Yu's invitation and began working with the Kweilin Forestry Bureau, the source of FineWood's products, with the goal of becoming the sole US broker, in spite of being a small business, for the new Chinese wood product, the Tiger Barrel. He initiated a preliminary analysis of the quality of the Chinese wood by sending pieces of the wood to be scientifically studied at one of the French Cognac Houses. The results showed that the wood was of high grade with many aroma qualities, much like Eastern European oak which is considered almost as good as French. In fact, the laboratory mistook the Chinese wood for Eastern European oak due to the similarity of its physical structure to French oak. With this in mind, Lynn informed Yu that the Chinese company would need to follow French, not American, wood stave-making procedures by splitting, not sawing the wood. He told Yu that if the Chinese were serious about selling their product, they would put aside split oak immediately so that it could air dry in time for the upcoming year's barrel production. Pleased with his interest in the Tiger Barrel, Yu sent a letter of intent to work with Lynn on an exclusive basis.

At Yu's request, Lynn called his contacts in France and for a few months worked on sourcing barrel-making machinery to use in the Chinese barrel-splitting mill. Lynn devoted much time to research and the writing of numerous proposals only to be informed later by Yu that the Chinese had already reverse-engineered and manufactured all the wood splitting equipment they would need.

In the following summer of 2000, Director Wang Chan, the second most senior person at the Kweilin Forestry Bureau, asked Lynn to come to China to assist in the making of the barrels. Wang assumed Lynn would pay his own way since he was to be the distributor but Lynn thought the opposite as he was providing value to the Chinese by helping them with the barrel making. Lynn replied that he would come only if they paid to bring both him and a cooper, a professional in the barrel-making field. They haggled for three months with the Chinese winning in the end: Lynn would pay for the trip to China on his own. This quarrel postponed the planned trip three months at which time the French barrel master Lynn had lined up to work with him in China would now not be available.

Upon Lynn's arrival in Beijing, a young student translator, a relative of a manager in Kweilin, and a chauffeur helped him around Beijing the first day. He was booked into a Chinese hotel, located a block off the main avenue, not in one of the major western-style hotels situated conveniently in the center of town. The next day he traveled by plane to the farthest part of Eastern China, a four-hour flight; then he was driven seven hours by a plain-clothed, non-English speaking driver to the headquarters of the Kweilin Forestry Bureau. Upon Lynn's departure from the factory to the airport five days later the same driver showed up in his People's Republic of China (PRC) party military outfit.

Lynn had been notified by the Chinese that he would find a "surprising abundance of food" in China which was a way of introducing him to the lush agricultural region in which the Forestry Bureau was located. Wang and Yu, who continued to act as a liaison, greeted Lynn upon his arrival to headquarters and escorted him for the five days Lynn had budgeted to spend in China.

Lynn offered as a gift to Wang his American Consolidated Barrels baseball cap which Wang wore with pride many times during the visit. He was interviewed on local television and given tours of the town, which included a hospital, schools and stores run by the Forestry Bureau. Wang arranged for a professional video to be made of the five-day visit which he gifted with pride to Lynn upon his departure.

The busy days began at 7 in the morning and were highlighted by lavish banquets each day at both noon and in the early evening which lasted for hours each. Large amounts of spirits and rich foods were consumed. During the highly ceremonious meals, the Chinese officials toasted Lynn often, underlining the importance of the new union of friendship and trust between themselves and the small American business and the prosperity that would soon follow. The atmosphere was very friendly but very businesslike at all times.

Numerous meetings were held with many managers and officials of the state to discuss points of the business deal. Lynn did not know who the endless stream of managers and officials were but was told that one director was in charge of the Foreign Relations Department. Later Yu explained that this person was the government PRC party representative. Upon being questioned, Lynn discovered that the man knew little of foreign affairs. Many meetings seemed only to be formalities as topics and principles were discussed in a very general nature.

51

At the barrel-making factory during work hours, Lynn noted that although the laborers worked hard to assemble a barrel, the equipment was subpar and often quite dangerous. He was amazed by the number of people, at least 10 at any time, who worked on a single barrel, each holding one part of the whole barrel as it was assembled. Normally one person made a barrel in France. The major flaw he was not prepared for was that although the wood had been split as requested, a large amount would not meet the quality standard he needed. Accompanied by a translator, he toured the wood park with the barrel workers, explaining to them why barrels leaked and how leaks could be predicted from poor choice of wood. He helped the workers to sort the wood by proper grain structure. Notes for future use were taken copiously by Wang's personal secretary although her English was very rudimentary. In the end, Lynn was impressed by the crude but effective way barrels were being made. He was convinced the Chinese could match the workmanship of the French coopers.

Wang asked Lynn to assist in translating the notes taken by Wang's secretary into production guidelines which would later be used as a training tool for the employees once Lynn departed. Lynn saw no harm in doing this as he was confident his training was sufficient enough to be able to provide guidelines, and because the Chinese knew he was not a professional cooper.

Lynn, suffering jet lag the whole five days, struggled to keep up with the demanding schedule of entertainment, sightseeing, and dining. Not able to speak Chinese, he felt awkward most of the time and counted the days to his departure. Much friendliness was exhibited during banquets and sightseeing, but a very forceful, aggressive stance was displayed during discussions in Wang's office with the ever present hordes of staff members and managers hovering over the single American.

At one evening banquet soon before Lynn's departure, Wang, Zhang Xiancheng, the head director of the Forestry Bureau, and another Director, somehow more important than Wang, were present. Lynn was reminded that this was the first time all three Directors were at the same meeting and that he should feel highly honored.

On the last day of his visit, Lynn came to Wang's office and found six other plant managers seated around the room on couches. Wang suddenly began discussing very specific issues, like future sales amounts and pricing. Shifting dramatically from his cordial style of the first four days, he ranted and waved his arms, attempting to convince Lynn that his cost structure required that the barrels be sold at his suggested price. From Lynn's point of view, however, the high price Wang proposed put him at a real disadvantage. Wang presented his position as though it were a concession to Lynn: he would be willing to sell the barrels to Harrop for $410 delivered to Napa, California. He explained that his wood costs were high and that there was more waste splitting the wood than he had originally thought.

A contract was drawn up after Wang and Lynn reviewed what Lynn could sell at the various price levels. Wang argued heavily that he could not accept lower prices and that his labor costs were not much different than those in America and France. Lynn decided to accept the price even though he knew labor costs were much lower in China. There was no discussion of possible currency fluctuations that could push prices up or down as was already the case with Lynn's Duxon and Parrelle products.

Wang agreed to pay for part of the costs to exhibit the barrel at the January Sacramento Unified Symposium, a wine industry trade show. However, Wang insisted that for Lynn to be reimbursed expenses incurred, he had to take it from future sales because the laws in China did not allow money to leave the country. This seemed preposterous to Lynn but Wang would not budge. Feeling obliged after all the lavish attention the Chinese had bestowed upon him, and in an effort to build trust, Lynn conceded this point even though he did not agree to it.

The contract was written in Chinese and then translated to English by Wang's assistant for Lynn to sign. Yu informed Lynn that the contract would not hold him accountable to buying the barrel quantity stated but that it was simply a formality needed by Wang to show his superiors that the project had true potential. Contracts in China, Yu explained, are a reference point to continue further discussion and are not intended to be binding the way Americans understand them. an and to later show them their mistakes in planning. Based on the relationship he felt he had established with Wang and other Chinese officials and wanting to cement exclusivity as a dealer, Lynn figured he was fairly safe. He agreed to sign the contract, feeling there were enough exclusions to allow him a way out if necessary. Besides, if the contract truly was only a formality, details he was not pleased about could be worked out later. In addition, he needed to wrap things up; the barrels needed to be ready to market in California for the upcoming harvest.

Yu told Lynn repeatedly that he need not worry; he could return the barrels at any time for any reason, but an order needed to be placed now. The investment of $16,400 he risked, a major amount for his small business, Lynn reasoned, could be recovered in sales. He ordered his first 40 barrels feeling really excited about his new product.

Returning to Napa in September 2000, excited by the Tiger Barrel in spite of the dubious outcome to the negotiation in China, Lynn set out to sell his first 40 barrels for $430 a piece, even though he intuitively felt this was too high a price for the market. He hoped to deliver them upon their arrival to California in December, only 3 months after his visit to China. Knowing that he would take a loss on the first shipment of these few barrels, he justified this as a long-term investment in the project. Lynn reasoned that he could convince Wang to come down in price after testing the market.

Lynn's goal had been to offer the Chinese barrel at a point lower than the price of an Eastern European barrel price since those barrels were gaining respect with winemakers due to the flavors they contributed to the wine. The first forty Chinese barrels, however, he felt he could sell by their uniqueness alone. He placed a full-page advertisement in two of the major wine journals in January 2001 and took a sample barrel to the Unified Symposium where he immediately was exposed to an audience of 5,000 industry contacts. Lynn also secured a lead story about the Tiger Barrel project in a September issue of a weekly Web-based journal, the *Wine Business Weekly*, which drew a lot of calls from interested winemakers. The successful advertising and article brought in one of the largest wine companies in California as well as many other new customers for his small business.

The first four of forty barrels were delivered in December 2000, but by January Lynn discovered they had significant quality problems. He stopped delivering and quickly withdrew the first four barrels from the market due to their unacceptable quality so as not to ruin his reputation as a quality supplier. Lynn was not surprised when the local cooper who repaired the barrels confirmed that the barrels themselves were made acceptably but the wood selection was poor. The Chinese barrel makers simply required more training; Lynn still believed there should

53

Prepared by Erica Louise Harrop, Sarah Louise Dove, Duane Dove, and Wingham Liddell of Sonoma State University the basis for class discussion rather than to illustrate either effective or ineffective handling of an administrative situation. Reprinted with permission from Erica Louise Harrop, Sarah Louise Dove, Duane Dove, and Wingham Liddell. Copyright 2003 by Erica Louise Harrop, Sarah Louise Dove, Duane Dove, and Wingham Liddell. All rights reserved.

be an experienced technical expert hired to teach them properly.

In February, Lynn wrote two letters to Yu, the first in which Lynn outlined several problems and their solutions, and the 2nd in which he outlined a better way of setting pricing to correct what he saw as a major hurdle for future sales. In both letters he attempted to appeal to the Chinese business style he had recently read about by explaining that he needed to correct problems in order to *save face*. Lynn had counted on the testimonials of customers who had used the barrels to obtain new orders for August 2001 sales, but since the barrels had been faulty, he'd not been able to cultivate these product recommendations and had therefore lost the selling season. He would have at least his 40 repaired barrels to work with in 2001.

May, 2001, Napa Valley restaurant revisited

Lynn thought to himself after the lunch meeting that there were still significant gaps in his business plan with the Chinese. He had had been totally convinced in the Chinese workers' abilities to build a wine barrel. He had invested a lot of development time and advertising money as a small business owner in this venture which had paid off with impressive press articles so that he would have something unique to make winemakers take notice. Instead, the project had turned into an expensive disaster, perhaps more than his small company could weather.

He was now more concerned if he would be reimbursed for the faulty barrels than in seeing his commitment to the Chinese through for the following year. However, if the barrels he had already sold brought in good results, he was still positioned to proceed with the deal. Unfortunately, his momentum was long gone. He wondered what went wrong. How could he have averted some of the problems he now faced? What could he now do to try and save the deal? Based on the pressures he felt during the visit in China, he wondered if the Chinese were really sincere about making the barrels the right way in order to produce consistent quality down the road?

References

Adler, Nancy J. (2002). *International Dimensions of Organizational Behavior* (*Fourth Edition*). Cincinnati, Ohio: South-Western Publishing.

Anon. (1997). *Culturegram '98. People's Republic of China.* Brigham Young University, Provo, Utah.

Blackman, Carolyn (2000). An Inside Guide to Negotiating. *The China Business Review*, 27, 44-48.

Chen, Min (1993). Tricks of the China Trade. *China Business Review*, 20, 12-17.

Harris, Philip R. and Robert T. Moran (1991). *Managing Cultural Differences (Third Edition.),* Houston, TX: Gulf Publishing.

Kaplan, Seth (November/December, 1999). A Practical Education. *The China Business Review,* 26, 42-46.

Li, Ji and Chalmer E. Labig Jr. (2001*).* Negotiating with China: Exploratory study of relationship-building. *Journal of Managerial Issues*, 13 (3), 345-359.

Pye, Lucian W. (1988). *Chinese Negotiating Style.* Westport, CT: Quorum Books.

Shi, Xinping (2001). Antecedent factors of international business negotiations in the China context. *Management International Review*, 41 (2), 163-187.

Zhao, Jensen J. (2000). The Chinese approach to international business negotiation. *The Journal of Business Communication*, 37 (3), 209-237.

Case Study 4

Ocean Adventures*

Introduction

Captain Kimo Kahana[1] wore red, yellow, and blue Hawaiian print shirts that were outlandish even by Hawaiian shirt standards. He wanted to be easily recognized to his potential customers. As co-owner of Ocean Adventures (OA) making sure that he was spotted by his customers was urgent because he was losing them to his competitor across the way. "I'm frustrated and angry at losing customers," he said to his long-time partner Sam. Sam agreed, saying, "Too often when we think we have a customer signed up, our competition intercepts him, offers a lower price and steals our bread and butter." Kimo continued, "Worse still, we fight back by lowering our price as well. Our profit margin has virtually disappeared, and I wonder if it is worth the effort to stay in business."

Kimo and Sam were in the ocean parasailing business providing thrill rides to their mostly tourist customers. The rider (or riders, for tandem rides) was strapped into a harness that was attached to a parasail. (See Exhibit 1.) The rope attached to the parasail was let out as the boat moved forward. Height was variable depending on how much line was let out and the speed of the boat relative to the speed and direction of the wind. Most rides included a slow-down where the rider was dipped into the ocean.

Kimo and Sam started OA in 1980 because of their love of the ocean and parasailing. Equally important, they saw a chance to make a living. OA was their major source of income, and for a number of years they were satisfied with the business. By offering parasailing excursions to tourists and local residents, they shared their love of the sport while providing themselves with a reasonable level of income. But competition changed all that.

THE PARASAILING BUSINESS AT WEST OAHU

OA was located at the Waianae Boat Harbor on the West Shore of the island of Oahu. (See map in Exhibit 2.) The harbor was run by the State of Hawaii, Department of Transportation (Harbors Division). The State gave OA and a younger up-start competitor, Blue Hawaii Parasails (BHP) concessions to operate their businesses out of

---

* By Jack P. Suyderhoud of the University of Hawaii. This case was prepared by the author for the sole purpose of providing material for class discussion. It is not intended to illustrate either effective or ineffective handling of a managerial decision. The author thanks his colleagues Steven Dawson for helpful comments on earlier drafts and Nicholas Ordway for comments on legal issues. Anonymous referees made very useful suggestions for improvements. The names and nature of the businesses have been disguised at the request of the owner of "Ocean Adventures." Reprinted by permission from the Case Research Journal. Copyright 2003 by Jack P. Suyderhoud and the North American Case Research Association. All rights reserved.
[1]Kimo (pronounced Key-moh) is Hawaiian for "Jim."

the harbor. [2] This was the only location on the west side of the island from which such businesses were allowed to operate. (See Exhibit 2 for other sites.) OA and BHP functioned in very similar ways. Both used boats with a U.S. Coast Guard licensed captain and a crewmember on standby to serve the customers.

When Captain Kimo and Sam started OA in 1980, they were alone in the market and the business was less sophisticated than now. They bought an 18-foot outboard motorboat and the required equipment and set up their "sales office" in a parking area of the harbor using a folding table and an umbrella to protect themselves from the sun. In 1984, OA added a second boat and crew to serve a growing demand for its services.

During their first few years of business, Sam and Captain Kimo gained valuable experience in running their operations and understanding the market. For example, at the beginning, their excursions were 30 minutes in duration with heights up to 150 feet. However, it was found that because of the motion of the parasail and some customers' fear of heights the experience was not pleasant to a large portion of the customers. This hurt business since word-of-mouth advertising was essential. Most customers preferred a 15-minute ride with somewhat lower height and this seemed to make the experience positive for the vast majority of customers. As a result, the 15-minute ride became the market standard for operations from Waianae boat harbor. Longer rides with higher heights remained an option at a higher price.

The vast majority of OA's customer base was from tourists who generally found out about the activity through ads placed by OA in tourist publications. Exhibit 3 provides data on tourism on the island of Oahu. Most tourists stayed in hotels in Waikiki and came as part of a group or on a package tour. OA's customers tended to be independent travelers who liked to visit the rural West Shore as a change of pace from the more developed Waikiki hotel area. At one time, OA benefited from being included in a popular-press book used by tourists to plan their activities in Hawaii. This was a serendipitous occurrence that Captain Kimo appreciated but had no opportunity to replicate since it was at the whim of the book's authors. While about ½ the tourists are repeat visitors to Oahu, Captain Kimo noted there is very little repeat business. However, word-of-mouth referrals were important since the customers told other tourists about the good experiences they had with OA.

OA's business was affected by seasonal patterns in Hawaii's tourist market. The seasonal peaks coincided with school breaks (Christmas, Easter, and summer vacations) when families were more likely to travel to Hawaii for vacations. Another complicating factor was that the tours could only go out during limited (daylight) hours and when the weather was favorable.

OA was the market leader. On average, OA sold about 40 rides per day at average revenue of $35 per ride.[3] BHP averaged about 30 rides per day at a somewhat lower average revenue.[4] Captain Kimo believed that if the two companies cooperated so that they could have average revenue of $60 per ride the market demand would have

---

[2] The State allowed multiple concessions to encourage competition.

[3] These are annual average figures. For example, during the peak season the number of rides per day was higher while during the off-peak period it was lower.

[4] BHP's average revenue per ride was difficult to determine because of their pricing practices. Sometimes they would discount their prices significantly.

decreased to about 50 rides per day (from 70) with each company having about the same market share as before (57% OA and 43% BHP).

Exhibit 4A shows OA's major costs. The boats were owned outright. Captain Kimo is the marketing person, and Sam performs the maintenance. They cover all other costs such as taxes, insurance, boat storage rental, maintenance, capital charges and their own compensation out of any residual that may be generated. When the average revenue was $50 – 60 per ride, Kimo and Sam were comfortable with the net income they were earnings from the business. However, at $35 per ride the revenue was barely enough to covering their total costs and they were receiving very little to compensate them for the opportunity cost of their time and capital investment.

A History of Rivalry and Conflict

In the early days when it had no direct competition, OA raised prices every two years or so as Hawaii's tourism industry grew. (See Exhibit 5.) By 1988, OA had raised prices to the point where potential competitors found the market attractive. The first competition came from Lynelle, a former employee who thought she could get a share of the market. She set up a table near OA and competed for the customers by under-pricing OA, which by then was selling a ride at $25. Through some investigation, Kimo and Sam found out that Lynelle paid her boat owner $18 per ride (including captain, crew and equipment). OA responded by lowering its price to $16 per ride and Lynelle was forced out of business within six weeks.

Lynelle's departure did not end the threat of competition. The captain whose boat and equipment she used, Edward, decided that he would stay in the market. He created Blue Hawaii Parasails (BHP). BHP entered the market on a small scale and with some product differentiation. Edward's initial target market was experienced parasailers who wanted higher and longer rides. He also took them away from the ocean area where OA operated. In this way, BHP initially did not compete directly with OA.

Both companies benefited from harbor improvements done by the State of Hawaii, including to the parking lot where OA and BHP were located. In 1993 the state built dual booths from which both companies operated. These booths were situated across from each other separated by 10 yards of covered seating space for waiting customers. Both companies operated within the confines of this physical location where they faced each other, could see each other's customers come and go, and could hear each other's conversations.

The combination of adjoining locations and similar businesses led to an increasingly competitive environment. After three years of sticking to its niche, BHP started to compete directly for the same customer base as OA. Captain Kimo was extremely agitated at an apparently underhanded move by Edward to change the name of BHP to one close to that of OA. Captain Kimo was able to stop that, but only by resorting to legal action. Yet, the intense competition continued. According to Captain Kimo, Edward and BHP harassed OA employees and were very aggressive in trying to take customers in the parking lot. Captain Kimo surreptitiously videotaped some of these activities.

Because of the competition, OA was forced to reduce prices after 1992. (See Exhibit 5.) In 1996, the situation changed once again as Edward sold BHP to another owner/operator who brought in an outside investor. With the additional resources, BHP bought a second boat with equipment. However, Edward remained as BHP's main captain and as an important player in determining the competitive strategies of the company.

The prospect of OA and the new owners of BHP competing for the limited market prompted both groups to think about alternative strategies. In late 1996, they agreed to a cooperative arrangement. Both listed their rides at $70. (With coupon discounts that were in the market, rides averaged $60.) They also decided to share revenues and proposed other forms of cooperation such as renting each other's equipment. But the agreement did not last. Captain Kimo expressed doubts that BHP was abiding by the arrangement and felt that BHP was stealing customers from OA. By mid-1997 in an atmosphere of mistrust the agreement broke down.

OA'S Competitive Tactics

After the breakdown of the 1996-97 arrangement the rivalry and conflict persisted with both OA and BHP engaged in price and non-price competition. At one time, BHP promoted rides for as little as $19. However, this is for a 10-minute ride at a lower height.

The pre-agreement practice of trying to entice customers away from the other returned. Whenever a potential customer arrived in the parking lot, a sales representative from each company met the individual and offered his/her own company's services. However, the representatives frequently offered a lower price than the posted price. At times this competition was mean-spirited, and tensions ran high on almost a continuous basis. Captain Kimo found this "stealing" of customers especially frustrating. "I spend $4,000 per month advertising our services in tourist magazines on Oahu. BHP does less advertising and often runs no ads at all. When a tourist travels the 35 miles from Waikiki to Waianae, it is due to my ads. Then the other guys grab the customer away at the last moment." Sometimes Captain Kimo's co-owner Sam (who is physically a large person) showed up to discourage customer "theft" with his mere presence.

Advertising through tourist publications was OA's major marketing effort. There were several of these publications on Oahu and they were made available free to tourists on racks placed at the airport and in or near hotels. Generally, the publications were monthly and OA placed quarter-page ads indicating the nature of the activity, their rural location, the phone number, and the price per ride. OA ads urged potential customers to "See Captain Kimo."

In order to compete with BHP's pricing practices OA wanted to lower prices but not to damage its limited brand image. To do so, in 1998 OA created a new and separate smaller company called Ocean Sail Hawaii that offered prices at $35 per ride (compared to $50 before). Since the "new" brand was operated from the same locale and with the same boats and crew as Ocean Adventures, the name "Ocean Sail Hawaii" did not establish itself in the minds of the customers as a separate product. However, the $35 price became the market benchmark and remained so.

Captain Kimo also tried to work with hotel concierge and activities desks to increase OA's visibility. Tourists used the services of these desks to identify activities in which they might have been interested and to make reservations for those activities. As an incentive to remember OA to customers, OA offered the employees of these desks free ride coupons. There was only lackluster response to this. Few hotel employees took advantage of the opportunities and Kimo was unable to identify an increase in the number of customers from this initiative.

Brand recognition was a challenge to OA. In many cases tourists made the drive to Waianae but forgot whose ad they saw or what company they talked to. To keep customers "in the fold" once they saw OA's ad, they were encouraged to call ahead to make reservations. They were also encouraged to call one hour before the reservation to confirm weather conditions. At all times, the customers were reminded to "See Captain Kimo" upon arrival at the harbor parking lot. To make sure that potential customers were not missed, OA retained an answering service that routed calls to Captain Kimo wherever he happened to be.

Captain Kimo also tried to differentiate his product. He has told customers about OA's safety record and OA's 20 years of experience. This type of information seemed to have little impact on consumer choices.

Captain Kimo tried several tactics to compete without setting off adverse reactions from BHP. For example, OA's price was posted on a permanent, painted sign, unlike that of BHP which was attached with Velcro to a banner. Captain Kimo also stated in his ads that he would beat or match any parasailing price. Captain Kimo paid his sales person a commission of $2 per ride while BHP paid its sales person a commission of up to $10 per ride plus up to 20% of the price of the ride.[5] None of Captain Kimo's tactics brought peace between the rivals.

The State Department of Transportation informally tried to mediate the disputes. They had some experience with this. For fifty years flower lei sellers were provided adjoining spaces at the Honolulu International Airport to sell their traditional Hawaiian floral greetings to tourists and residents meeting new arrivals. Although there were periodic episodes of the type of competition used by the parasailing companies of this case, the lei sellers seemed to have less of a history of this behavior. This was due in part to long-held understandings that the sellers not be involved in "barking," or leaving their stands to solicit sales. However, the State was unable to get the parasailing companies to be similarly restrained.

Captain Kimo considered requiring reservations to be guaranteed with a credit card. However, this is not a common practice among tourist service providers in Hawaii, and he felt that this would turn off some customers or cause them to use BHP.

Captain Kimo and Sam also thought of buying out BHP. At one time an opportunity presented itself when the outside investor in BHP wanted to get out of the business. However, he sold his share to Edward, and Edward had no intention of selling. Further, even if OA bought out BHP Kimo noted that, "Another company could easily enter and we are back to where we were before."

---

[5] It is estimated that on average BHP sales representatives earned $8 per ride sold.

While Captain Kimo and Sam resented their situation, they could not and would not give up their business. Neither were they inclined to try to resurrect cooperative efforts. The history of past betrayals, distrust, and bad feelings seemed impossible to overcome. Yet, they needed to do something to return their business to adequate profitability.

Exhibit 1: Parasailing in Hawaii

Exhibit 2: Map of Oahu

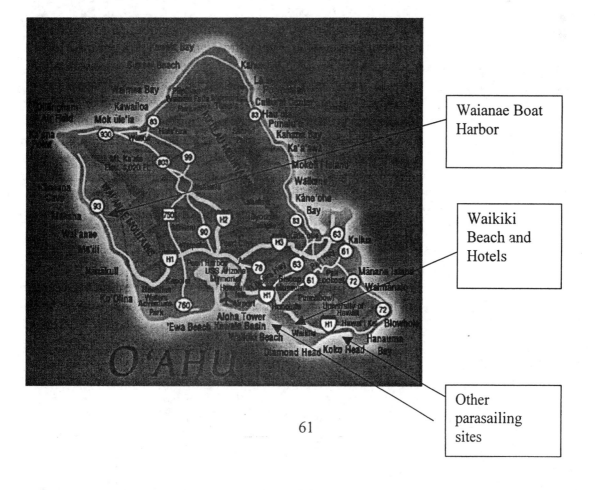

Waianae Boat Harbor

Waikiki Beach and Hotels

Other parasailing sites

Exhibit 3: Oahu Visitor Characteristics, 2000

	Total	Domestic	International
Total Visitor Days	31,077,256	18,734,118	12,343,138
Total Visitors	4,719,244	2,485,058	2,234,186
VISIT STATUS			
First-Time	2,191,624	1,007,622	1,184,002
Repeat	2,527,620	1,477,436	1,050,184
Average # Trips	3.75	4.58	2.82
TRAVEL METHOD			
Group Tour	1,583,087	265,712	1,317,375
Package	2,645,683	891,505	1,754,178
Group Tour & Pkg	1,490,987	214,498	1,276,488
True Independent	1,981,461	1,542,339	439,122
ACCOMMODATIONS			
Hotel	3,655,449	1,687,137	1,968,312
...Hotel Only	3,396,186	1,490,455	1,905,731
Condo	484,988	315,692	169,296
...Condo Only	352,091	220,178	131,912
Timeshare	127,362	104,189	23,173
...Timeshare Only	87,100	68,645	18,455
Apartment	56,886	38,897	17,989
Bed & Breakfast	42,811	33,798	9,013
Cruise Ship	82,469	69,163	13,306
Friends or Relatives	385,560	339,996	45,564

Source: Hawaii State Department of Business, Economic Development and Tourism, "Annual Visitor Research Report 2000," Table 41.

Exhibit 4A: OA Major Cost Items (2001)

Harbor lease to State of Hawaii	$	2,000	Per month
Advertising	$	4,000	Per month
Answering service	$	500	Per month
Use fees to State	$	1	Per ride
Fuel	$	1	Per ride
Licensed boat captain (on average 2 captains per day)	$	70	Per captain per day
Plus variable pay	$	3	Per ride
Crew member (on average 2 crew per day)	$	50	Per crew per day
Plus variable pay	$	3	Per ride
Sales representative/receptionist (one per day)	$	50	Per day
Plus variable pay	$	2	Per ride

Notes: The boat captains, crew members, and sales representative/receptionist were paid on a per-day basis if they were called into work, even if there were no rides sold that day. As noted in the text, taxes, insurance, maintenance, depreciation, and the compensation to the owners were paid from net revenues after the costs listed above.

Exhibit 4B: Estimated BHP Major Cost Items (2001)

Harbor lease to State of Hawaii	$	2,000	Per month
Advertising	$	1,000	Per month
Answering service	NA		Per month
Use fees to State	$	1	Per ride
Fuel	$	1	Per ride
Licensed boat captain (on average 2 captains per day)	$	70	Per captain per day
Plus variable pay	$	3	Per ride
Crew member (on average 2 crew per day)	$	50	Per crew per day
Plus variable pay	$	2	Per ride
Sales representative/receptionist (one per day)	$	50	Per day
Plus variable pay	$	8	Per ride

Notes: The costs are estimates based on what is known about BHP's operations. The compensation of the employees works the same as for OA. The variable compensation of the sales representative/receptionist is an estimated average per ride sold.

Exhibit 5: History of List Prices for Ocean Adventures

Year	Price per Ride
1980	$ 16
1982	$ 18
1984	$ 20
1986	$ 23
1988	$ 25
1990	$ 30
1992	$ 35
1994	$ 30
1995	$ 32
1996	$ 45
1997	$ 60
1998	$ 50
1999	$ 35

References

Besanko, David, Dranove, David, and Shanley, Mark, *Economics of Strategy*, 2nd Edition, New York: John Wiley & Sons, Inc., 2000.

Cheeseman, Henry R., *Business Law*, 4th Edition, Prentice Hall, 2001.

Clarkson, Kennetn W. Miller, Roger LeRoy, Jentz, Gaylord A., and Cross, Frank B., *West's Business Law*, 8th Edition, West, 2001

Oster, Sharon, *Modern Competitive Analysis*, 2nd Edition, New York: Oxford university Press, 1994.

Rao, Akshay R., Bergen, Mark E., and Davis, Scott, "How to Fight a Price War," *Harvard Business Review*, March - April 2000, pp. 107 – 116.

Shepherd, William G., *Public Policies Toward Business*, 7th Edition, Homewood, Illinois, 1985.

R & S Enterprises, LLC
Part A

It was January of 2003 and Herbert Sherman and Daniel J. Rowley, the two major shareholders of the recently formed R & S Enterprises, LLC, were reviewing their current business situation. This would have seemed to be a normal situation for any two business partners, yet for Sherman and Rowley, this was a strange occurrence indeed. It was not that Sherman and Rowley did not get together to discuss work for they had worked with each other for years on numerous projects and had developed a long standing friendship. Yet this type of work, real estate management, was clearly undiscovered country for these two novice landlords and undoubtedly outside of their field of expertise; classical literature.

Yet Sherman and Rowley were basking in their perceived success of their new startup venture. The cabernet, like the rent from their six properties, was flowing and the conversation was upbeat and quite jovial. "I find it rather easy to portray a businessman" jested Sherman while taking on the air of a rich and pompous aristocrat. "Being bland, rather cruel and incompetent comes naturally to me." Rowley nearly choked with laughter and could hardly keep himself from falling out of his chair. "Milton, perhaps Oscar Wilde?" queried Rowley. "No" replied Sherman sternly yet whimsically in his best imitation of a haughty British nobleman, "John Cleese of Monty Python!"

Academics Turned Landlords

In August 2002, when the Dow Jones Industrial Average dipped under 8000, Rowley and Sherman, friends and coauthors, were lamenting their ever shrinking retirement funds. Neither was getting any richer on a faculty member's salary nor expected any windfalls from relatives, their book sales, or lottery tickets. As Sherman was fond of saying "America believes in education: the average professor earns more money in a year than a professional athlete earns in a whole week."[1]

By Herbert Sherman of Southampton College and Daniel J. Rowley of the University of Northern Colorado. Reprinted by permission from Herbert Sherman and Daniel J. Rowley. Copyright 2003 by Herbert Sherman and Daniel J. Rowley. All rights reserved.

[1] http://www.quotationspage.com/search.php3, August 27, 2003.

After a long discussion, they decided that they could not longer bear "the slings and arrows of outrageous fortune"[2] and consequently needed to become masters of their own economic fate. Rowley had done enough preliminary research on the real estate market in their area and convinced Sherman (who had a bad experience renting his house several summers ago) that there was money to be made becoming what Sherman half jokingly called "slum lords."

The basic premise behind their business was quite simple. New starter homes (3 bedroom, 2 bath) in their area sold for about $175,000 and could be purchased with as little as a 5% down payment. Rowley was working with a real estate agent who noted that there were numerous families looking to get into these starter homes who either did not have enough cash for the down payment and/or had a poor credit history and could not qualify for a mortgage. These families lived in either mobile homes or apartments and were paying rents ranging from $1100 to $1400/month. These families would be willing to sign a three year lease on a new home with an option to buy. The three years would allow these families to build up a positive credit history and/or a down payment.

Given the very low 30 year mortgage rate of 6%, the mortgage and taxes combined on a starter home would cost about $1000/month, yielding a small but positive cash flow. Homes in the area accrued in value at about 5% each year and therefore the home would resell for about $ 200,000. Rowley and Sherman figured that an investment of $ 8750 (the down payment) would yield at least $ 25,000 over a three year period; they would be earning what was about equal to their initial investment per year, and trebling their money. In September of 2002, they formed a LLC, with each investing $50,000, with the idea of buying a total of 10 homes by the following year.

Rowley and Sherman, with the assistance of Rowley's real estate agent, found six families in three months and worked with these families to find them homes in the $175,000 price range that the families would be happy to lease and eventually purchase. The deal was so attractive that they even had a waiting list for new tenants. Rowley and Sherman easily qualified for these mortgages but found that the interest rates were higher because the homes were purchased as rental properties and not primary residences. They decided to put 10% down and to use a three-year adjustable rate mortgage in order to drop the interest rate and their monthly expenses to about $900/month. They also found that they needed to invest another $10,000 into each home for real estate brokerage fees, appliances, interior design, and landscaping. The six homes had gobbled up their initial investment of $100,000 and required an additional $80,000 (which Sherman loaned the company) although their monthly cash flow yielded a net profit of $ 1,500/month.

Why, Then the World's Mine Oyster;[3] Or Is It?

After a few more repartees, with a blatant disregard for the treatment of Chaucer and the Bard, Rowley and Sherman diminished their merriment and turned to a discussion of the business. "You were right about the positive cash flow" remarked Sherman "and I am

[2] Hamlet (III, i, 56-61)
[3] The Merry Wives of Windsor (II, ii, 2-3).

truly impressed that we are actually seeing an immediate return on our investment. I am assuming that we are banking this money to build up an emergency fund, just in case we have a problem with a renter or have a problem with one of our homes that is not covered by the builder's warranty." "Indubitably, my dear Sherman." Rowley mimicked the speech and mannerisms of his favorite fictional character, Sherlock Holmes, and then quoted Holmes directly. "One should always look for a possible alternative and provide against it. You can never foretell what any one man will do, but you can say with precision what an average number will be up to. Individuals vary, but percentages remain constant."[4]

"Quite so" jabbed Sherman. "Of course there is no formula for success except perhaps an unconditional acceptance of life and what it brings.[5] I am greatly concerned, however, that not only has our initial investment been spent, but that we have had to use the Bank of Sherman to bridge our cash needs. We need to figure out a way that we can raise more capital without dipping into our own pockets in order to purchase four more homes. We have the customers waiting, now we need some capital! And please, do not talk to me about the plans of mice and men since it is not in the stars to hold our destiny but in ourselves."[6]

Rowley nodded his head in agreement, became quite contemplative, and took a final swig of wine, emptying his glass and finishing off the bottle. "As noted by Heraclitus, it is better to hide ignorance, but it is hard to do this when we relax over wine.[7] There may be a way to reduce our need for more capital but right now I can't think of any. Let me think about our problem for awhile, talk with our real estate agent and our mortgage loan officer, and see what I come up with."

Figures Don't Lie but Liars Figure

Rowley and Sherman got back together a week later to discuss Rowley's research. The meeting this time was anything but a celebration, and Rowley moved quickly into lecture mode as he presented his findings to Sherman. "I think there is a way to pull money out of each of these homes quite quickly and recoup a good portion of our initial investment; here is the plan. We know that property in this areas goes up 5% a year so that a $200,000 home, that we would have put 5% down on, is worth $ 210,000 a year after it is purchased." "But we do not own $200,000 homes" exclaimed Sherman. "I know" retorted Rowley "I'm using this example because it makes the numbers easier – just hang on and I'll eventually get to my point." Rowley knew that Sherman was an impatient fellow and that he would put the kibosh on any scheme that at all seemed fool hardy. He also knew that if he presented Sherman with the bigger picture, that he was astute enough to bridle his impetuousness.

---

[4] http://calibercomics.com/SHERLOCK/sherlock_holmes_maxims.htm, August 27, 2003.
[5] http://www.quotationspage.com/subjects/success/, August 27, 2003.
[6] http://www.quotadstionspage.com/search.php3, August 27, 2003.
[7] http://www.quotationspage.com/search.php3, August 27, 2003.

"Assuming that we had put 5% down on this house" Rowley continued "that $10,000 could be recovered by refinancing the property in one year at its higher assessed value, thus pulling out our initial investment, minus closing costs of course. Yet this plan doesn't work since we have put 10% down and would have to wait a second year in order to pull out the additional property value."

Sherman was huffing and puffing to himself, and getting very fidgety in his seat. Rowley knew that he had to get to the bottom line soon or Sherman was going to explode like a volcano. Rowley quickly moved on. "What does work though is the following. All of these homes have unfinished basements. Some of these homes have been framed for basements, others have not. Having looked at the framing, we could easily put in two additional bedrooms, one den/office, and one full bath. This would convert our 3 bedroom, 2 bath homes into 5 bedroom, 3 bath homes and add another 800-1000 square feet of living space to a 1300-1400 square foot home. The values of these homes, according to my real estate broker, would rise about $30,0000."

Sherman was clearly in distress. He was no longer fidgeting, but rather pacing the floor and pounding his right fist into his left cupped hand. He was starting to mumble to himself and it was evident to Rowley that Hodgett's fuse had been lit and it was just a matter of time as to when he was going to explode. And explode he did!

"Let me see if I'm following you correctly and review our current situation" quipped Sherman. "We originally planned to invest a total of $100,000 into this little venture to the tune of $10,000 per home. So far, we have invested $180,000, or about $30,000 per home and, at this rate, we will need another $120,000 to pay for our next four homes. Our plan, no, I should say your plan, was off by 200%. I can live with that, plans are not perfect." Sherman paused for dramatic effect, an action not unnoticed by Rowley.

"But now" Sherman roared "but now" he repeated "your brilliant idea is that we finish off the basements, which really means spending more money. I've heard of spending money to make money but this sounds insane!"

The Plot Thickens

Rowley's reaction to Sherman' comments, hilarity, quite unsettled Sherman yet allowed Sherman some time to cool down and think. Rowley controlled his laughter after a few minutes and retorted using a famous quote from Oscar Levant "There's a fine line between genius and insanity and I have erased this line.[8] To paraphrase our good friend Oscar Wilde, you, my dear Sherman, are wonderfully tolerant. You forgive everything except genius.[9] Now if you would be so kind as to let me finish, perhaps I can respond to all of your objections."

"First off, let me tell you that the builders for our six homes have priced a finished basement out at about $15,000. That includes architectural plans, heat, air-conditioning,

---

[8] http://www.quotationspage.com/search.php3, August 28, 2003.
[9] Ibid.

and painting. You can see that we can would clear $15,000 per house if we refinanced these homes after completing the basements. Secondly, when we finish those basements renters would be charged an extra $100-$200/month. I have spoken to several of our renters and they are quite excited about the possibility of getting allot more house for a little more rent. They are also thrilled that when they go to purchase the home that they would be purchasing a fully finished home."

Sherman was calmer but unconvinced. "O.K., so we get a little more rent money. Assuming $200/month for 36 months, this still does not pay for the basement renovation nor does it immediately put allot of cash back in our hands. We still have to lay out 15 G's! Again, where does this money come from?"

"You're right as always" answered Rowley "but let me finish the rest of my analysis. To make the math easy and to match my earlier example, let's assume that our $175,000 home is now assessed at $200,000. Now this home will be worth $210,000 at the end of the first year's lease, $ 220,500 at the end of the second year, and $ 231,525 at the end of the third year. The home at $175,000 would be worth only $ 202,584 in the third year, a difference of nearly $30,000. So, this $15,000 investment would yield a little over $7000 in rental fees and $30,000 in increased home value. That's more than doubling our money in a three year time period.! More importantly, we would have pulled an additional $25,000 out of the house through refinancing in the first year – again, assuming a very conservative real estate assessment."

Sherman' demeanor had changed and he seemed to have cheered up, at least a little. "I get it – you put more money into the house, you get more money out of it, both upfront and overall. What I still don't understand is, where is the money for the basement refinishing going to come from?"

The Light at the End of the Tunnel, or Just Wishful Thinking?

Rowley had the answer that he knew would win Sherman over and minimize his protestations. "That's the least of our problems – some of the builders would be willing to bill us after we have re-mortgaged the house but would charge us a thousand dollars extra. Several local banks would be willing to allow us to open up a personal credit line, although the rates would be at least 3-4 points higher than a mortgage if the credit line was unsecured. We could even borrow more money from the Bank of Sherman on a short term basis, knowing that the funds would be returned about a month to two months later."

Rowley smirched when he made the reference to using more of Sherman's money. He knew that Sherman was opposed to lending more funds to this venture but would do so as a last resort if the other sources of capital for these projects did not work out and if he would get his money back quickly. Sherman in the meantime had been very contemplative during Rowley's last set of comments, and didn't even react when Rowley jibbed him about using more of his funds. Rowley wondered what Sherman was thinking but knew that he would not keep silent for long. Sherman then spoke quite calmly and to the point.

"I've thought about your proposal and although I have not had a chance to sit down and study all of the numbers, here's what I have come up with. If we can net $10,000 for our six homes through refinancing immediately after we have completed the basements then we will have accumulated $60,000. Assuming that each home will require a $30,000 investment, based upon our past experience, we would be $60,000 shy of the $120,000 we would need to be able to buy four more homes. We would have to borrow an additional $ 60,000. By finishing off those new homes (four basements) we could raise another $40,000, still leaving us borrowing $20,000."

"Your right again" Rowley answered. "But if we could pull out $15,000 per house, we would make an additional $5,000 per home or $ 50,0000 – assuming we finish the basements of all ten homes. We would then have an immediate net profit of $30,000. That's money we could use to pay back part of your loan to the company! And even if we could only pull out $10,000 per home, certainly it would be easier to manage the additional $20,000 loan if we finished off the basements than to borrow another $120,000 for down payments for our last four homes."

Sherlock or Shylock?

"This is all well and good" Sherman sarcastically commented. "But this scheme of yours is dependent upon the good graces of our tenants. Would they really allow us to finish off the basement, increasing the value and therein the selling price of their homes?"

"But my dear Sherman" retorted Rowley, again taking on the demeanor of his favorite fictional character, Sherlock Holmes "it is elementary. There is nothing more deceptive than an obvious fact.[10] You forget that these are our homes, our property, and we can do with them as we like. I agree that we would prefer the cooperation of our tenants, as well as their additional rent, and we would even desire both their good graces and their aspiration to purchase the home in the long run, but business is business and we have to do what is best for our company and ourselves. To quote Mr. Holmes, 'what you do in this world is a matter of no consequence. The question is, what can you make people believe that you have done?'[11] I believe that we can make a very persuasive argument, buttressed with perhaps some economic incentives, to assist our current tenants into making the right decision. The new tenants, on the other hand, will have to understand that this is just part of the rental agreement."

Sherman, who despised the idea of being a landlord in the first place, went along with Rowley's original idea for the business because he felt that assisting low income families in buying their first homes had a strong social value. A landlord who was benevolent was a rare commodity indeed! But now he could not believe his own ears. His face turned white as if he had just seen the Ghost of Christmas's Yet to Come. Images of Charles

---

[10] http://www.bcpl.net/~lmoskowi/HolmesQuotes/q.detection.html, August 29, 2003.
[11] http://calibercomics.com/SHERLOCK/sherlock_holmes_quote_philosophy.htm, August 29, 2003.

Dickens' most famous works and his most insidious characters (Scrooge from *A Christmas Carol;* Uriah Heep from *David Cooperfield;* Miss Havisham from *Great Expectations*; Fagin from *Oliver Twist;* Ralph Nickelby from *Nicholas Nickleby,* and the Marquis St. Evremonde of *The Tale of Two Cities*) passed before his eyes and they beckoned him to come join them in their evil games.

He thought to himself, "Did my good friend, business partner, and colleague just say what I thought he said? Could he really mean to deal with our tenants in this manner?" A paraphrase of two of Shakespeare's most famous quotes stumbled softly, barely audible, through his cracked and barely opened lips. "For if you prick them do they not bleed? If you tickle them do they not laugh? If you poison them do they not die? And if you wrong them, shall they not revenge?[12] For is it not enough to speak but to speak true?"[13]

---

[12] http://quotations.about.com/cs/shakespearequotes/tp/10_shakespeare.htm, August 29, 2003.
[13] Ibid.

CASE STUDY 6

BIG SKY BREWING COMPANY

At 7:00 A.M. on Wednesday May 23, 2001 Neal Leathers and Bjorn Nabozney, two of the three founders of Big Sky Brewing Company (BSBC), sat at the long cherry conference table at the offices of Montana Business Capital Corporation. BSBC was a craft-brewing company based in Missoula, Montana that experienced $729,309 sales growth (57 percent) over the past year and was trying to acquire the expansion capital necessary to develop in-house bottling capabilities. Montana Business Capital Corporation, a boutique[1] investment-banking firm, was retained eight months earlier to assist BSBC in its efforts to acquire the capital through the United States Department of Agriculture's (USDA) Business and Industry Guaranteed Loan Program. Tom Swenson, the president of Montana Business Capital Corporation, called Leathers and Nabozney the night before and requested a special meeting to discuss the status of their loan application.

Swenson entered the conference room and explained the situation:

"Thanks for coming in so early guys. As I told you yesterday, the bad news is that the USDA loan was not approved. The good news is that I was told that we could reapply…and that there is a chance that we could still get the loan. However, we are going to have to move quickly because your company may no longer qualify for this USDA program once the new census data is approved. I am thinking that approval of the new census data could come as early as next week. The guy that I spoke with over at the USDA indicated that the application documentation did not provide enough evidence that the expansion was needed at this time or that the expansion made good financial sense. One specific area that they noted is the 4 page summary business plan that we submitted with the application. They said it wasn't adequate. Given that information, I propose that we review the information we included in the original application, conduct a more thorough analysis of the company and the project, and develop a more compelling set of arguments for expansion and document them for the new application. So, I would like to start at the beginning by asking you why you think you should go ahead with the project."

[1] Montana Business Capital Corporation described itself as a "boutique" investment banking firm because it provided highly specialized financial services and products for businesses located in rural parts of the northwestern United States.

Leathers and Nabozney, clad in shorts and company t-shirts, watched as Swenson walked up to the flip chart in the room and reemphasized the urgency, "Gentlemen, we have until Friday afternoon to develop and document our arguments". Swenson loosened his tie and began outlining what they should try to accomplish during the meeting. The thirty-one year old Nabozney remarked, "Whatever you need us to do, we'll get it done. I'm surprised that they seem to be giving us a hard time. We've had tremendous growth, we're turning away orders, we're earning a profit, and, in a business where every penny counts, we shouldn't be cornered into outsourcing our bottling."

The Beer Industry in the United States

In 2000, *Beverage Industry* estimated that beer was an $83 billion industry in the United States and that the beer industry was projected to grow 1 percent annually through 2003. Companies competing in the U.S. beer market were classified into four industry segments: national, import, regional, and microbreweries. The four largest national breweries (Anheuser Bush, Miller, Coors and Pabst) accounted for 87 percent of the total U.S. beer production in 2000. Anheuser Bush, the largest player in this segment, produced five of the ten most popular brands, held a 48 percent market share in the U.S., and was the largest brewery in the world. National breweries generally realized profits by using inexpensive ingredients and taking advantage of large purchasing, production, and distribution economies of scale.

Before the introduction of microbrews, imports were considered premium beer products. In comparison to the products sold by national breweries, imported beers were brewed using higher quality ingredients, were available in a wider variety of styles, were usually more flavorful, and were shipped into the country, thus incurring higher per unit distribution costs. As a result, imported beer was often priced at a rate double the per unit price of beer sold by national breweries.

The *Institute for Brewing Studies* defined regional breweries as those breweries with an annual 15 thousand barrel to 2 million barrel brewing capacity (1 barrel = two kegs = 13.78 cases of beer). Regional breweries were similar to national breweries in that their products were widely available to consumers, had considerable advertising budgets, and earned profits by producing large quantities of inexpensive beer. However, regional breweries limited their distribution to a specific geographic region and leveraged their image of a "local" company in advertising to differentiate their products from those offered by national breweries. Generally, regional breweries produced a beer that was very similar to national breweries although their smaller size allowed more freedom to produce specialty brews as well.

The microbrewery segment consisted of breweries that produced less than 15 thousand barrels of beer annually. Because their distribution centered on the brewery itself, microbreweries tended to be a truly local product. By brewing small batches and using only top quality ingredients, microbreweries produced beers with quality equal to the imports. However, local production and distribution resulted in a product that was much fresher than imported beers. In addition, smaller batch production afforded microbreweries with greater flexibility and resulted in the production of a wider variety of beer styles. Over the past six years, this segment of the industry experienced significant consolidation.

The craft-brewing industry was comprised of microbreweries and those regional breweries that produced high-quality, flavorful beers. After experiencing rapid sales growth of 30 to 50 percent per year from 1990-1994, the rate of sales growth declined to single digits over the next six years. Despite the declining rate of sales growth, this segment accounted for 3 percent of the total U.S. beer market sales in 2000. More recently, the industry grew 4.1 percent in 2000, more than doubling 1999's 1.9 percent increase over 1998 (Exhibit 1), and brought total annual sales for the segment to more than 5.9 million barrels. Craft-brewing sales generally came from four different sources. In addition to the regional brewery and microbrewery sources described above, sales in the craft-brewing industry were also comprised of sales from contract brewing companies and brewpubs.

Contract brewing companies provided brewing and bottling facilities for smaller craft brewers who did not have sales sufficiently high enough to warrant the capital expenditure associated with acquiring their own facilities and equipment. As a result, these smaller companies outsourced brewing and bottling activities to contract brewing companies. Craft beers were also brewed onsite by brewpubs and sold as draft beer to their patrons. Sales levels for each of the four sources of the craft-brewing industry are presented in Exhibit 2.

Getting the Product in the Consumer's Hands

Leathers and Nabozney described the malt beverage industry as being structured into a three-tier system: 1) brewers produced the product and then sold it to distributors, 2) distributors then sold the product to individual or chain retail outlets, and 3) retail outlets then sold the product to the consumer. As a result of this structure, breweries had to meet the demands of three distinct groups of customers. *Distributors* were generally looking for high sales volume brands that pulled other brands into their portfolio. Developing a portfolio of strong brands and having an efficient distribution system were essential for distributors to gain and maintain control in their target market.

Retailers were also interested in high sales volume brands that pulled consumers into their stores. High sales volume in retail outlets was critical due to finite shelf space and the low margins associated with this industry. Products that did not sell in high volumes were considered a waste of valuable shelf space.

The third tier consisted of the *consumers* who drink beer products. Leathers and Nabozney suggested, based on their review of industry research, that microbrew consumers were generally seeking products that offered high quality, provided a consistently good taste, and projected a favorable image on the individual. Leathers and Nabozney broke this tier into two segments: on-premise consumers and off-premise consumers. On-premise consumers purchased microbrews, usually served as draft beer, at bars and/or restaurants and were generally between the ages of 21 and 27. Because beer served draft style was not readily identifiable, the management team believed that taste and quality were a greater concern for these individuals than was image.

Off-premise consumers purchased microbrews in bottles from retail outlets for consumption at home or at a social function (picnic, sporting event, etc.). Because these beers were identifiable during consumption through the labeling provided on bottles, the management team believed that image was as important for these individuals as taste and quality. Purchasers in this segment were generally between the ages of 21 and 45.

Big Sky Brewing Company

Big Sky Brewing Company (BSBC) was founded in 1993 and began producing and selling craft-brewed ales in mid-1995. In its first six years, the company grew to become the largest brewery in the Northern Rockies region, which included Montana, Idaho, and Wyoming. This was despite the fact that until March 1, 2000 the company's ales were only available in kegs. Even before selling bottled beer, BSBC sold more beer than any of the other forty-plus breweries located in the Northern Rockies. With the addition of bottled beer sales in early 2000, BSBC sold more than three times as much beer as any other brewery in the region. The company realized strong sales growth from the beginning, with annual growth rates of 52% in 1997, 30% in 1998, 18% in 1999, and 57% in 2000. The slower than average growth in 1999 was caused by the entry of New Belgium Brewing's Fat Tire Ale into the Montana market.

Nabozney believed that BSBC's initial and continued success was primarily the quality of its beer:

"There have always been quality issues in the craft brewing and micro-brewing. That's why we focus much of our efforts on quality. Simply put, we don't skimp….if something is bad, we pour (discard) it. Fortunately, this has only happened two times in our brief history. But we have a simple rule here…if it (the beer) doesn't meet specs (specifications), then we don't sell it. However, we're not beer snobs. There is a serious side around here, but we like keeping a fun atmosphere."

By May of 2001, BSBC sold its various ale products throughout Montana, Idaho, Wyoming, Washington, Oregon, Alaska, North Dakota, and South Dakota. For 2001 BSBC expected continued revenue growth of 104% for the year, with on-premise and off-premise purchases accounting for about 45 and 55 percent of BSBC's total sales respectively. Exhibits 3-8 provide historical financial statements for BSBC and select financial ratios for a peer group for the years 1998 through 2000.

The founders established the main brewery and distribution center near the Orange Street Bridge in downtown Missoula, Montana. This location was selected based on its easy access for distributors' and suppliers' vehicles and the fact that it would allow the founders to maintain their permanent residences. The facility was designed with offices in the front and a 5,000 square foot manufacturing space in the rear that provided the capacity necessary for the brewery to meet its production projections for all keg beer for the near future. However, the brewing facilities were not sufficient for brewing enough beer for the company's bottled beer projections, and there was no space available on the company's small lot for the necessary additional bottling equipment. Moreover,

BSBC management expected that the product mix would change from the 44 percent keg beer sales, 55 percent bottled beer sales, 1 percent taproom beer sales that they experienced in 2000 to about 28 percent keg beer sales, 70 percent bottled beer sales, and 2 percent taproom beer sales in the next two years.

Big Sky Brewing Company Enters the Bottled Beer Market

In order to penetrate the bottled beer market without expanding brewing its own site or opening a bottling facility, BSBC examined several northwestern contract brewing companies. BSBC eventually signed a contract with Portland Brewing Company (PBC) on March 1, 2000. PBC was selected primarily based on the fact that it had enough excess capacity to meet BSBC needs. Under the contract, BSBC products were to be brewed and bottled in PBC's plant in Portland, Oregon. Nabozney recalled the decision to enter the agreement with PBC:

"Portland Brewing Company provided an inexpensive opportunity for us to test the bottled beer market without having to take on the debt necessary to finance the new equipment and larger facility required for us to bottle our own beer. We (senior management) agreed that if the market demonstrated enough demand for our bottled ales, we would look into the possibility of bottling our own beer in-house."

During the first ten months bottled beer sales surpassed draft sales by nearly ten percent. By January 2001, BSBC had contracts with 56 distributors and several hundred retail outlets. Major retail chain outlets carrying BSBC products included Safeway (350 outlets throughout Montana, Washington, Idaho, and Oregon), Costco (BSBC is its #1 microbrew product in the only two states that currently sell BSBC products – Montana and Idaho), Albertson's, Tidyman's, Fred Meyer's, Rosauers, QFC, Brown and Cole, Topcut, Larry's Markets, Yokes, Smith's, and many others. Leathers was clearly excited about how fast BSBC's product was moving off the shelves, "We're selling an average of 4-6 cases per week in each store…the industry average is only 2 cases per week for other microbrew brands! This puts us in a great position to continue expanding."

Nabozney had mixed emotions about the demand for BSBC's products. "It's great to see that our product is in such high demand. But we're being forced to turn down orders from some of the largest retail chains because we don't have enough capacity in our contractual arrangement with Portland Brewing (Company). Costco, for example, recently placed an order for 100,000 cases for its California stores but we can't fill such a large order…PBC simply doesn't have enough excess capacity to give us." The management team projected that its bottle sales could increase to as much as 80 percent of its total sales in the near future. BSBC based these revised projections on a combination of actual sales realized and the number of orders that could not be met because of the constraints imposed by the contractual arrangement with PBC. The contract required a six-week lead-time for orders, minimum orders of 1,750 cases, and only allowed bottling to take place every third week. As a result of these constraints, BSBC was unable to meet market demand, particularly during the peak demand months of June, July, and August.

BSBC sold a variety of beers in draft and bottled form. The vast majority of BSBC's beer sales came from four brands: Moose Drool Brown Ale, Scape Goat Pale Ale, Powder Hound Winter Ale, and Slow Elk Oatmeal Stout (see Exhibit 9 for a description of the brands). Together, the four brands made up over ninety-seven percent of BSBC's beer sales with its Moose Drool brand accounting for nearly 80 percent of the total. BSBC has experienced overall sales growth since its introduction to the market, rising from just over 2,000 barrels in 1996 to over 15,000 barrels in 2000 (Exhibit 10).

In addition, BSBC generated revenue through the sale of branded merchandise in its own store as well as in retail stores throughout Montana and the surrounding states. Based on industry data, Leathers and Nabozney believed that BSBC quite possibly sold more branded merchandise than any other craft brewery in the USA. In addition to increasing the company's income, these items also served as advertising mediums for the brewery. T-shirts, drinking glasses, and hats were the most popular items with BSBC's customers. In 2000, BSBC sold over 15,700 barrels of beer, $380,000 in merchandise, and generated over $2.0 million in gross revenue.

BSBC's main craft-brewing competitors in its primary marketplace were: Bayern (Missoula, MT), Deschutes (Bend, OR), and New Belgium (Boulder, CO). In the Western Washington area, other breweries including Redhook, Pyramid, and Full Sail were also strong competitors. In its home state of Montana, BSBC sales in 2000 surpassed the combined sales of all other craft-breweries. The only downturn in BSBC's local sales growth was caused by the entry of New Belgium Brewing's Fat Tire Ale into the Montana market in early 1999. In 2000, BSBC beer outsold New Belgium by more than two-to-one in Montana, indicating a reversal in the trend. BSBC beer has experienced similar results in 2000 in other markets. In Idaho, BSBC was ranked in the top five craft breweries in terms of overall sales. BSBC's sales ranked the company in the top 20 craft-breweries in the Washington market. Statistics for the nation's top craft-breweries in 2000 are provided in Exhibit 11.

The key characteristics of BSBC's closest competitors are summarized in Exhibit 12. Bayern was BSBC's only true Montana based competitor, but BSBC sales have grown to almost three times Bayern's. The Alaskan Brewing Company continued to brew and bottle all beer in Juneau, Alaska and has built strong levels of brand equity and customer loyalty in the Pacific Northwest region. "We're committed to use the Montana mystique as a unique selling point," Nabozney noted, "and bottling in Montana instead of Oregon would allow us to leverage that even further". Like Alaskan Brewing and BSBC, the Deschutes Brewery relied heavily on image-based branding, building its brand image based on its association with the natural pristine beauty of the Oregon high plateau where the beer was brewed.

New Belgium was the largest of the seven competitors identified by Leathers and Nabozney, and its success story offered BSBC several insights. Leathers suggested that, "Both our and New Belgium's initial success are the result of our original flagship brands (BSBC: Moose Drool and New Belgium: Fat Tire) rather than to the introduction of several brands". New Belgium invested heavily in marketing and was rumored to have spent over $130,000 (mainly on neon signs) when it entered the Missoula market. According to Nabozney, "Although Boulevard and SLO Brewing do not sell in our markets and are unlikely to do so in the near future, we follow both companies closely." Boulevard and SLO were similar in size to BSBC's present position and recently invested approximately $2.5 million each into new bottling facilities. Both companies increased sales and gained market share over the past year. Among all of these competitors, BSBC was the only brewery that did not bottle in-house.

In comparison to most of its craft-brewery competitors, BSBC's products were usually priced at a level similar to Deschutes and New Belgium. A survey of prices in Montana supermarkets (Exhibit 13) illustrated that BSBC products typically sell for $6.49 per 6-pack.

BSBC had four employees on its initial management team. All four managers were with BSBC since production began, and three were the company's founders. The company added several key employees over the past few years and planned to add a controller within the next year. The current management team consisted of:

Neal Leathers – President and Founder. Neal was involved in brewing since 1985 and was the President and one of the founders of BSBC. In the 15 years Neal was involved in the micro-brew industry, responsible for literally every aspect of the business – from brewing to marketing to financing. At BSBC, Neal was responsible for company oversight, long-term planning, financial projections, industry relations, and project management. Neal held a B.A. in Telecommunications from Michigan State University.

Bjorn Nabozney – Vice President and Founder. While a student in business school at the University of Montana, Bjorn wrote the original business plan for BSBC. He then spent the next four years trying to raise the initial seed capital to make his dream a reality and start the business. As a founder and vice president of BSBC, Bjorn has spent the past six years performing all the various functions required to grow the business into the largest brewery in the Northern Rockies. Throughout the process of growing the business, Bjorn has shown the same enthusiasm, passion, and resourcefulness he did as a student writing the plan and raising the initial capital. Bjorn was primarily responsible for beer sales and marketing, project implementation, equipment evaluation and purchasing, and long-term planning. Bjorn's talent in sales and marketing were illustrated by his acquisition of major accounts such as Safeway and Costco. He has been a Vice President since 1997. Bjorn has a B.S. in Finance from the University of Montana.

Kris Nabozney – Vice President. Kris was employed by BSBC since production began in the summer of 1995. Kris was primarily responsible for production operations, quality assurance, and long-term planning. Kris has been a Vice President since 1999. Kris was working towards his B.S. in Management at the University of Montana.

Brad Robinson –Founder. Brad has been involved in brewing since 1985 and was one of the founders of BSBC. Brad was primarily responsible for advertising, retail and wholesale merchandise purchasing and management, public relations, and long-term planning. Brad has a B.A. in Zoology from the University of Montana.

Matt Long – Head Brewer. Matt has worked at BSBC for nearly five years. Matt was named Head Brewer at BSBC in 2000. Matt earned a B.A. in Microbiology from the University of Montana, and has graduated from an intense six-month brewing course offered by the American Brewers' Guild. During Matt's tenure at BSBC, the company has won numerous awards for its hand crafted beers.

Kevin Keeter – Bottling Line Manager. Kevin has been a professional brewer for over ten years. During that time, Kevin has been involved in a major expansion that included purchasing and installing a bottling line for a Washington based craft brewery. He also was the lead on that bottling line for over two years. Because of his experience installing, maintaining, and operating a bottling line, Kevin is playing a major role in the upcoming expansion of BSBC.

Chad Hania – Regional Sales Manager. Chad was an experienced regional sales manager within the beverage industry. Prior to coming to BSBC, Chad worked for four years as the regional sales manager of A&W Bottling Co. of Spokane, WA. During that period Chad was largely responsible for the tremendous increase in sales of SoBe products in the four-state region of Montana, Idaho, Washington, and Wyoming. Also, during those four years, Chad made numerous contacts within store chains in BSBC's primary geographic region, which will prove invaluable in getting BSBC's bottled products on grocery and convenience store shelves.

BSBC's constraints on growth during 2000 forced management to consider an in-house alternative to the contract brewing arrangement with PBC. All of BSBC's bottled beers were brewed and bottled at PBC's 130,000 total barrel capacity facility in Portland. Although PBC provided contract brewing services for several smaller companies, most of its capacity was devoted to production of its own portfolio of beers. Accommodating its contract brewing and bottling services required carefully arranged schedules for the facilities and frequent meetings with breweries. BSBC's 18,000 barrel maximum production contract with PBC, for example, stated that orders needed to be placed a minimum of six weeks in advance, allowed access to the bottling line every third week, called for minimum orders of 1,750 cases, and required bi-weekly visits to Portland by one or more of BSBC's management team. One or two management team members traveled to PBC every second week at a cost of $1,000 per manager in addition to the lost work time during travel to and from PBC. Nabozney expressed his concerns about this arrangement: "These constraints are difficult for us. We're still in the process of pegging rapidly growing demand levels in each market we enter. Our current arrangement doesn't allow for much flexibility. This amount of travel is also difficult on our families."

Leathers noted that there were additional constraints regarding accounts payable and inventory handling costs:

"The contract with PBC stipulates payment terms of net 20. This means that we need to pay for all of our bottled beer orders within 20 days of production. Meanwhile, our contract with our suppliers for in-house brewing calls for payment terms of net 30. By bringing bottling in-house we will have ten extra days to pay suppliers at no additional cost. We also have to pay penalties to PBC for long-term storage of our products. These penalties can really add up, so we've worked hard to avoid them".

These constraints, coupled with the initial success in the bottled beer market, led the management team to develop plans for bringing bottling activities in-house. This was consistent with the management team's original plan to discontinue outsourcing these activities once the company's sales volume reached a point at which they believed in-house bottling and brewing would afford significant economies of scale and thereby reduce the high per unit costs associated with outsourcing these activities.

The project being considered involved constructing a 30,000 square foot facility that, combined with its existing 8,000 square foot facility, would provide enough room for the company to expand production fourfold before requiring additional external expansion. In addition to moving much of BSBC's current production equipment to the new site, over $1.3 million dollars of brewing equipment would be purchased and installed in the new facility. This equipment would allow BSBC to brew more than twice as much ale per day as its current facility and contract with PBC permitted, as well as allowing BSBC to package its ales in bottles. All of the equipment to be purchased was selected based on its ability to allow continued expansion as BSBC's production needs grow. The project included enough land to allow BSBC to more than double the building's size for future expansion. In addition, an option was negotiated that would permit BSBC to purchase additional adjoining acreage within the first two years. This 2.5-acre parcel would make it possible for BSBC to more than double its brewery's size and ensured that this location would remain BSBC's long-term home.

Leathers looked optimistically toward the new facility, "We expect to gain significant flexibility as a result of this project. For example, we're going to be able to bottle every week, produce smaller orders of 450 cases, and we'll be able to reduce our lead time on orders from 6 weeks to 2 weeks." A comparison between existing operations and operations with the new facility is provided in Exhibit 14.

Nabozney and Leathers were proud of BSBC's human resource record; only one employee had left the organization since the company was founded. Nabozney estimated that the expanded facilities would create an additional 22 jobs (an increase from 14 currently employed to 36 employees once expansion is completed), most of which would be well-above the state's average income level per capita. Moreover, Nabozney argued, "In a sparsely populated state like Montana, expansion by a business like ours has significant spillover effects into other industries. For example, due to the amount of paper we use for cardboard case boxes and six-pack holders, we will become one of the largest users of paper in the state. We're excited about being able to help these suppliers while we expand."

Finding Financing – A Job for Montana Business Capital Corporation

BSBC founders were drawn to Montana Business Capital Corporation based on the company's reputation for helping Northwestern United States businesses find more attractive financing alternatives than readily advertised by commercial lenders. Swenson described his company as "a boutique investment banking and consulting services company". As he put it, "we provide consulting services regarding optimal funding strategies to expanding businesses. Once a strategy is developed, we package the funding request and act as an agent for the borrower".

Swenson's company excelled when working with clients who could benefit from some level of government enhancement. The company's Web site highlighted these specialized skills:

> "We are uniquely adept at applying these government augmentation
> products to commercial credits. There are many details and exceptions
> inherent to these applications, which can make the difference between a
> successful application and a denial. Montana Business Capital Corporation

supplies "high touch" services to its clients. This complete and thorough suite of services includes extensive work with the client on business plans, projections, pricing, management techniques, etc. Montana Business Capital Corporation's services also include utilizing an extensive background in the usage of various programs, as well as dedicating time to client specific research related to the implementation of these programs."

One government program that Swenson had been particularly successful in using was the USDA's Rural Business-Cooperative Service Business Program (RBS BP). This program worked in partnership with the private sector and community-based organizations to provide financial assistance and business planning to projects that create or preserve quality jobs. As RBS BP described the program, "the financial resources of RBS BP are often leveraged with those of other public and private credit source lenders to meet business and credit needs in underserved areas". In fiscal year 2000, the program disbursed a total of 721 loans and 473 grants totaling over $1.1 billion. This resulted in over 73,000 jobs either being created or saved, and over 2,500 businesses assisted in rural America. Swenson planned to use RBS BP's Business and Industry Guaranteed Loan Program for BSBC. This program provided guarantees up to 90 percent of a loan made by a commercial lender. Loan proceeds were to be used for working capital, machinery and equipment, and buildings and real estate.

BSBC's expansion project required a total of $2.6 million. Swenson determined that this amount would be raised through $350,000 from an equity infusion from current investors, $2.0 million from a USDA RBP BP Business and Industry Guaranteed Loan, $150,000 from a Missoula Area Economic Development Corporation loan that was already approved but contingent upon approval of the loan from the USDA, and $100,000 from BSBC's cash reserves. The loan was to be used to purchase land, build the new brewery, and purchase and install new brewing and bottling equipment. Exhibits 15-17 provide projected financials obtained from information in the original loan application. The expansion project was expected to result in total company sales of $6.8 million and net income of $581,000 by 2004. Throughout the first three years BSBC expected to maintain a positive cash flow. Expected operating cash flows for 2002-2005 are provided in Exhibit 18.

There was also a brief discussion about the appropriate cost of capital to use in evaluating projects. The new loan would have a blended interest rate of 3.125%. Swenson believed that if BSBC did not obtain the loan a more traditional loan would carry a minimum interest rate of about 10%. Swenson also added that more traditional lenders would most likely not approve the loan because the company was already highly leveraged. As a result, if the company was unable to acquire the loan from the USDA's program, BSBC would have to rely on more expensive equity financing. Currently the owners thought that they should earn about 30% on equity investments. One team member argued that based on his research of competitors, a cost of capital of 15% would be appropriate for BSBC. Another opposing position argued that venture capitalists typically seek an expected return of 35% or more for new ventures.

Finally, Swenson suggested that a break-even analysis should be conducted to illustrate any increases in operating risk associated with in-house bottling. In-house bottling would increase fixed costs such as interest expense, depreciation and other salary and maintenance expenses associated with bringing bottling in-house. Swenson examined BSBC's cost structure and determined that depreciation, interest expense, and general administration expense were predominately fixed costs in the near term. A large portion of BSBC's sales costs were also fixed in the short term. Finally a portion of manufacturing costs, (predominately rent, leases, salaries, maintenance and some utilities), were also categorized as fixed. Exhibit 19 illustrates the breakdown of fixed and variable costs for BSBC from 2001 to 2002.

As the four hour meeting began to wind down, Swenson, Leathers, and Nabozney summarized their conclusions. Swenson's remarks captured the essence of their conclusions:

> "I think that the USDA was right in terms of what we were lacking in the original application…especially in terms of the supplementary documents. We know that the expansion makes sense but we need to do a better job of convincing them. In the original document you only included a four-page summary of the business and the expansion plan. We need to use the information we discussed today to convince them that the combination of your team, the market opportunity, and their financing will lead to success. To do this, we need several things. First, we need to assess what components we might be missing on the team. They (the USDA) indicated that they are not convinced that you have all the pieces in place to pursue such a large expansion. Second, we need to do a better job of analyzing the market. You've provided some data regarding the market, but we need to analyze in greater depth and in a more organized way. And third, we need to provide evidence that this expansion is necessary at this time. This means that we need more analysis regarding the expected hard and soft results from pursuing the expansion project. The hard results entail analyzing the value of the project, breakeven points, etc. The soft results include what you believe will be gained operationally from expanding".

As the three rose from the table, Swenson reminded Leathers and Nabozney that they had three days to get the new application and analysis together. They knew that completing this work within such a short time-frame posed a real challenge, but realized that the alternative of not getting the USDA guarantee would likely pose even greater challenges for obtaining the necessary financing for expansion.

Exhibit 1: Annual Growth in Craft Beer Market (percentage growth in sales)

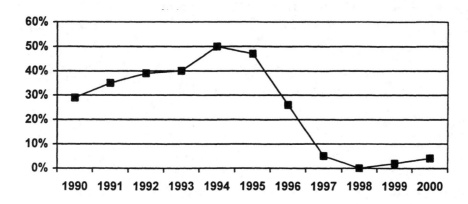

Exhibit 2: Craft Beer Sales (in barrels)

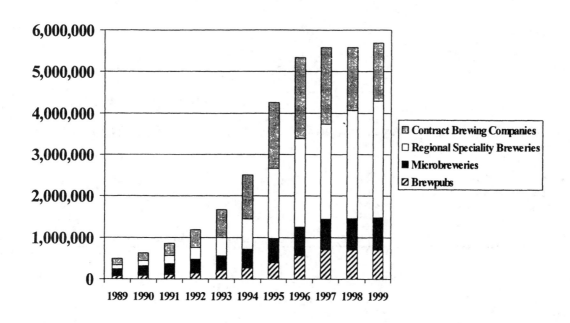

Exhibit 3 - Big Sky Brewing Historic Income Statement
Years 1998-2000
(In full dollar amounts)

	1998	1999	2000
Revenues	$1,091,480	$1,290,903	$2,020,212[1]
Costs of Goods Sold	716,148	731,656	1,030,708
Gross Profit	375,332	559,247	989,504
Total Sales and Admin Expense	389,497	446,203	745,192
Earnings Before Interest and Taxes	-14,165	113,044	244,312
Interest Expense	18,755	47,035	51,812
Earnings Before Taxes	-32,920	66,009	192,500
Taxes[2]	0	0	0
Net Income	$-32,920	$66,009	$192,500

[1] This was the first year that BSBC sold bottled beer. The following represents the breakdown of sales for 2000:
Wholesale beer = $798,160
Bottled beer = $997,700
Taproom beer = $18,140
Merchandise and Other revenue = $206,212

[2] BSBC paid no taxes in 1998-2001 because of loss-carry-forwards accrued in previous years.

Exhibit 4 - Big Sky Brewing Historic Balance Sheet
For Years 1998 to 2000
(In full dollar amounts)

	12/31/1998	12/31/1999	12/31/2000
Assets			
Current Assets			
Cash	$5,647	$69,922	$71,010
Accounts Receivable	61,268	75,852	187,562
Inventory	38,155	39,379	71,333
Other Current Assets	15,917	11,547	10,706
Total Current Assets	$120,987	$196,700	$340,611
Fixed Assets			
Gross Fixed Assets	835,317	1,100,439	1,369,138
Accumulated Depreciation	-411,394	-480,364	-574,592
Net Fixed Assets	$423,923	$620,075	$794,546
Other Assets	$5,354	$4,717	$3,946
Total Assets	**$550,264**	**$821,492**	**$1,139,103**
Liabilities & Equity			
Current Liabilities			
Accounts Payable	$72,333	$65,290	$144,719
Line of Credit	0	0	0
Other Current Liabilities	24,657	18,351	16,603
Current Portion of LT Debt	35,000	0	0
Total Current Liabilities	$131,990	$83,641	$161,322
Long-term Liabilities			
Loans	$238,452	$469,020	$492,450
Other LT Liabs	0	23,000	47,000
Total Long-term Liabilities	$238,452	$492,020	$539,450
Total Liabilities	**$370,442**	**$575,661**	**$700,772**
Stockholder Equity			
Capital Stock	510,355	510,355	510,355
Earnings	-330,533	-264,524	-72,024
Total Equity	**179,822**	**245,831**	**438,331**
Total Liabilities & Equity	**$550,264**	**$821,492**	**$1,139,103**

Exhibit 5
Big Sky Brewing Company
Historical Statements of Cash Flow
Years 1999 and 2000
(In full dollar amounts)

	1999	2000
Cash from Operations		
Net Income after tax	$66,009	$192,500
Plus Depreciation	68,970	94,228
Accounts Receivable Decrease (Incr.)	-14,584	-111,710
Inventory Decrease (Incr.)	-1,224	-31,954
Other Current Assets Decrease (Incr.)	4,370	841
Accounts Payable Increase (Decr.)	-7,043	79,429
Accrued Expenses Increase (Decr)	-6,306	-1,748
Total Cash from Operations	110,192	221,586
Cash from Financing		
Long Term Debt	230,568	23,430
Other Long Term Liabs.	23,000	24,000
Notes Payable	0	0
Current Portion LTD	-35,000	0
Paid in Capital	0	0
Total Cash from Financing	218,568	47,430
Cash from Investing		
Property, Plant & Equipment	-265,122	-268,699
Other LT Assets	637	771
Total Cash from Investing	-264,485	-267,928
Change in Cash	64,275	1,088
Beginning Cash	5,647	69,922
Ending Cash	$69,922	$71,010

Exhibit 6
Common Size Income Statement Data For Malt Beverage Industry
Provided By Robert Morris Associates*

	Peers
Revenues	
Total Revenue	100%
Total COGS	<u>62%</u>
Gross Profit	38%
Total Sales and Admin Expense	<u>32%</u>
Earnings Before Interest and Taxes	6%
Interest Expense	<u>2%</u>
Earnings Before Taxes	4%
Taxes	<u>NA</u>
Net Income	NA

* Peer data obtained from Robert Morris Associates Annual Statement Studies 2001-2002. Peer Group is classified as Malt Brewing Industry and includes 29 companies ranging in size from below $1 million in sales to over $25 million in sales.

Exhibit 7 - Common Size Balance Sheet Ratios For
The Malt Beverage Industry Provided by Robert Morris*

	Peers*
Assets	
Current Assets	
Cash	10.00%
Accounts Receivable	8.80%
Inventory	11.50%
Other Current Assets	3.50%
Total Current Assets	33.80%
Fixed Assets	
Net Fixed Assets	49.40%
Other Assets	NA
Total Assets	**100.00%**
Liabilities & Equity	
Current Liabilities	
Accounts Payable	8.60%
Line of Credit	3.30%
Other Current Liabilities	NA
Current Portion of LT Debt	3.90%
Total Current Liabilities	22.80%
Long-term Liabilities	
Loans	27.10%
Other LT Liabs	NA
Total Long-term Liabilities	NA
Total Liabilities	**56.40%**
Stockholder Equity	
Capital Stock	NA
Retained Earnings	NA
Total Equity	**43.60%**
Total Liabilities & Equity	**100.00%**

Exhibit 8 - Malt Beverage Industry Peer
Financial Ratios From Robert Morris Associates*

	Peers
Gross Margin	38.40%
Operating Margin	6.20%
Asset Turnover	1.5
Inventory Turnover	11.3
Days Sales Outstanding	22.95
Fixed Asset Turn	2.2
Payables Period	28.29
Leverage	3.00
Debt Ratio	66.67%
Times Interest Earned	3.3
Current	1.60
Quick	0.70

* Peer data obtained from Robert Morris Associates Annual Statement
Studies 2001-2002. Peer Group is classified as Malt Brewing Industry
and includes 29 companies ranging in size from below $1 million in sales
to over $25 million in sales.

Exhibit 9 – Description of a Sample of Big Sky Brewing Company Products

MOOSE DROOL Moose Drool is our Brown Ale. Far and away the best selling draft beer brewed in Montana, Moose Drool is chocolate brown in color with a creamy texture. Our brown ale is a malty beer with just enough hop presence to keep it from being too sweet. The aroma also mostly comes from the malt with a hint of spiciness being added by the hops. Moose Drool is brewed with pale, caramel, chocolate, and whole black malts and Kent Goldings, Liberty, and Willamette hops. It has an original gravity of 13 degrees Plato, and is 4.2% alcohol by weight, 5.3% by volume.

SCAPE GOAT Scape Goat is our award-winning Pale Ale. It is a very smooth, refreshing, and well-balanced brew. Scape Goat took home the Gold Medal from the 1997 North American Brewers' Association competition as the best English style Pale Ale brewed west of the Mississippi! Scape Goat is brewed with pale, crystal malts, and Kent Goldings and Crystal Hops. Scape Goat is 3.8% alcohol by weight and 4.7% by volume.

SLOW ELK Slow Elk is our Oatmeal Stout. It is a malty, creamy, and very smooth drinking beer. This is one stout that even people who "don't like dark beers" can love. By the way, a "Slow Elk" is a nickname for a cow, a few of which are mistaken for elk during hunting season every year! Slow Elk is brewed with pale, crystal, chocolate, and black malts, rolled oats, and Kent Goldings hops. Slow Elk is 3.9% alcohol by weight and 4.9% by volume.

POWDER HOUND Powder Hound is our Winter Ale. Available from November through March, Powder Hound is a deep golden colored ale brewed in the tradition of English Old Ales. It is a strong beer designed to warm up the coldest winter night, yet not so full bodied that you cannot enjoy a couple runs down the mountain. Powder Hound is brewed with Hugh Baird's Pale and Crystal malts, and then hopped with Kent Goldings and Willamette hops. Powder Hound is 4.6% alcohol by weight, 5.7% by volume.

Exhibit 10
BSBC Sales Growth

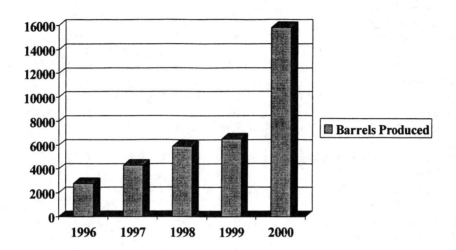

Exhibit 11 - The Top 22 Craft Breweries Ranked by Share of Segment in 2000

Company	2000 shipments	% change in 2000	Share of segment	Change in share
1. Sierra Nevada Brewing Co.	498,986	+14	8.44	+ 0.76
2. New Belgium Brewing Co.	165,000	+12	2.79	+ 0.18
3. Deschutes Brewery (2)	95,000	+10	1.61	+ 0.07
4. Alaskan Brewing Co.	81,300	+16	1.37	+ 0.14
5. Harpoon Brewery (2) *	63,100	+18	1.07	+ 0.13
6. Gordon Biersch Brewing Co. (packaging brewery only)	60,237	+13	1.02	+ 0.08
7. Boulevard Brewing Co.	46,060	+17	0.78	+ 0.08
8. Brooklyn Brewery*	35,100	+10	0.59	+ 0.03
9. BridgePort Brewing Co. (subs. of Gambrinus Co.)	30,720	+17	0.52	+ 0.06
10. Hops Restaurant, Bar and Brewery (74) (subs. of Avado Brands)	27,387	+18	0.46	+ 0.05
11. Gordon Biersch Brewery Restaurant Group (25-all brewpubs)	26,502	+17	0.45	+ 0.05
12. Magic Hat Brewery	26, 100	+21		
13. Kalamazoo Brewing Co.	24,600	+16	0.42	+ 0.05
14. Otter Creek Brewing Co.	24,500	+10	0.41	+ 0.02
15. Rogue Ales	23,687	+31	0.40	+ 0.08
16. Odell Brewing Co.	20,592	+12	0.35	+ 0.03
17. SLO Brewing Co. (2) *	20,600	+56	0.35	+ 0.13
18. Mac and Jack's Brewery	20,163	+26	0.34	+ 0.06
19. Anderson Valley Brewing Co.	17,737	+10	0.30	+ 0.01
20. Lagunitas Brewing Co.	17,099	+16	0.29	+ 0.03
21. Ram/Big Horn Brewery (20) (C.B. & Potts/ Humperdink's)	16,306	+18	0.28	+ 0.04
22. Big Sky Brewing Co.*	15,741	+57	0.27	+ 0.14

Notes: Figures in parentheses indicate number of breweries/brewpubs operating during 2000, if more than one. Shipments also refer to taxable removals at brewpubs. * Denotes all or partially contract brewed during 2000.

Source: Association of Brewers

92

Exhibit 12 - Key Characteristics of BSBC's Major Craft-brewing Competitors

	In-House Bottling	# Barrels (2000)	Focal Markets	% sales increase (2000)	Differentiation
Big Sky Brewery	No	15,741	Regional Northwest	57%	In 2000, achieved the largest increase in sales (57% growth) of any of the top 50 craft brewers. For the fourth straight year, Big Sky Brewing Company sold more beer than any other Montana Brewery. Moose Drool continues to be the best selling draft beer brewed in Montana.
Alaskan Brewing	Yes	81,300	Regional Pacific Northwest	16%	In 1986 they were the only brewery in Alaska. They use pure malt, premium hops, glacier-fed waters and continue to brew all beer in Juneau, Alaska.
Deschutes Brewery	Yes	95,000	Regional Pacific Northwest	10%	Deschutes was named for the wild and scenic Deschutes River. Produce handcrafted, traditional style ales and lagers.
New Belgium Brewing	Yes	165,000	Regional Western	12%	Its brewing facility is a nationally recognized paradigm of efficiency. 1998 NBB made the financial commitment to make its facility the first wind powered brewery in America.
Boulevard Brewing	Yes	46,060	Regional Midwest	17%	The brewery is in a historic district of Kansas City, Missouri, in a turn-of-the-century building which had originally housed the laundry of the Santa Fe Railroad. The beer has distinctive hop characteristics.
SLO Brewing	Yes	20,600	Regional West Coast	56%	Fourth largest brewery in California. Pushing draft sales in restaurants and bars helped SLO Brewing triple its accounts in Northern California to 60 in the past year.
Bayern	Yes	5,600	Regional to Montana	0.94%	They are the only German brewery in the Rocky Mountains. Bayern does not contract brew or bottle outside its own brewery and they brew strictly according to the German Law of Purity of 1516. Big Sky's largest Montana based competitor.

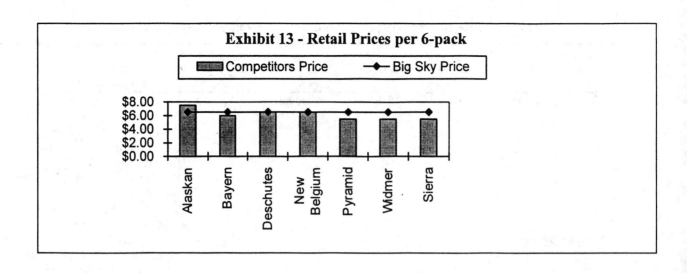

Exhibit 14 – Improvements from bringing bottling in-house

Parameter	Current Operations	Operations After Expansion
Bottling	Every three weeks	Every week
Minimum size orders	1,750 cases	450 cases
Lead time for orders	6 weeks	2 weeks or less
Payment terms	Net 20 on all orders (can surpass $150,000 payable per order)	Net 30 is standard
Total Capacity	34,000 Barrels 18,000 at PBC 16,000 at BSBC	Up to 100,000 Barrels

Exhibit 15 - Big Sky Brewing Forecasted Income Statements
For Years 2001-2004
(In full dollar amounts)

	2001[1]	2002	2003	2004
Revenues				
Beer Revenue				
Wholesale Beer	1,215,000	1,302,750	1,552,500	1,721,250
Bottled Beer	2,440,944	2,915,902	3,925,199	4,328,932
Taproom Beer	63,800	84,400	84,400	92,200
Other	12,500	12,000	12,000	12,000
Merchandise Revenue	425,000	500,000	550,000	605,000
Total Revenue	**4,157,244**	**4,815,052**	**6,124,099**	**6,759,382**
Cost of Goods Sold:				
Manufacturing				
Wholesale, bottled, taproom Beer Costs	2,433,469	2,433,491	3,029,977	3,339,625
Excise Tax	63,000	163,800	217,000	239,750
Depreciation	159,720	274,020	296,736	314,652
Total Manufacturing COGS	2,656,189	2,871,311	3,543,713	3,894,027
Total Retail Sales COGS	265,625	312,500	343,750	378,125
Total COGS	**2,921,814**	**3,183,811**	**3,887,463**	**4,272,152**
Gross Profit	**1,235,430**	**1,631,241**	**2,236,637**	**2,487,230**
Selling and Admin Expense				
Sales Costs	515,045	616,200	742,200	803,000
General and Admin Expense	360,870	438,901	531,888	547,996
Total Sales and Admin Expense	**875,915**	**1,055,101**	**1,274,088**	**1,350,996**
Earnings Before Interest and Taxes	**359,515**	**576,140**	**962,549**	**1,136,234**
Interest Expense	90,000	130,743	142,620	132,855
Earnings Before Taxes	**269,515**	**445,397**	**819,929**	**1,003,379**
Taxes	60,580	187,068	344,372	421,420
Net Income	208,935	258,329	475,557	581,959

[1] Note: As mentioned in the case, BSBC experienced a significant product mix shift between 1999 and 2001. 1999 data represents a product mix that did not include bottled beer. In the 2nd quarter of 2000, BSBC entered its bottling agreement with PBC and began selling bottled beer. And, 2001 represents the full year in which BSBC was selling bottled beer as part of its product mix. It should also be noted that the revenue generated per barrel of beer is much higher when sold in bottles versus when sold in kegs. Correspondingly, the cost of goods sold is higher for bottled beer than for keg beer.

Exhibit 16 - Big Sky Brewing Forecasted Balance Sheets
For the Years 2001-2004
(In full dollar amounts)

	12/31/2001	12/31/2002	12/31/2003	12/31/2004
Assets				
Current Assets				
Cash	19,297	384,134	781,169	1,346,448
Accounts Receivable	152,264	177,264	202,264	227,264
Inventory	126,333	146,334	166,335	186,336
Other Current Assets	8,064	8,064	8,064	8,064
Total Current Assets	305,958	715,796	1,157,832	1,768,112
Fixed Assets				
Gross Fixed Assets	4,046,014	4,056,014	4,256,014	4,406,014
Accumulated Depreciation	-734,312	-1,008,332	-1,305,068	-1,619,720
Net Fixed Assets	3,311,702	3,047,682	2,950,946	2,786,294
Other Assets	6,917	6,917	6,917	6,917
Total Assets	**3,624,577**	**3,770,395**	**4,115,695**	**4,561,323**
Liabilities & Equity				
Current Liabilities				
Accounts Payable	83,145	108,145	133,145	158,145
Line of Credit	35,000	35,000	35,000	35,000
Other Current Liabilities	78,887	77,887	77,887	77,887
Current Portion of LT Debt	126,783	122,980	119,291	115,713
Total Current Liabilities	323,815	344,012	365,323	386,745
Long-term Liabilities				
Loans	2,403,496	2,270,788	2,119,220	1,961,467
Other LT Liabs	0	0	0	0
Total Long-term Liabilities	2,403,496	2,270,788	2,119,220	1,961,467
Total Liabilities	**2,727,311**	**2,614,800**	**2,484,543**	**2,348,212**
Stockholder Equity				
Capital Stock	760,355	760,355	760,355	760,355
Retained Earnings	136,911	395,240	870,797	1,452,757
Total Equity	**897,266**	**1,155,595**	**1,631,152**	**2,213,112**
Total Liabilities & Equity	**3,624,577**	**3,770,395**	**4,115,695**	**4,561,323**

Exhibit 17 - Big Sky Brewing Forecasted Statement of Cash Flows
For Years 2001 to 2002
(In full dollar amounts)

	2001e	2002f	2003f	2004f
Cash from Operations				
Net Income after tax	208936	258329	475557	581959
Plus Depreciation	159720	274020	296736	314652
Accounts Receivable Decrease (Incr.)	35298	-25000	-25000	-25000
Inventory Decrease (Incr.)	-55000	-20001	-20001	-20001
Other Current Assets Decrease (Incr.)	2642	0	0	0
Accounts Payable Increase (Decr.)	-61574	25000	25000	25000
Accrued Expenses Increase (Decr)	62284	-1000	0	0
Total Cash from Operations	352306	511348	752292	876610
Long Term Debt	1911046	-132708	-151568	-157753
Other Long Term Liabilities	-47000	0	0	0
Notes Payable	35000	0	0	0
Current Portion LTD	126783	-3803	-3689	-3578
Paid in Capital	250000	0	0	0
Total Cash from Financing	2275829	-136511	-155257	-161331
Property, Plant & Equipment	-2676876	-10000	-200000	-150000
Other LT Assets	-2971	0	0	0
Total Cash from Investing	-2679847	-10000	-200000	-150000
Change in Cash	-51712	364837	397035	565279
Beginning Cash	71010	19297	384134	781169
Ending Cash	19297	384134	781169	1346448

98

Exhibit 18 - Project Cash Flows Resulting from Expansion
Operating Cash Flows for the Years 2001 to 2002
(In full dollar amounts)

	2001	2002	2003	2004	2005
Project Investment	$-2,600,000				
Operating Cash Flows with Expansion		$663,092	$914,913	$1,029,466	
Operating Cash Flow w/o Expansion		$504,521[1]	$554,973	$610,470	
Marginal OCF		$158,571	$359,940	$418,996	$439,946[2]
Total Project Cash Flows 2001-2005	$-2,600,000	$158,571	$359,940	$418,996	$439,946

Calculation of OCF With Expansion (2002-2004):	**For 2002**
Net Income:	$ 258,329
Plus: Depreciation:	$ 274,020
Plus: Interest	$ 130,743
Total Operating Cash Flow	$ 663,092

Calculation of OCF With Out Expansion (2001):	**For 2001**
Net Income:	$ 208,935
Plus: Depreciation:	$ 159,720
Plus: Interest	$ 90,000
Total Operating Cash Flow	$ 458,655

[1] Assumes that OCF will increase at a rate of 10% a year from 2002 to 2004 if BSBC does not expand and continues to outsource.

[2] Marginal operating cash flows beyond 2004 are calculated assuming a constant 5% growth rate.

Exhibit 19 - Breakdown of BSBC costs into Fixed and Variable Costs 2001-2004

	2001	2002	2003	2004
Forecasted Revenues	$4,157,199	$4,815,052	$6,124,099	$6,759,382
Fixed Costs	$1,189,631	$1,664,624	$1,938,857	$2,046,993
Variable Costs	$2,763,298	$2,892,099	$3,709,686	$4,130,430
Variable Costs as Percent of Revs.	66%	60%	61%	61%

CASE STUDY 7

CHRONIC ILLNESS IN THE WORKPLACE

Monday morning had not started well. Louise, the accounting clerk at Property Management, Inc., had just received a call from the bank telling her that the company account was overdrawn. Louise told the bank that this was impossible since a very large deposit of cash and checks had been made on Thursday afternoon. However, the bank had no record of the deposit. Louise was perplexed. She had given Annette, the office manager, the deposit to make on the way to lunch on Thursday. Annette had said explicitly that she was going to the bank first and then to lunch. Louise decided to call Annette on her cell phone and see what had happened.

Property Management, Inc. was a property management company in South Florida. The company managed offices and took care of all service needs such as maintenance and upkeep for condominium properties. Property Management also provided customized software programming for managing the accounting and tracking maintenance requests for each condominium complex they supervised.

Todd Dolan, President, and Peter Krauss, Vice President, started the company in 1978. As of 2004, they managed 15 condos and maintained accounting for each condo's association dues. The other four condos had accounting only. Todd handled management of the condos and while Peter wrote the computer programs and managed the main office staff. The office staff included Louise in accounting, Annette as the office manager/administrative assistant, Kara as the clerical person and Sabrina as receptionist. One of the 19 condominiums had a staff member on site; four maintenance men rotated among the 15 properties they managed handling routine maintenance and repairs.

Louise was an elderly woman in her seventies. She enjoyed working and getting to be around people. She was very organized and gave 100% to every task that she performed. She ensured that everything was done according to the book and would not deviate in anyway from the instructions that were given to her during training. Her high task orientation met the needs of the President, Todd, quite well. They were completely in sync with one another, and sticklers for detail. A precise and detailed process or method existed for almost every task in the office, even including how to take messages. Louise was responsible for receivables, accounts payable, assisted in answering the phones, and served as the bookkeeping interface with the accountant.

Annette was in her late forties. She was a workaholic and barely spent any time outside the office. She held a Master Degree in Business Administration and was clearly overqualified for the job of office manager. Her one downfall was that she had trouble delegating and often took on more work than she could humanly handle in one day. She was a constant source of frustration to Louise. While Annette was physically present for long hours at the worksite, she did not accomplish very much. She spent a lot of her time getting little accomplished. Frequently she was distracted, and often needed to take naps to restore here energy.

Lately, Annette has had a difficult time focusing on work. She was diagnosed ten years ago with fibromyalgia. Fibromyalgia is an increasingly recognized chronic pain illness characterized by widespread musculoskeletal aches, pain and stiffness, soft tissue tenderness, general fatigue and sleep disturbances. The most common sites of pain include the neck, back, shoulders, pelvic girdle and hands, but any body part can be involved. Fibromyalgia patients experience a range of symptoms of varying intensities that wax and wane over time. It is estimated that approximately 3-6% of the U.S. population has fibromyalgia. Although a higher percentage of women are affected, it does strike men, women and children of all ages and races. Because of its debilitating nature, Fibromyalgia has a serious impact on a patient's family, friends, and employers, as well as society at large.

The disease has many different symptoms. Pain is profound, widespread and chronic. The severity of the pain and stiffness is often worse in the morning. It can also be aggravated by weather conditions, anxiety and stress. Fatigue is another symptom but it is more than just being tired. It is an exhaustion that can interfere with the simplest daily activity. Many patients often complain of sleep problems that prevent them from getting a deep restful sleep. Additional symptoms include irritable bowel and bladder, headaches and migraines, restless legs syndrome (periodic limb movement disorder), impaired memory and concentration, skin sensitivities and rashes, dry eyes and mouth, anxiety, depression, ringing in the ears, dizziness, vision problems, raynaud's syndrome, neurological symptoms and impaired coordination.

The disease had become debilitating for Annette although she did find some relief from medication. The problem was that the medication left Annette with some memory loss and extreme fatigue. Sometimes she needed to nap in the break room. The owners were very understanding, especially since Annette was married to Todd. The problem was that Annette had been making some serious mistakes. She seemed to be on edge and often became defensive with her co-workers. She had been working on site at one of the condominium offices but the tenants had complained so much about her that Todd decided to bring her back to the office. However, now, when a tenant called with a problem, she often treated them rudely and once again there have been complaints.

Property Management had a high turnover of personnel. In the prior year, before Annette began working at the office, the company had trouble staffing the administrative assistant position. There were four different people hired and subsequently let go within a 12 month period. The trouble was that the position never had clear cut guidelines. Although the employees were given job descriptions, additional tasks were sometimes added. The job seemed to overwhelm all the previous employees because they could never finish their work before more was piled on top of them. In addition, the procedures for doing various tasks often changed depending on who trained the employee. One day the procedure for tracking maintenance calls was one way and then a call would get missed and the next day the procedure would change. This often made for much confusion. Now, since Annette had filled this role, turnover was no longer an issue. She had been doing the job for over six months. The issues now were fostering harmony among the office staff, maintaining the customer base and Annette's forgetfulness.

Louise called Annette on her cell phone. Although it was almost 10 AM in the morning, Annette had not made it into the office. Annette made her own hours and often came in late and then stayed late into the evening. When Louise reached Annette she was at the condo that Property Management staffed to pick up time records. Annette was on her way into the office at that moment. Louise explained the situation about the bank calling and the missing deposit. Annette looked into her briefcase, saw the bank bag, and realized she had forgotten to make the deposit! She promised Louise that she would go to the bank immediately and make the deposit.

Louise did not know what to do. The bank was going to charge them for every check that bounced. She knew about Annette's medical condition and certainly did not want to stir up trouble. But, she knew something had to be done. The small staff was beginning to talk about Annette and speak badly of her. They complained that she was often napping, coming in whenever she felt like it, making mistakes and then blaming them on someone else. The owners at the condos would call with problems and if she answered the phone she was often rude to them. Louise was convinced that she needed to talk to someone, and soon, before anything else went wrong.

Considering that Annette was the wife of the President of Property Management, Louise knew that Todd would be the one who would have to make the decision. Louise scheduled her meeting with Todd, presented her concerns, and detailed the costs and inefficiencies resulting from Annette's lack of performance in the job. As she left his office, Louise turned to Todd and added a parting comment, "I don't envy you this decision, Todd. It's difficult to deal with family. We all love Annette, and understand how much the fibro hurts, but business is business. You have to do something."

As the door closed, Todd winced. What was he going to do?

Monthly Financial Information
Property Management, Inc.

Monthly Income (15 properties at $1800.00 per month)	$27,000
Operating Expenses*	$14, 570.
Net Income	$12,430

*Includes the following monthly expenses:

Salaries	$11,600
Rent	$ 1,000
Electric	$ 400
Taxes	$ 200
Telephone	$ 600
Cell phones	$ 150
Pagers	$ 60
Misc. office supplies	$ 200
Advertising	$ 360

Appendix

Brief Questions & Answers Related to FMLA, Social Security, and Sections 503 and 504 of the Rehabilitation Act of 1973

Family Medical Leave Act
[Material excerpted from *US Department of Labor e-laws – Family and Medical Leave Act Advisor – August 10, 2004*]

Q. How much leave am I entitled to under FMLA?

If you are an "eligible" employee, you are entitled to 12 weeks of leave for certain family and medical reasons during a 12-month period.

Q. How is the 12-month period calculated under FMLA?

Employers may select one of four options for determining the 12-month period:

- The calendar year;
- Any fixed 12-month "leave year" such as a fiscal year, a year required by state law, or a year started on the employee's "anniversary" date;
- The 12-month period measured forward from the date any employee's first FMLA leave begins; or
- A "rolling" 12-month period measured backward from the date an employee uses FMLA leave.

Q. Does the law guarantee paid time off?

No. The FMLA only requires unpaid leave. However, the law permits an employee to elect, or the employer to require an employee, to use accrued paid leave, such as vacation or sick leave, for some or all of the FMLA leave period. When paid leave is substituted for unpaid FMLA leave, it may be counted against the 12-week FMLA leave entitlement if the employee is properly notified of the designation when the leave begins.

Q. Which employees are eligible to take FMLA leave?

Employees are eligible to take FMLA leave if they have worked for their employer for at least 12 months, and have worked for at least 1,250 hours over the previous 12 months, and work at a location where at least 50 employees are employed by the employer within 75 miles.

Q. Do the 12 months of service with the employer have to be continuous or consecutive?

No. the 12 months do not have to be continuous or consecutive; all time worked for the employer is counted.

Q. Do the 1,250 hours include paid leave time or other absences from work?

No. The 1,250 hours include only those hours actually worked for the employer. Paid leave and unpaid leave, including FMLA leave, are not included.

Q. Will I lose my job if I take FMLA leave?

Generally, no. It is unlawful for any employer to interfere with or restrain or deny the exercise of any right provided under this law. Employers cannot use the taking of FMLA leave as a negative factor in employment actions, such as hiring, promotions or disciplinary actions; nor can FMLA leave be counted under "no fault" attendance policies. Under limited circumstances, an employer may deny reinstatement of work – but not the use of FMLA leave – to certain highly-paid, salaried ("key") employees.

Q. As an employer, are you engaged in commerce or in an industry or activity affecting commerce?

Note: Employers who employ 50 or more employees for each working day in 20 or more calendar weeks of the current or preceding calendar year are deemed to be engaged in commerce or in an industry or activity affecting commerce. In counting the 20 or mre calendar weeks, you cannot count weeks that crossover from one calendar year to the next.

Serious Health Condition defined:

Serious health condition means an illness, injury, impairment, or physical or mental condition that involves:

Any period of incapacity or treatment connected with inpatient care (i.e., an overnight stay) in a hospital, hospice, or residential medical care facility; or

A period of incapacity requiring absence of more than three calendar days from work, school, or other regular daily activities that also involves continuing treatment by (or under the supervision of) a health care provider; or

Any period of incapacity due to pregnancy, or for prenatal care; or

- Any period of incapacity (or treatment therefore) due to a chronic serious health condition (e.g., asthma, diabetes, epilepsy, etc.); or

- A period of incapacity that is permanent or long-term due to a condition for which treatment may not be effective (e.g., Alzheimer's, stroke, terminal disease, etc.); or

- Any absences to receive multiple treatments (including any period of recovery that follows) by, or on referral by, a health care provider for a condition that likely would result in incapacity of more than three consecutive days if left untreated (e.g., chemotherapy, physical therapy, dialysis, etc.).

For the definition of a serious health condition see Regulations 29 CFR Part 825.114.

For information regarding the employee's ability to perform the functions of the position of the employee, see Regulations 29 CFR Part 825.115.

The Americans with Disabilities Act Public Law 101-336
[Excerpted from US Department of Labor, Office of Disability Employment Policy, www.dol.gov/odep, August 10, 2004.

Employment Requirements

Employers, employment agencies, labor organizations and joint labor-management committees must:

Have non-discriminatory application procedures, qualification standards, and selection criteria and in all other terms and conditions of employment.
Make a reasonable accommodation to the known limitations of a qualified applicant or employee unless to do so would cause an undue hardship.

Exceptions

The bill makes exceptions regarding the employment of a person with a contagious disease, a person who illegally uses drugs or alcohol, employment of someone by a religious entity, and private membership clubs.

Public Accommodations

Included in any entity licensed to do business with, or serve, the public such as hotels, theaters, restaurants, shopping malls, stores, office buildings and private social service agencies. They must:

Assure that criteria for eligibility of services do not discriminate. Auxiliary aids and services are required unless the result is an undue burden or fundamentally alter the nature of the goods or services.
Remove barriers from existing facilities when such removal is readily achievable. If not, alternative methods of making goods and services available must be provided.

Make altered facilities accessible to the maximum extent feasible. In major structural renovations, a path of travel to the altered area, including restrooms and other services, must be accessible.

New facilities must be accessible. Generally, other than health-care facilities and multilevel shopping malls, elevators need not be provided in buildings with less than three floors, or less than 3,000 square feet per floor.

Disability Defined

Anyone with a physical or mental impairment substantially limiting one or more major life activities; has a record of such impairment; or is regarded as having such an impairment, is considered a person with a disability.

In terms of employment, the law defines a "qualified individual with a disability" as a person with a disability who can perform the essential functions of the job with or without reasonable accommodation.

Rehabilitation Act of 1973, Sections 503 and 504

This law protects qualified individuals from discrimination based on their disability (section 504) and requires that affirmative action be taken to employ and advance in employment qualified individuals with disabilities (section 503) by any contractor or sub-contractor entering into a contract with the Federal government that is valued at $10,000 or more.

RIVER BEND TRADING[1]

It was Friday in Columbus, Montana (population 2,000)—about 6:30 p.m. in January 2002. Columbus was nestled in the foothills of the towering Beartooth Mountains along the Yellowstone River in Stillwater County. It was located 40 miles west of Billings (population 85,000), Montana's largest city, on the western edge of the Northern Plains in Montana's Big Sky Country. Although it was dark, the lights in and around the Apple Village Plaza at the Interstate 90 exit illuminated the light snow blowing in lazy undulating patterns across the surface of the ground in the subzero Fahrenheit weather.

Mary Blankenship and Lois Frerck ("frair ic") were locking the doors of River Bend Trading, which was located in the plaza. As usual, the partners were not taking work home. Mary pulled up her collar against the chill and asked Lois, *"Is Jenny roping this weekend?"* Lois replied, *"She has a rodeo in Bozeman* (indoors, 100 miles west). *By the looks of this snow, we'd better get an early start in the morning. I hate hauling horses on icy roads!"* As they crossed the paved parking area to Lois's pickup and Mary's sports utility vehicle, Mary said, *"I hope the first quarter is better this year!"* Lois replied, *"Me too, for nine months we go hard, then we flat line in the first quarter—the near death experience in retail! We must watch our costs! Sometimes I feel we're trying to do the impossible, but I'm still going to have a life!"*

Background

River Bend Trading (http://www.riverbend@riverbendtrading.com) opened in June 2000. At yearend, December 31, 2000, it reported a pre-tax six-month net income of $47,370 on sales of $241,197 (Exhibit 1). The net worth of the business was <$33,842> (Exhibit 2). In June 1997, Lois and Mary had purchased a similar business called Haddy's Shack. After a three-year struggle, they closed Haddy's Shack and reopened as River Bend Trading in a different location. The negative net worth of <$32,792> on June 30, 2000, came from operating Haddy's Shack.

At yearend, December 31, 2001, River Bend Trading reported a pre-tax annual net income of $74,527 on sales of $425,068 (Exhibit 3). The net worth of the business was <$12,414>. Lois and Mary's concern was cash flow—paying their bills (e.g., their creditors, employees, and vendors), making a reasonable living, and increasing the value of the business (Exhibit 4). Occasionally they thought about someday selling the business. As Mary said, *"We don't want to do this forever!"*

By Patricia Holman and Tom Hinthorne of Montana State University-Billings. Reprinted by permission of the Case Research Journal. Copyright 2002 by Patricia Holman and Tom Hinthorne and the North American Case Research Association. All rights reserved.

[1] This case was prepared as a basis for class discussion rather than to illustrate either effective or ineffective management.

River Bend Trading offered a mix of clothing lines with a "classy, sporty" look for men and women. Woolrich™ was one of their most popular brands. Several of the clothing lines carried the River Bend Trading logo—often featuring a moose silhouette. Mary and Lois were also in the initial stages of developing their own clothing line, "River Rags"—a go-anywhere, stylish, unisex line of jackets, sweatshirts, t-shirts, etc. in basic colors.

River Bend Trading (2000 square feet) and the Montana Silversmiths™ Factory Outlet (800 square feet) were adjacent stores. They had separate entrances but were joined inside by a 16-foot wide opening. Mary and Lois staffed and managed both stores (Exhibit 5). The outlet carried a large inventory of first-line Montana Silversmiths™ jewelry and gift items owned by Lois and Mary. The sale of the first-line Montana Silversmiths™ products accounted for about 50 percent of River Bend Trading's total sales—about $200,000 annually. The outlet also carried a large inventory of discounted (outlet) jewelry owned by Montana Silversmiths™. Mary and Lois received no direct compensation—no revenue—from the sale of the discounted jewelry. In late 1999, to secure the right to manage the outlet, they verbally agreed to this arrangement. By January 2002, they were considering how they might modify the informal agreement and reduce their dependency on Montana Silversmiths™.

Columbus, Montana

As Interstate 90 dropped out of the foothills to Columbus, an exit to the Stillwater Valley and Yellowstone National Park, travelers could see the "new town." In January 2001, Dan Burkhart, a Stillwater County resident and feature writer for the *Billings Gazette* wrote:

> *This is a tale of two towns in one, separated by just a dozen blocks, yet by almost a century and by a new version of economic opportunity. The first Columbus is downtown, comprised partly of stately buildings dating to the early 1900s. It developed from the days when towns were platted near natural thoroughfares, like the Yellowstone River and then by the iron artery of the railroad.*
>
> *The other Columbus is a new town ... mushrooming where the modern artery, Interstate 90, feeds it. ... It looks like a town to itself and in many ways it is. And in many ways, it's the oldest story along the country's interstate system. As the interstates bypassed town after town, the communities either wilted or adapted. Columbus adapted. ... Still, a good number of downtown buildings are empty.*

Interstate 90 bordered the "new town" on the north. Pasture bordered it on the east. Baseball fields and residential housing bordered it on the west (Exhibit 6). On the east side of the road leading south to the "old town" there was a Town Pump convenience store, restaurant, and truck stop, a Super 8 motel, a Lucky Lil's Casino, a McDonald's restaurant, and some other buildings. Most of the area was paved; and there was a large parking area for "18 wheelers."

Across the road there were several buildings known collectively as the Apple Village Plaza, which took its name from one of its principal establishments—the Apple Village Café & Gift Shop. The plaza was suspended in an "almost finished" stage of development. About 30 percent of the parking area was paved; the rest was gravel. Landscaping in the "new town" was limited to a small area on two sides of McDonald's (e.g., grass and small trees).

The Montana Silversmiths™ Factory Outlet, River Bend Trading, Art Is Everywhere, and the Village Laundry faced north along the south side of the plaza and occupied, east-to-west, a new single-story building measuring 40 x 116 feet. The building had a light-colored log cabin façade, a sloping deep-blue steel roof, and 8 x 6 foot tinted windows across the front and down the east side of the building. It also had a four-foot covered board walkway across the front and down one side. Other businesses in the plaza, included Eagle's Nest Floral, Outdoor Supply, The Otters Den, Stillwater Copy Center Plus, Subway™, Dr. Jay, and a video store.

Outdoor Supply was River Bend Trading's only local competitor. Poorly positioned in the plaza, it lacked the highway exposure of River Bend Trading. The store's clothing lines and gift items differed from those carried by River Bend Trading, and it carried less inventory. It framed paintings and prints and appeared to be a competitive threat to Art Is Everywhere.

Downtown Columbus—"old town"—was less than half a mile away. As Dan Burkhart had noted:

The old town still has active businesses, almost a Noah's ark of survivors: two pharmacies, two auto parts stores, two car dealerships, two hardware stores and two financial institutions. The county library, the historic New Atlas Bar, and a combination jewelry-carpet business remain here, too.

The businesses that have popped up near I-90 would welcome an old town revival. "It was a difficult decision to move out here," said River Bend owner Mary Blankenship. She and her partner, Lois Frerck, had their clothing business downtown until a year ago. ... "We would have liked to stay where we were, but there just wasn't the traffic."

Lois and Mary were close friends and their personalities complemented each other. Lois was friendly but reserved; Mary was outgoing with a quick sense of humor. Lois was a single parent with three children. Her youngest child, Jenny, was a senior in high school. Coley, was a junior at Montana State University-Bozeman; he had a full-ride rodeo scholarship. Willy, was a foreman for Barnhart Construction. Mary and Kevin's only child, Theresa, was a junior in high school, and she and Jenny were close friends. Kevin, with a partner, built and remodeled houses.

Haddy's Shack

Lois and Mary's first retail venture, Haddy's Shack, was located on Front Street, the main street of "old town." In fiscal year 1996, the previous owners of the business lost $9,000 on sales of $107,000. In May 1997, the business went up for sale. Lois and Mary had been thinking about starting a business and had looked at several businesses. They ran their ideas past Pat, Lois's sister, and she encouraged them to "run the numbers" on their options. Pat had co-owned and operated Columbus Building Supply, Inc. for 12 years.

Pat was concerned when they proposed an equal partnership. She knew from experience partnerships were difficult to manage successfully, so she encouraged them to discuss the issues typically affecting partnerships and to sign a partnership agreement drawn by legal counsel. This they did. Looking back in 2002, Mary and Lois felt the partnership was working very well:

We are equal partners, and we draw money from the business in equal amounts on predetermined paydays. Occasionally, one of us may be a little short of cash ahead of payday; and we'll ask the other, "Could I, you know, maybe two days early?" We are best friends. We complement each other. Could men do this as well? No, because men don't talk to each other.

Lois and Mary wrote their business plan in the first week of June 1997 and received bank financing on June 7th, the day after submitting their plan to the bank. They purchased the assets for $11,875 (e.g., racks, display cases, a cash register, and a 15-year old point-of-sale system). They purchased the poor-quality inventory at cost for $55,000. To avoid creating bad feelings in the small town, Mary and Lois did not argue the value of the inventory. Their families each contributed $10,000 for a total of $20,000, and the bank financed a $48,000 long-term SBA-guaranteed loan and a $12,000 shorter-term loan. The total capital acquired was $80,000 of which $66,875 was spent on assets leaving a working capital balance of $13,125.

Their bankers, Don and Danny, liked the business plan and partnership agreement. In the plan, Lois and Mary stated they each planned *"to work 60 hours a week in the business."* They also stated, *"Both partners are hard working, self disciplined, dedicated, motivated, and have an excellent rapport with people."* Mary and Lois were well known and liked. They owned Haddy's Shack for three years—three tough years. As Lois explained:

We dumped the poor-quality inventory and took the loss. We didn't get the traffic downtown. The building was old. The parking was terrible. At times, derelicts were hanging around. We made money the first year, but it went downhill from there. We worked hard to keep each other going! Our "lifelines" were the Montana Silversmiths' product line, our credit cards, and our bankers.

Apple Village Plaza

In October 1999, Donna Godwin, the owner of Apple Village Plaza, was planning to construct a new building in the plaza; and she agreed to lease space to Mary and Lois and Montana Silversmiths™. Mary and Lois sold Montana Silversmiths™ first-line products in Haddy's Shack, so they asked the CEO of Montana Silversmiths™ if they could manage the planned factory outlet. He agreed, and Don and Danny agreed to finance the new venture. In November 1999, they opened the outlet in a temporary location behind the Apple Village Plaza. Then, for eight months they ran two stores—Haddy's Shack and the outlet in its temporary location. In June 2000, they closed Haddy's Shack and opened River Bend Trading and the Montana Silversmiths™ Factory Outlet in the new building. (For a chronological list of the important dates and events, see Exhibit 7.)

The Local Economy

In January 2002, the Columbus area economy was growing at about two percent per annum, and the unemployment rate was about five percent. Interstate 90 was the principal east-west highway through Montana. Yellowstone National Park and Glacier National Park were the two primary destinations of the nearly ten million tourists who visited the state each year. Tourist traffic on Interstate 90 increased in May, peaked in July and August, and decreased in September. Retail sales were typically slow in the January-March period.

The Stillwater Mining Co. (SMC) was the primary employer in Stillwater County (population 8,200). It was also the only producer of platinum and palladium in the U.S.A. In 2000, it produced more than 330,000 ounces of palladium and 100,000 ounces of platinum. It employed about 150 people between its headquarters and refinery in Columbus and about 1,300 people in its Nye and new East Boulder mines. Employment would increase to about 1,800 people, as the new mine expanded. As Lois explained:

> *SMC has been a good corporate citizen. It prepaid taxes to develop an infrastructure that would support the mining community—schools, roads, etc. In 2000, it paid 48 percent of the taxes in Stillwater County—over $9 million! It runs buses from Billings and Columbus, three shifts a day, seven days a week, to keep its employees off the roads and reduce accidents. The miners make good money, but they tend to spend it in Billings, not at River Bend Trading!*

Idaho Consolidated Metals was planning to develop its platinum and palladium resources in Stillwater County. However, the economic slowdown in 2001—propelled in part by the World Trade Center bombing on September 11, 2001—sent palladium and platinum prices crashing. Between 1996 and 2001, palladium prices rose almost $950 per troy ounce—from roughly $100 to $1,050 per ounce. By November 2001, palladium prices were hovering around $325 per ounce. Russia, who produced about two-thirds of the world supply of palladium, had flooded the market with palladium after withholding supply early in the year. In late October 2001, Dan Burkhart quoted SMC's CEO, Francis R. McAllister, as saying, *"A strategic partner, a merger, a buyout, a change in operations—all are under review. ... Obviously, we have some tough decisions to make."* By January 2002, palladium prices were about $400 per ounce.

Some of the local realtors anticipated growth in the "new town." However, Lois and Mary saw two trends. First, there was turnover in the "new town." Some businesses closed; new businesses started up; and occasionally, there was some vacant retail space. Second, despite the modest growth of the area and the business turnover in the "new town," the sales of River Bend Trading and the Montana Silversmiths™ Factory Outlet were increasing.

Montana Silversmiths ™ Factory Outlet

Montana Silversmiths™ produced silver jewelry and related products. Most of its product lines targeted western and rodeo lifestyles (e.g., belt buckles), although other product lines were being developed. The head office and a manufacturing facility were located in the "old town" in Columbus. Another manufacturing facility was located in Billings. At the head office, a telephone caller was greeted by an automated answering service. On talking to a person, the caller with a retail question usually received the telephone number of the Montana Silversmiths™ Factory Outlet in Columbus regardless of the geographic origin of the call.

The interior of the factory outlet reflected the "log cabin" façade of the building. The sales counter and cash register were toward the back of the store. The outlet had a bathroom and a heating and air conditioning unit. About 90 percent of the 800 square feet (20 x 40 feet) was usable retail space (Exhibit 8).

An Unusual Arrangement

Montana Silversmiths™ leased the space, paid the utilities, etc. Mary and Lois sold the products. The products in the outlet included: (1) first-line products owned by Mary and Lois and (2) discounted (outlet) jewelry owned by Montana Silversmiths™. First-line products met Montana Silversmiths'™ quality standards. The discounted jewelry was flawed or discontinued. Unlike some factory outlets, Montana Silversmiths™ did not minimize the defects with slogans like, *"You wouldn't notice the slight imperfection, but we* (the implied experts) *know where it is!"*

Mary and Lois received no revenue from the sale of the discounted jewelry. They paid the labor costs of selling the first-line products and the discounted items. Each day, they deposited the revenue from the sale of the discounted jewelry in a Montana Silversmiths™ account. One day Mary overheard a person from Montana Silversmiths™ who was stocking the outlet say to a person who was with her, *"They have it good and don't need to make anything on the discounted jewelry."*

Product Lines

Montana Silversmiths™ first-line products accounted for about 50 percent of River Bend Trading's total sales—about $200,000 annually. These were sold from display cases, tables, and racks and met all of Montana Silversmiths™ quality standards. The first-line jewelry was displayed in the front of the outlet store on shelves in two locked glass cases measuring about four feet wide by five feet high by two feet deep. It was purchased on normal terms, sold at a 50 percent markup, and carried a full unconditional guarantee against defects in workmanship. Mary and Lois had to stock the full complement of Montana Silversmiths™ lines including jewelry, bits and spurs, collectors' dinnerware, statues, and trophy belt buckles.

Montana Silversmiths'™ markup to the retailer was 50 percent, and the retailer's markup to the customer was 50 percent. Thus, an item that cost $25 to manufacture sold to the retailer for $50 and to the customer for $100 (i.e., markup percentage at retail = [retail selling price - merchandise cost] ÷ retail selling price).

The discounted jewelry was displayed in five similar cases; four of the cases were located at the back of the outlet store; and one was located near the front of the store. The items in three cases were discounted 30 percent; the items in another case were discounted 40 percent; and the items in the last case were discounted 50 percent.

Promotional taglines capitalized on the Montana mystique, for example, "Montana Brands – The Mark of the West," "Step Into the Night with Montana Silver," and "Wear the Legend." A mirror next to a display of belt buckles focused the viewer's attention on his or her mid-section—subtle comparative promotion!

Similarly, brand extensions capitalized on the Montana mystique. Watch displays carried taglines, such as "Montana Time," "Hard Workin' Watches," and "When It's Time to Get Tough." Racks displayed the Bit & Spur™ product line whose components were endorsed by Professional Rodeo Cowboys Association (PRCA) champions such as Fred Whitfield, John Lyons, Clinton Anderson, and Martha Josey. A display of Kow Boy Kids™ birthstones carried the tagline, "Every Kid is a Keepsake." Gift items, such as dishes, frames, and statues, were displayed on benches and tables and carried tag lines such as, "Montana Lifestyles" and "Western Home décor." Prices on the various Montana Silversmiths™ products varied (e.g., see the River Bend Trading Web site), but the product lines could generally be described as mid-line to up-scale, and the products were priced accordingly (e.g., $25-$250 each).

Montana Silversmiths'™ newest line of silver jewelry—B-Fussy™—was launched in May 2001. B-Fussy™ did not carry the Montana Silversmiths'™ name. The target market was women 12-18 years of age. The styling of the jewelry was simple, and it was lightweight. The promotional taglines were "Express Yourself" and "Jewelry that Screams with Independence." With a 60 percent margin, retail prices ranged from $4 to $14. There was no warranty. Mary and Lois felt the B-Fussy™ line had a "different look" that complemented the other jewelry. It proved to be a popular line.

Promotion

Montana Silversmiths'™ rented two billboards—one on either side of the Columbus exit on Interstate 90—at a cost of $500 per month. The billboards directed travelers to the outlet and enabled River Bend Trading to intercept the outlet bound customers. As Lois explained:

> *About 75 percent of our customers are travelers on Interstate 90; the rest are local people. The travelers typically have money and like to stop and shop in small towns. They're looking for gift items, outdoor clothing, and t-shirts. The women are typically the decision makers, and more than half of our customers are women. Last summer, several tour buses stopped in the plaza. I think the plaza storeowners would like to develop that market.*

115

Soliciting Customer Input

Montana Silversmiths™ asked the sales person to have first-time customers complete a survey at the outlet cash register. The survey asked, "How did you learn about our store?" Among other things, the responses over a 12-month period showed that 27 percent of the respondents learned about the outlet from a billboard on the interstate (Exhibit 9).

Performance Reviews—Making the Numbers

In late 1999, Mary and Lois secured the right to manage the Montana Silversmiths™ Factory Outlet; and they enthusiastically developed the business. A year later, they got a reality check:

> We thought we were really doing a good job; then, we had our first annual review in November 2000. We met Dick, the CFO, and Dennis, the CEO, for lunch at a restaurant. Dick had been encouraging, but Dennis said, "We'll have to watch this closely. If the right things aren't happening, we'll have to make some changes." We don't have a formal agreement with Montana Silversmiths™, so we're really concerned they might pull their outlet stock or decide to take over the first-line Silversmiths' part of the store.

Dennis's comments alarmed Mary and Lois. However, someone said Dennis was a "numbers" CEO and suggested they *"get their numbers together"* and *"present their case"* at the next review. Someone else suggested a *"relationship building"* strategy in which River Bend Trading would *"reach out"* to the employees at Montana Silversmiths™ and their spouses with impromptu *"special offers"* on clothing and gift items. The objective was to create personal relationships with people—especially senior managers—who might speak on Lois and Mary's behalf at Montana Silversmiths™ and who might counter the CEO's emphasis on Lois and Mary's "making their numbers" (e.g., people like Dick, the CFO).

Mary often made several trips a day to the manufacturing facility in Columbus to pick up special orders (e.g., engravings) while the customer waited in the store or visited other stores in the plaza. In June 2001, the facility's office manager told Mary she could only pick up special orders at three times during the day because *"it disrupted the office staff's operation too much."* Some customers refused to wait, and Mary lost those sales. She documented the lost sales.

In November 2001, Mary went to the manufacturing facility in Columbus to pick up an order. Dennis saw her and asked her to come to his office. There, he asked several questions. How were she and Lois doing? Did she think the billboards were effective? Had she heard any comments about the quality of the Montana Silversmiths™ jewelry? He also indicated they were thinking about doing a customer satisfaction survey. As Mary was leaving, she met a friend who said, *"I saw you in Dennis' office. Is everything okay?"* Mary said, *"Sure, what's going on?"* Her friend said, *"Oh, I thought you knew. Dick quit!"* When Mary asked what happened, her friend said, *"They'd have my head if I told you."*

Mary told Lois what happened. A few days later, they met at Pat's house to talk things over. After a long discussion, Pat summed things up by saying:

Look, Montana Silversmiths™ is a big part of your business, but look at their options. What can they do? They can move the factory outlet to some other place (e.g., Billings), but the local Montana Silversmiths™ retailers would be angry. A Billings retailer was furious over the opening of the factory outlet in Columbus. They could keep the present location and replace you—either by hiring someone to manage the outlet or by selling the outlet. If they hired employees, they'd need, say, one employee for12 hours/day at $10/hour for 350 days a year plus another employee for the busy season for eight hours/day at $8/hour for 120 days. They might find these options were more expensive than they thought! They might also find it's good business to support local business in small communities—especially two women who have lived in the community for a long time! Lastly, they might move the outlet to a larger store in the plaza, perhaps with new owners!

When you started selling Montana Silversmiths™ jewelry, you didn't know anything about jewelry. Now, you know how to sell jewelry! You could sell any kind of jewelry—Black Hills gold, Mexican silver, or Montana sapphires! Diana is recovering from cancer, and she is selling her store in Billings (the store, Bull Sessions, sold high-end Western clothes and gear). She and Steve want to travel and sell from a booth at the big shows like the National Finals Rodeo in Las Vegas. They have been doing these shows for years; but if she sells her store, the vendors probably won't sell to her. Also, for years she and Steve have been going to Mexico and buying silver jewelry. It has good margins! Maybe you could buy merchandise for her, and they could buy Mexican silver jewelry for you?

Evaluating the Sales of Montana Silversmiths™ Discount (Outlet) Jewelry

In anticipation of a November performance review, Mary and Lois started getting their "numbers" together. Among other things, they examined their sales of the discounted (outlet) jewelry owned by Montana Silversmiths™. Time passed; and by January 2002, Dennis had still not requested a meeting. The 2001 sales of discounted (outlet) jewelry came in at $156,818—up $10,340 from $146,478 in 2000. Pat and Lois analyzed the numbers and concluded that Montana Silversmiths™ was, as Mary put it, *"making out like a bandit!"* (Exhibit 10).

Selling on the Internet

River Bend Trading was the only Montana Silversmiths™ Web retail outlet that Yahoo's search engine recognized in January 2002. As Lois and Mary explained:

We put our business card with its Web address in every customer's package unless they're local. About five percent of our Montana Silversmiths™ sales come from the Web, but the volume is growing. Only first-line products are sold on the

Web. We're getting about 200 hits a week, and we're receiving orders from all over the U.S. and even England, France, Holland, Japan, and Malaysia. We want to develop a secure site for order entry and credit card transactions. If we lost the Montana Silversmiths™ line, we'd have to redesign the Web site. A lot of our clothing lines and gift items with their short life cycles and limited stock wouldn't work on a Web site. However, the River Rags line might work online.

River Bend Trading

River Bend Trading occupied 2,000 square feet (50 x 40 feet). Necessary features (e.g., office, dressing rooms, bathroom, furnace and air conditioning, and a rear exit hallway) spanned the back of the store. A counter and the cash register were in the center of the store surrounded by glass cases displaying gift items and jewelry. About 70 percent of the 2,000 square feet was usable retail space (Exhibit 8).

The "log cabin" façade of the building extended to the interior of River Bend Trading where three-way peeled pine display racks and clothes trees gave the place a warm friendly ambiance with traces of the rugged Montana outdoors. The central theme featured moose— moose dolls, moose clothes trees, moose clothing logos, and moose silhouettes. Associated features accented trees, canoes, streams, and log cabins. Warm yellow pine accented doorframes, window frames, and dressing rooms. Customers tended to linger and browse, and the average customer purchased about $85. Men found the pine display racks intriguing. They asked, *"Are these really horseshoe nails?"*

Product Lines

As a customer entered the store, s/he would see women's clothing on the right (about 800 square feet) and men's clothing on the left (about 300 square feet). A small "kid's corner" (about 40 square feet) bordered the men's clothing. Gift items were displayed in one corner, around the cash register, and scattered throughout the clothing areas (about 210 square feet). The scattered gift items were "little finders and keepers." "Waterfall" racks displayed women's clothing along two walls (e.g., jumpers, blouses, shirts, tops, etc.), and the windows, walls, and counter tops were used to display merchandise. A small display of Lewis and Clark memorabilia would be expanded as the bicentennial celebration of the 2004-2006 expedition approached. A local radio station played country-western music in the background. As Christmas approached, Mary and Lois played Christmas music. Rotating screen savers on the computers at the cash registers replicated the paintings of Charlie Russell, one of Montana's famous artists (e.g., scenes of cowboys, Indians, horses, and mountains).

Mary and Lois followed common practice and used the retail-selling price to calculate markup (Exhibit 11). They monitored sales and gross profit by department (Exhibit 12). The gross profit (i.e., sales less cost of goods sold) showed the amount of revenue available to cover operating expenses. The residual revenue went to the partners.

Merchandising in retail was a challenge, but Mary and Lois felt they met the needs of the tourists and local clientele. As Mary and Lois explained:

Women's clothing turns the fastest. In women's clothing, the racks near the door carry the popular more expensive items—the impulse items! We continually change these racks. The sale items and the standard items, like slacks, go in the back of the store. The jumpers and other semi-impulse items display nicely along the two walls. We'd like to use the space effectively, but we don't want shoppers to be frustrated because they can't get around.

The balance between women and men's clothing is good. Men don't shop here much. For them, we have shorts and t-shirts and Wranglers™, button front shirts, underwear, and socks. That's all men need! However, the men really love the little kids camouflage outfits! They'll buy them!

Vicky, a salesperson, felt the store gave customers an opportunity to "mix and match." She showed customers how to combine items to create unique outfits. As she noted, *"It's a fun store with a classy sporty look! I'm the color coordinator. Here, everything works together."*

Purchasing Merchandise at Market

Lois had 20 years of retail clothing experience, and she did most of the buying. Mary—who was an excellent salesperson—accompanied her on buying trips. As Mary quipped:

Sometimes we disagree on colors. I like yellows and greens, so she has to control me. If she let me do the buying, I couldn't afford to buy the leftover inventory. Lois is good at "layers." She puts together coordinated outfits men and women will buy right off the display.

Lois and Mary went to the Billings "market" four times a year. It was the largest market for men and women's clothing, gift items, and western tack and clothing in the surrounding six-state region. They also attended a Montana market once a year in Great Falls, Montana, where they purchased Montana-made products. At market, they found out how other retailers were managing their businesses, merchandising their product lines, and so forth. Going to market, was also an opportunity to visit other retail firms to gain new merchandising insights.

Mary and Lois generally purchased men and women's clothing about six months in advance. However, they purchased their Woolrich™ line—their major line in men and women's wear—about 12 months in advance. As Lois explained, *"Woolrich™ is a great company to do business with. Many of our customers eagerly wait for each new shipment."* Women's clothing lines included Rocky™, Bacca™, and Citicraze™. Men's clothing lines included Wrangler™ and Nocona™. Mary and Lois usually purchased gifts items about two months in advance. Jewelry and gift lines included Ron Yazzie™, a Native American silversmith, Kay's Jewelry™, Peg Montana™, and Will Creek Trading Company™. Lois and Mary had established their credit worthiness and rarely had to pay in advance. Accounts were paid 30 to 90 days after receiving the product, and there were generally no incentives for early payment. Mary and Lois financed their short-term credit needs with credit cards rather than use their higher-cost bank line of credit.

The summer stock was typically in by the end of April. The winter stock began arriving in July and was usually in by the end of October. As soon as stock arrived, it went on display. As Lois explained, *"You can't sell it if it's in the back room!"* The wrinkles were steamed out of all clothing items before they went on display.

Promotion

Lois and Mary used different means of promoting their products. Lois said, *"Advertising is the hardest part of managing the business."* They advertised in Montana magazines and the *Stillwater County News*. For example, with the start of hunting season in October 2001, they ran a 4x5-inch ad stating, *"They hunt ... You shop!"* The best results came from making and mailing flyers with coupons. In mid-November 2001, they ran an advertisement in the *Stillwater County News* and sent a flyer to 4,200 households in Stillwater County inviting people to *"celebrate the season with wine & cheese and register to win great prizes"* on the evening of November 20th. The flyer announced special drawings and discounts on the Thursday evenings before Christmas and wished everyone *"Happy Holidays"* from *"Lois and Mary and the crew at River Bend Trading."* At times during the summer, Lois and Mary promoted the store with free barbecued hot dogs and hamburgers; and Mary dressed as a clown and painted faces on the kids. The Chamber of Commerce included their brochure in its information packets.

Customer Service

Mary and Lois believed they had the ability to "read" customers. Pat recounted a situation in which two men in their late forties came into the store. They were returning to their out-of-state homes from a fishing trip and had to catch a plane in Billings. They had forgotten to buy gifts for their wives and children, and they did not have much time to shop. As Pat explained:

> *Mary and Lois quietly and assuredly worked with the two men to help them find what they needed for their families. They showed them things, made suggestions, and let them make their own decisions. In less than 20 minutes, they bought over $200 worth of stock—Montana Silversmiths™ jewelry and other gift items.*

As Lois explained:

> *Customer service is what we do best. We look after our customers. For example, men will call us up and say, "Tomorrow is Valentine's Day, and I want something nice for my wife. You pick it out. Gift wrap it. Oh yes, would you please deliver it?" We deliver, and we try to remember what people like. Then, we call them when we get new things in we think they would like. We keep notes on people. Notes are everywhere!*

Occasionally, shoplifting was a problem. Lois thought it cost them one to two percent of their inventory annually. As she explained:

It's hard when there are only three of us working and a shoplifting team enters the store. Three will engage the employees over purchases, and the others will move through the store. We have two entrances, adding to the problem. We have our jewelry in cases, but some of the small items are on display and vulnerable. A skilled shoplifting team really makes it difficult to protect the merchandise.

Soliciting Customer Input

Lois and Mary knew some of River Bend Trading's sales came from intercepting people who initially intended to shop at the outlet. They did not know if the shopper was attracted by the Montana Silversmiths™ brand or by the idea of an outlet store or by some combination of the two. Therefore, they initiated a survey in River Bend Trading in June 2001. The sales person asked first-time customers to complete the survey while their purchases were processed. By January 2002, nearly 90 customers had completed the survey (Exhibit 13). The survey results appeared to validate Lois's view that, *"Customer service is what we do best."*

The Point-Of-Sale System

Mary and Lois's extensive use of notes contrasted sharply with their Retail Inventory Control System™ (RICS), which was a management and point of sale (POS) computer system. Kathleen, Mary's sister-in-law, managed the office and worked about 32 hours a week. She implemented RICS, and she maintained it as well as the QuickBooks™ accounting system. RICS and QuickBooks™ were not electronically integrated. As Mary bantered:

I'm the messy one! I'm not even allowed in the office! Lois is the visionary and the organized one. In the past, when we went to market, Lois used an open-to-buy worksheet she'd created by hand. She still uses clipboards for tracking vendors, and she keeps notes on pads of paper. Neither of us likes computers.

The point-of-sale system had an excellent report generation capability. In May 2001, Pat asked for a report that identified River Bend Trading's best selling brands and compared the sales per brand to the corresponding inventory (Exhibit 14). She said, *"The key to success in retail lies in using the POS system to identify cost reduction and value creation opportunities."*

Shortly thereafter, Kathleen told Lois the store needed better control over purchasing new merchandise. One evening they met at the store, and Kathleen developed a monthly "open-to-buy" report. Kathleen told Lois to print the report prior to a buying opportunity. It answered a key question: What was the projected availability of cash for purchasing new merchandise? By August 2001, Lois and Mary were using the open-to-buy report. At the end of each day, they also used the point-of-sale system to see what was selling (i.e., to manage inventory turns) and to monitor gross profit. Yet, to Kathleen's concern, they did not show much interest in the monthly income statement, balance sheet, or cash flow statement.

Employees

The store and the factory outlet were open seven days a week. Mary and Lois had about ten employees, including Kathleen. Three to five women worked in the store on any given day. Jenny and Theresa, their daughters, worked 10-15 hours a week in the store during the summers. During the school year, they worked on weekends as their sports schedules allowed. They sold merchandise and created and distributed flyers, direct mailers, and other promotional pieces. Lois and Mary put family first and encouraged their employees to do the same. For example, when River Bend Trading had its grand opening, Jenny was roping in a high school rodeo, so Lois went to the rodeo and missed the grand opening. None of the employees worked full time, and they were encouraged to cover for each other. As Mary and Lois explained:

> We hire women who like to talk to the customers. Most of our employees are women who want to work part-time and love to work with the customers. Their skills add value; they don't just wait on customers. We select our employees. We have never advertised for help in three years! We pay about $6.00 to $8.50 per hour and offer a 40 percent discount on clothing and gift items.

> Vicky maintains the log cabin ambiance. Theresa Lehman created the ambiance. One day Theresa told us to take her off the schedule. No one quits or gets fired at River Bend Trading! They just get taken off the schedule! Theresa developed the Montana Tess line of hand soaps, body lotions, etc. we carry in the store. Lynn manages the Web-site correspondence. Darlene owned an antique shop. She knows everyone, and she helped us keep the local clientele when we moved from Haddy's Shack. Marla took a leave of absence from teaching in Iowa to complete her straw cabin in the Beartooths. Jolene (Lois's niece) designed our Web site. She and her husband raise cattle and horses on a ranch in the Missouri Breaks.

Mary and Lois felt fortunate to have attracted competent people, even though they could not afford to provide medical, dental, or retirement (e.g., 401k) benefits for their employees or themselves. Lois said, "Our bankers have given us phenomenal support! Pat has helped us 'think through' and 'do the numbers' on our ideas. Our friends have really supported us!" Sometimes they got a little extra help—Mary said, "Every so often miracles happen. We had an employee who wasn't working out. We didn't want to fire her. Then, God sent a divorce and she moved! Thank you, God!"

Thinking About the Future of the Business

The daily operation of the business took most of Lois and Mary's time. There was little time to think about the future of the business. They were starting to develop a new clothing line, "River Rags"—a go-anywhere, stylish, unisex line of jackets, sweatshirts, t-shirts, etc. in basic colors.

They were applying for a registered trademark and evaluating potential suppliers of clothing and logo embroideries. Lois said, *"River Rags would work on the Internet because it isn't seasonal or vulnerable to fashion trends."* Recently, a friend had asked Lois and Mary:

> *What images come to mind when people hear or see the words "River Bend Trading"? I see the wild horses, whitewater rapids, awesome mountains, vivid sunsets, and rugged people featured in the movies about Montana—A River Runs Through It, Horse Whisperer, Legends of the Fall, and Lonesome Dove. How does "River Rags" fit the image? How can you capitalize on these images?*

Lois and Mary had considered expanding the Woolrich™ line http://www.woolrich.com. They had a good relationship with Woolrich™; it was a strong brand; the margins were good; and the brand image was consistent with the Montana mystique. One problem was lack of space; but if Art is Everywhere vacated its space—about 800 square feet—River Bend Trading might be able to expand into that area. Yet, as Lois noted, *"Her frame cutting saw seems to be operating all day. She seems to be doing okay."*

"Flat Lining" in the First Quarter

In January 2002, Pat stopped at the store on her way home from work to ask how Jenny had placed in the rodeo. She walked in and asked, *"What's up?"* and Mary said, *"Our after-Christmas sale was a big success! Since then, things have been slow. Oh yah, guess what? The Montana Silversmiths™ performance review may be next week! It's time for a strategy session!"* Pat said, *"How about now?"* Lois said, *"I can't tonight. I've got horses to feed, and Jenny has homework."* Mary added, *"I better not, Kevin probably has dinner ready by now."*

Later, as Lois was feeding her horses she reflected on the business. How could they improve the cash flow? How could they modify the informal agreement with Montana Silversmiths™? How could they reduce their dependency on Montana Silversmiths™? How could they improve their relationship with Montana Silversmiths™? Then in her mind, she heard Mary's laughter as she said, *"We're going to be all right!"* Lois laughed quietly to herself and said, *"And I'm going to have a life!"*

CASE STUDY 9

A Kona Condo for My Island Bed and Breakfast Inn

"Get a condo in Kona and take advantage of your good name. You'll leverage the reputation you've built, get some extra income, and gain a valuable asset." That well-intentioned advice from My Island Bed and Breakfast Inn's accountant kept coming to mind as Gordon and Joann Morse went over the figures and pondered whether to add an accommodation on the other side of the island. As the operators of a successful bed and breakfast in Volcano Village on the Island of Hawaii, they regularly were asked by guests about a place to stay in Kona. Lacking either a bed and breakfast unit in Kona or the necessary State Property Manager's License to collect a referral fee, the Morses were passing up a likely new source of revenue. It was late at night as the Morses sat at the handsome wooden breakfast table where twenty-one guests staying at their historic house and eight other nearby units would soon be gathering for breakfast. They knew this was going to be a tougher decision than their accountant foresaw. Not only would a condo be located a hundred or so miles away, but it would be their biggest investment since they bought the historic Lyman Missionary Family Home and turned it into Volcano Village's largest bed and breakfast.

Morse Family Businesses

Starting and operating a business came naturally to the Morses. Over a 41 year period they created four successful "mom and pop" businesses. All were begun with very little money down and without large bank loans to finance growth. One of Joann's oft repeated sayings is "Just as the least said is soonest mended, the least borrowed is soonest repaid." One startup, for example, was a motor home and vehicle rental company centered on the Big Island, as the Island of Hawaii was commonly called. It filled a niche left open by car rental companies such as Avis, Hertz, and National and the Morses developed with it their preferred way to finance a business. Start with one vehicle and pay off the loan before getting another. Once there were two vehicles clear of debt the cash flow would be enough to cover the loan on a third. The ratio of two cash generators to one unit still in debt, while not expanding faster than could be safely financed, worked well. Holding rigorously to it meant the business did not grow faster than the ability to finance it.

With their four children grown, an offer to sell three of their businesses and go into retirement was too tempting to pass up. It was exciting for the Morses to see the

By Steven M. Dawson, University of Hawaii. Management assisted in the field research for this case, which was written for the purpose of stimulating student discussion. All events and individuals are real. I gratefully acknowledge suggestions from Nicholas Ordway and financial support from the UH Center for Entrepreneurship and E-Business.

annual income produced by the businesses converted into the much larger value the purchaser paid. Unfortunately for the new owners all three businesses went bankrupt soon afterwards. Why? "Simply," the Morses believed, "because the businesses were solvent and successful, the owners became too complacent and forgot to pay attention to their limits." The new owners saw the amount of profit and the non-existent debt, formed ideas for growth beyond practicality, and expanded too quickly. Without crunching the numbers, and growing the business over a number of years, they overextended themselves. The motor home business owner, for example, couldn't pass up an opportunity to also rent cars. He had bought a fleet of fifty cars from another vehicle renter who was going out of business. Not being used to the high prices and way of doing business in Hawaii, he couldn't stand buying what he considered overpriced parts from Big Island parts suppliers. Therefore, he started his own supply business, importing parts from Seattle to service his vehicles. The additions to the rental fleet meant a big increase in debt payments and the parts department required a large capital outlay. It wasn't long before more money was going out than coming in. Then when competition arose, and a downturn in the economy came about, he couldn't make it. Lacking was an understanding of the Morses' "mom and pop" concept of business, namely to maintain a profitable business for providing income for the family with "the wolf never coming to knock on the door." "Don't risk the family's economic future." Instead, "let other people speculate and try to burn up the world."

There was another business concept the new owners did not see. In all the Morses' businesses their creed was to give more value and service than the client paid for or expected. This resulted in having more repeat customers than most businesses could expect, and word of mouth advertising that allowed for drastic reductions in advertising expense. The Morses felt that the new owners who went bankrupt would not think of doing more than expected of them. Generally their short-sighted philosophy was "there are millions of customers out there. If one is dissatisfied, there are always more who will pay for what we offer."

With the funds from the sales of the businesses safely in the bank, the Morses "retired" to VolcanoVillage where Gordon wrote and published tour books, children's books, and novels for teenagers, and Joann went into real estate and painting.

The My Island Bed and Breakfast Inn

It wasn't long before the Morses saw a new business opportunity in Volcano Village. Because the one hotel in the nearby Volcano National Park was small, poorly run, and couldn't be expanded since it was located in the National Park, bed and breakfasts (B&Bs) were opening up in nearby Volcano Village. If they could find a suitable property, the Morses could have a go at yet another business venture. After some delay, and considerable courtship of the trust which owned the Lyman House, the historic summerhouse built in 1886 by the Lyman Missionary family, the Morses bought the old house and had the property they needed for a bed and breakfast.

Long interested in the history of Hawaii, the Morses could hardly believe what they now owned. In 1868, a huge tidal wave and earthquake had devastated villages on the south side of the Big Island. The Lyman family in Hilo had sent a wagon of relief supplies. Near what would become Volcano Village, the axel broke and the Lymans fashioned a new one from a tree. Because it was late in the day, they spent the night sleeping under the wagon. Years later they asked King Kamehameha III if they could buy this piece of land for a summerhouse. When the Morses bought the house they got the original deed, a piece of paper Gordon liked to point out was possibly worth more than the house itself since it had the original signatures of King Kamehameha and the Lymans. Operating a B&B in a historic house would provide needed income, and give the Morses the opportunity to share their passion for Hawaii with tourists. The Morses, and their daughter Kii, who had moved back from the mainland to help manage the B&B, were each one-third owners.

Surprisingly many of the principles learned by experience worked in the B&B. The Morses paid careful attention to guest satisfaction, employee morale, and careful expansion. Guests were treated to a tasty breakfast in the dining room. When they arrived, Gordon gave them copies of his suggestions of how and what to see. When the Morses traveled, they made it a point to stay at least once a week in a B&B to see how they felt as guests and to pick up new ideas. Just as with the motor home rentals, business grew gradually. Being careful not to expand too fast, three new "garden units" were added on the seven acres of land that came with the house and an additional five-offsite houses owned by others were added. The Morses built the three on-site rental units with their own money, and a lot of their own labor, as cash flow was available.

In checking the financial merit of the new units, the Morses looked at what they thought they could take in from rentals in the first full year of normal operations, less the cash expenses, and divided it by the funds they invested up front building and furnishing the units. Their accountant said this was called a "cash on cash return." Requiring that an outlay produce an expected positive cash flow avoided cash drains and provided the reliable family income source the Morses wanted from their businesses. Using the first full year meant not relying on lengthy forecasts. Based on the experience with their original B&B units, it looked even before construction of the new units started that there would be a positive cash return and the return to the funds invested would beat the minimum 10 percent after tax return the Morses expected from their investment holdings. Sure enough, the first year exceeded projections and the occupancy figures were safely above the breakeven number of nights.

The five-offsite units were homes whose owners were often away. Instead of leaving their homes vacant, the owners one by one had arranged with the Morses to manage their units as B&Bs in return for sharing the rental income. The Morses handled reservations, cleaning, and breakfast for the guests. The big advantage of managing other people's homes was that there was no investment in property by the Morses. But there was a downside. Sometimes the owners would, on short notice, decide to come over and stay in their homes. This cut the revenues for the Morses and occasionally bumped guests with reservations who then needed accommodations elsewhere. Other times the homeowners would send over friends who would stay for free but the Morses, for public relations reasons, still provided the cleaning service.

The Condo in Kona

As the year 2001 began and the three new on-site units were all built, the Morses could look around with satisfaction at their very well regarded B&B Inn. The guidebook, *Hawaii Handbook*, referred to its "excellent reputation" and they were regularly turning away inquiries because they were already booked. Many guests asked the Morses opinion on where to stay on the Kona Coast on the other side of the Island. Hawaii. The Morses would give them a list of Kona B&Bs and condos with phone numbers and prices, and say "good luck." Several years earlier the Morses had referred guests to specific B&Bs in return for a commission, but they subsequently decided this wasn't worth the effort. A current real estate property manager's license was needed to legally collect referral fees. The State "puts a lot of monkeys on our backs," complained Gordon, by requiring the fees collected before service is provided are kept in a separate bank account which the State can inspect. Bad experiences with travel agencies going out of business and not returning customer deposits had made the State extra cautious. The paper work of referrals also put a burden on the office staff. The real clincher was that a number of B&Bs didn't pay the fees owed. "We didn't enjoy writing letters to friends telling them they owed us money." Kii, the Morse's daughter, decided "let's not do referrals anymore."

Just as it seemed they once again had it made, their accountant suggested they "get a Kona condo and book these guests into it. Put the profit into your own pocket, and at the same time have them pay for the asset." The Morses had been successful in business by not overlooking opportunities so they followed up on the accountant's suggestion. A condo would be a major investment and the Morses did their usual thorough investigation. To keep a good handle on customer satisfaction, the Morses' target market would be guests at their main B&B location who were looking for a place to stay in Kona, either before or after their stay at Volcano. A computer check of guests at My Island B&B Inn who requested a Kona accommodation over the past four years found that the majority were a couple, a couple with a third adult, or a couple with 1 or 2 under teen children. This pointed toward a one-bedroom unit rather than a studio or two bedroom. About twice a month the Morses made a trip to Kona to buy supplies at Costco. They used the trips to look at various condos, to stay in some of them overnight, and to talk to owners of some units. They learned that one bedroom units ranged in price from $90,000 to $160,000 with many having desirable locations. The lower price units had "garden" or "mountain" views. The typical one bedroom condo was better than the studios which usually felt confining, were located with less desirable views, and had an image as a "make do" accommodation instead of the ideal Hawaiian vacation rental. This did not fit what the guests of My Island expected.

After considering their savings and the risk of adding a new unit, the Morses decided not to invest more than $125,000, including buying expenses. Fortunately they found a suitable unit with swimming pool access and a partial ocean view. A $20,000 down payment and a 15 year mortgage for the balance of $100,000 at the current 8 percent interest cost would produce a $955.65 a month mortgage payment. The $20,000 down payment plus $3,000 estimated startup costs would come from their Merrill Lynch stock account and gradually be paid back. To avoid getting behind, the repayment would be $250 per month. Actually the Morses did not plan to keep the condo for the 15 year life of the mortgage. Five years was more like it. "The world of business changes and a successful business has to change with it. After 5 years we will consider selling the condo at whatever price it commands, pay the mortgage off, and if we want to continue to have a condo we will use the rest of the proceeds as a higher down payment on a newer and better condo unit that our business sense says we should have by then." Besides, "if we paid all fifteen years to the bank, we would have paid over $170,000 for the condo. Would the building even still be there?" Real estate agents told the Morses that for a five-year holding period, an average annual appreciation of 8% as reasonable for this market. Similarly a reasonable annual range from a low of 2 percent to a high of 12 percent. When the condo is sold, selling costs will be about 8 percent of the selling price. If a new condo is bought, a 1031 exchange, named for the IRS section it refers to, would mean no tax was due on the gain if they reinvested in a more expensive condo. That's convenient because the Morse's combined federal and state marginal tax rate is 35 percent. With any luck the condo appreciation would give the Morses the option of a nice new down payment ready to use.

During their investigation of the choices the Morses made a list of startup costs, revenues, and expenses:

Startup costs: $3,000.
Besides the furniture and supplies purchased with the condo, there will be redecoration, upgrading and "Hawaiianizing" of the apartment to meet the expectations of clients, and to give the guests the feeling that they are getting what they are paying for. From 17 years of decorating a B&B, the Morses knew guests expected quality pictures, paintings, and wall decorations that are of the Pacific, Hawaii, and Polynesia. Bed and bath linens must be of superior quality, and color-coded to the apartment's decor. Same with kitchen eating and cooking equipment. Every rental condo they inspected in Kona lacked all of these. The existing rental condos shout "This is a rental unit, and it is 'plain Jane' because we figure clients will misuse it."

Room rates: $90 per night, double occupancy. Twenty dollars more per extra adult. Fifteen dollars per extra child. Based on experience at My Island, the average nightly revenue per night of occupancy would be $98 and occupancy would range from 18 to 28 nights per month, with the average occupancy being 23 nights. In comparison, the typical visitor rental charges per night in Kona for a one bedroom, ocean-view unit was $75 to $120. Over time room rates will edge up, but so will expenses with the difference between the two remaining about the same

Management fee: 10% of rental revenue.
The building manager owns one of the condo units, and has a tiny office. She can do telephone answering, collect deposits up front, provide visitors with details regarding arrival and departures, and see that the unit is cleaned and ready for guests.

Condo monthly maintenance fee: $350.

Included are the basic building upkeep, grounds maintenance, swimming pool, electricity, air conditioning, water, cable TV service, trash removal, and parking.

Property tax and insurance (annual): $1200.

This is paid with the bank mortgage and includes homeowners insurance for personal property, state land tax, and special liability for guests.

Depreciation (annual): $2,564

The accountant told the Morses that residential property depreciates straight-line over 39 years. Twenty thousand of the $120,000 purchase price was allocated to land which does not depreciate.

Cleaning fee: **$33 per day of occupancy**.

Cleaning will cost a lot more than at My Island where it is about $15 per room and it will need to be watched carefully to be done well. The wiping, dusting, vacuuming, bed making, and kitchen and bathroom cleaning at a Kona Condo is okay, but it stops there. What a B&B needs also includes replacing expendable items such as toilet paper, light bulbs, paper towels, trash basket liners, soap, etc. What very seldom gets done, or not done at all are window cleaning and the presentation of the rooms. Fresh flowers go in rooms plus a selection of magazines and books (including visitor information pamphlets), the current TV guide, staples like coffee and filters, tea, sugar, salt and pepper, information on how to use the telephone, TV and VCR, island touring guide books and maps.

Replacements and repairs to condo: $1,000 every two years.

Once the condo is set up for operation, this becomes minor and is handled out of spare change now and then. Every two years or so there will be a major replacement of items running about $1,000.

Utilities: $19 per month

This is for telephone only as all else is paid in the maintenance fee.

Down payment payback: $250 per month.

As with the Morse's earlier businesses, providing income and not just growing the business is an important objective. To make sure the funds invested in the condo are repaid to the stock account, the Morses will write a check each month to themselves for $250.

"Let's sleep on this," Gordon said. "Knowing more than we do would help, but we'll need to go with the data we have. We can run the numbers tomorrow and see if we get our positive cash flow. Five-thirty will be here before we know it."

CASE STUDY 10

GLOBAL MARKET OPPORTUNITY IN THE OLIVE OIL INDUSTRY: THE CASE OF BASER FOOD

Altay Ayhan gazed out of his Istanbul office window in early January 2002, where the snow was falling slowly onto the streets below. As Sales and Marketing Director for Baser Food*, a wholly owned subsidiary of Baser Holding, a major Turkish industrial group, Ayhan was responsible for determining the future strategic direction of the company's olive oil business. He had a meeting in 2 weeks with his boss Mehmet Baser, and was expected to present his recommendations regarding growth strategies for packaged olive oil.

There were several options that occurred to Ayhan, each offering prospects for growth but with varying levels of risk. A fundamental question was whether Baser Food should focus on its domestic market or should it seek to expand its operations in its existing export markets. Since 1998, the company had embarked on an ambitious global effort, exporting its branded olive oils to the US, Russia and several other countries. This was due both to Ayhan's own efforts and the commitment of Mehmet Baser, who saw enormous potential in global markets. Alternatively, Ayhan could recommend a strategy of identifying potential new markets. Countries such as China and India with their large populations were attractive, although their unfamiliarity with the product meant that an expensive marketing campaign would have to be developed in order to change deeply held food habits. He could also focus on the major olive oil producing and consuming countries such as Italy, Spain, and Greece with whose brands Baser already competed in several markets. Ayhan anticipated that if he pursued the latter strategy, he would face an uphill struggle, since the local producers would fight hard to protect their home turf. Another factor he had to consider was the prolonged economic crisis that Turkey had been mired in since 2000. With a high annual inflation rate, and the resulting drop in real incomes, many Turkish consumers were switching to cheaper edible oils such as sunflower and corn oil. Ayhan realized that he was in for a difficult 2 weeks while he weighed his options and made his decision.

* We want to thank Mr. Altay Ayhan and Mr. Mehmet Baser for their valuable help in preparing this case. Prepared by Ven Sriram of the University of Baltimore and Zeynep Bilrin of Marmara University as the basis for class discussion rather than to illustrate either effective or ineffective handling of an administrative situation. Reprinted with permission from the *Case Research Journal*. Copyright 2002 by Ven Sriram and Zeynep Bilgrin and the North American Case Research Association. All rights reserved.

Background

Edible Oils

Edible oils, also called pourable oils, were liquid oils and formed a part of most diets around the world. Taste preferences varied regionally depending on the climate and availability of suitable seeds and vegetables. For instance, coconut oil was used in many parts of South-East Asia whereas in some African countries, cottonseed, peanut and palm seed oil were used. Similarly mustard, sesame, sunflowers, corn and soybean were also processed into edible oils in different areas. In the Mediterranean region, olive oil was an integral part of the cuisine although its use was spreading to other parts of the world as well. Olive oil was the only edible oil produced from a fresh fruit and was therefore not considered a vegetable oil.

Olive Oil

Olive trees grew best in warm climates with the right soil conditions. Each tree yielded on average about 15-20 kg olives -- about 3 to 4 liters of olive oil annually[1]. The major olive growing countries in the world -- Spain, France, Italy, Greece and Turkey in Europe; Syria, Lebanon and Israel in the Middle East; Morocco, Tunisia, and Algeria in Africa; Cyprus in the Mediterranean Sea; California in the USA – possessed these climatic and soil conditions. In Turkey, olive oil trees grew primarily along the southern coast of the Marmara Sea and along the Aegean coast.

Environmental and other conditions had a significant impact on olive yield, thus affecting the production of olive oil. Olive flies harmed the trees and decreased olive growth rates. In years when the climatic conditions were mild, output was high. In high productivity seasons and years, European buyers tried to cut the price[2].

Olive output was also affected by harvesting practices. This was especially so in countries such as Turkey, where olives were not picked mechanically. Instead, branches were hit with sticks in order to dislodge the fruit. It took at least a year for the damaged branches to regenerate and become productive again. Therefore, years with low volumes of production often followed high productivity years. In Turkey, climatic conditions had improved over the last 5 years, new olive trees had been planted, growers had been encouraged to increase olive production, and had also been trained in the care and watering of trees. As a result, production volumes had increased[3].

Production Process

Unlike other vegetable and seed-based oils however, olive oils were not commonly seen as a commodity for two major reasons. Firstly, much like wine, the weather, soil and other conditions determined the taste and flavor of the fruit, and as a result, the oil. Therefore, customers, particularly in the Mediterranean, have developed preferences for olives from specific regions. In fact, in countries such as Turkey, producers of packaged olives and olive oil frequently stated the place of origin on their labels. Secondly, olive oils were categorized based on taste, aroma and color. The best quality olives were crushed and pressed to yield oil, which, after filtration, was then ready for consumption. Extra virgin (called "sizma" in Turkey) and virgin (called "naturel" in Turkey) olive oils were processed mechanically or manually and did not involve any chemical processing. Extra virgin oil had an acidity level of less than 1.0% and was the premium product that commanded the highest prices and margins, whereas virgin had an acidity level of 1-2%. In the case of light, or refined, olive oil (called "rafine" or "kizartmalik" in Turkey), the product was refined, since the olives used would not be appropriate for consumption by merely crushing and pressing. A mixture of 85-90% refined olive oil and 10-15% extra virgin olive oil was called pure ("riviera" in Turkey)[456]. Pomace ("pirina" in Turkey), the lowest quality olive oil with a natural acidity level of over 2%, was refined, deodorized and bleached to reduce its acidity level. In most markets, it was not usually used for cooking but for other purposes such as in the manufacture of soaps and as animal feed.

Olive Oil and Health

Olive oil consumption has been increasing even in countries where it was not traditionally used. A major reason for its popularity was its health benefits. In countries such as the US, where there was a growing health-consciousness among some segments of the society, the industry had done a good job promoting the product's benefits: its effectiveness in lowering LDL cholesterol, raising HDL cholesterol, the fact that it was natural and rich in vitamins, etc. It was used both for cooking as well as a salad dressing[7].

Olive oil provided the basic fatty acids necessary for the body and also had a high caloric value; besides, some basic vitamins such as A, D, E, and K could only be dissolved in oil. It was the only natural fruit oil that could directly be consumed like fruit juice based on its natural odor, taste and color. Besides its health benefits, olive oil was believed to contribute to a soft, healthy and young looking skin[8].

Industry in Turkey

Market Conditions

Since November 2000, Turkey had been going through the worst recession in its history. The economic crises of November 2000 and February 2001 had shown the weaknesses of the economy and budget deficits had continued in a highly inflationary environment. For 2000, the wholesale price index rose by 51.4 % and the consumer price index by 54.9 %. For 2001, inflation rates were 88.6% for wholesale goods and 68.5 % for consumer goods[9].

The economy was highly unstable even after a year of attempts to stabilize it. Energy costs were increasing as a result of high government taxes, negatively affecting the structure of production costs. The overall domestic market shrunk by almost 10% in 2001.

Edible Oil Sector

For the olive oil sector, huge export opportunities existed in the Middle East and Turkic Republics. Lack of governmental support for the sector was a setback for Turkish olive oil exports in the year 2000[10].

Ayhan estimated the annual volume of domestic consumption of vegetable oils (e.g., sunflower, corn, cottonseed, and soybean) to be around 1 to 1.2 million tons[+] . The annual vegetable oil consumption was 17 kg per capita whereas around 1 kg of olive oil per person was consumed annually in Turkey. This contrasted with an annual per capita consumption in the EU of almost 4 kg. However, the EU figures masked the fact that per capita consumption in Mediterranean member countries such as Greece, Italy, and Spain was well over 10 kg annually. A comparison of the consumption of corn oil to sunflower oil revealed that the market share of corn oil had increased while the market share of sunflower oil was decreasing. This was partly due to the price difference resulting from the different rates of customs duties -- 38% for sunflower oil and 12 % for corn oil[11]. Ayhan's data showed that by volume, sunflower oil accounted for 81% of all edible oil consumption in Turkey in 2000, followed by olive oil with 10% and corn oil with 9%. By value, sunflower oil's share was 66%, followed by olive oil with 25% and corn oil with 8%. These differences in volume and value shares indicated that olive oil was more expensive than the other edible oils in Turkey.

In the period 1990/91 to 1994/95 an average of 81,000 tons of olive oil were produced annually, and in the period 1995/96 to 1999/00, the average annual olive oil production was 100,000 tons[12].

Table 1: Turkey's Olive Oil Exports by Type (Tons and US $ million)

Types	1997		1998		1999		2000	
	Tons	US $	Tons	US $	Tons	US $	Tons	US $
Extra Virgin	4,684	10,523	9,660	15,977	22,630	41,528	5,081	9,627
Virgin	4,362	8,797	3,755	5,966	11,819	16,243	1,453	2,587
Refined	23,980	47,592	14,751	22,420	26,144	44,143	1,844	3,747
Pure	6,636	14,775	18,096	27,845	36,291	64,066	6,250	13,077
OTHER	8,639	5,654	2,018	1,463	6,209	4,070	1,786	1,369
TOTAL	48,328	87,413	49,016	75,386	103,093	170,050	16,414	30,407

Source: Foreign Trade Department, www.igeme.org.tr

[+] Tons here and elsewhere in the case refer to metric tons, i.e., 1000 kg.

Turkey's Foreign Trade

Exports

Turkey's olive oil exports (Table 1) reflected some dramatic fluctuations from year to year. The reasons behind this were agricultural problems with olive growth, and as a result, olive oil production. Other important factors influencing Turkish olive oil exports were problems with marketing policy development and fluctuations in the supply of olive oil from other producing countries.

As a result of the increase in consumption and demand for olive oil in the world (see Table 4), new export market opportunities for Turkey had emerged. In total, Turkey exported olive oil to about 70 countries. The major importers of Turkish olive oil can be seen from Table 2.

Spain and Italy, which were also producers and exporters of olive oil, received a major share of Turkish olive oil exports between 1996-2000. Turkey's exports to these countries were dependent on their own production levels and demand structures. Turkish olive oil exports to these countries were mostly unbranded and in bulk form, and therefore, demand was high in periods when these countries were faced with agricultural problems and their own processing volumes were low. Bulk olive oil imported from Turkey was then processed and sold in these markets and/or re-exported to other markets under Spanish or Italian brand names. This meant that Turkish firms then were faced with competition from Turkish olive oil packaged and branded by re-exporters from other countries.

Table 2: Turkish Olive Oil Exports by Country (%)

COUNTRY	1996-2000	2000
USA	23.0	36.0
ITALY	31.0	6.0
SPAIN	24.0	14.0
SAUDI ARABIA	3.0	9.0
SWİTZERLAND	2.0	-
ARGENTINA	-	8.0
UNITED ARAB EMIRATES	-	4.0
OTHER	17.0	23.0
TOTAL	100.0	100.0

Source: Source: Foreign Trade Department, www.igeme.org.tr

Imports

Although Turkey was self sufficient in terms of olive oil to meet the domestic demand, there were also a small amount (1088 tons, US$ 2.06 million in 2000) of olive oil imports. Imports took place in seasons where the domestic production was insufficient. The major exporters to Turkey were Tunisia, Italy, Saudi Arabia, and Egypt.

<u>Competition</u>

Although Turkey was a major olive oil producer, olive oil only accounted for a small share of the total liquid oil market. While there were unbranded and unpackaged products, almost all branded sales went through supermarkets. The major brands were Komili (a Unilever Turkey brand), Taris (manufactured by a government cooperative) and others such as Kristal, Bizim and Luna. Ayhan estimated that Komili and Taris together accounted for about 60% of the market by value. Komili positioned their brand as healthy and as part of a modern life style while Taris was positioned as being more economical. Both had ongoing media campaigns and as a result, enjoyed some brand loyalty. However, partly as a result of Turkey's economic crisis, some olive oil consumers had been switching to cheaper brands (Taris' market share had been increasing while Komili's had been declining) while others were switching to less expensive cooking oils such as sunflower and corn. The high inflation rate was also a factor in making consumers more price sensitive and less brand loyal.

The World of Olive Oil

<u>Production</u>

Although olives could be grown in many parts of the world with the right temperature, soil, and climatic conditions, the bulk of world olive oil production was still concentrated in the traditional olive growing region, the Mediterranean rim. The EU and 6 other countries (Turkey, Syria, Morocco, US, Argentina and Egypt) accounted for almost 90% of world table olive production and almost all of world exports according to provisional 2000-01 data[13]. In the EU, the major producing countries were Spain, Italy and Greece.

Not surprisingly, the countries that were the largest olive growers were also the largest producers of olive oil (Table 3). The average global annual olive oil production between 1990-91 and 1997-98 was 1.992 million tons[14]. Of the EU total, Spain, Italy and Greece accounted for almost the entire production. The other olive oil producers included Israel, Lebanon, Cyprus, Iran, and Egypt.

Table 3: World Olive Oil Production ('000 tons)

	1995-96	1996-97	1997-98	1998-99	1999-00	2000-01
Algeria	51.5	50.5	15.0	54.5	33.5	50.0
Argentina	11.0	11.5	8.0	6.5	11.0	3.0
EU	1403.5	1754.5	2116.5	1707.0	1878.5	1919.5
Jordan	14.0	23.0	14.0	21.5	6.5	27.0
Morocco	35.0	110.0	70.0	65.0	40.0	35.0
Palestine	12.0	12.0	9.0	5.5	2.0	20.0
Syria	76.0	125.0	70.0	115.0	81.0	165.0
Tunisia	60.0	270.0	93.0	215.0	210.0	130.0
Turkey	40.0	200.0	40.0	170.0	70.0	200.0
Other	32.5	38.5	30.0	40.5	41.5	41.0
Total	1735.5	2595.0	2465.5	2400.5	2374.0	2590.5

Source: http://www.internationaloliveoil.org/eng/Eco-OliveOilProduction.html
Note: 2000-01 data are provisional

Consumption

As can be seen from Table 4, world consumption of olive oil had been increasing steadily. Interestingly however, the major producing countries were also the major consuming ones and this made Ayhan wonder whether cooking and eating habits could be changed so that consumers in non-producing countries would also switch to using olive oil, as they appeared to be doing in the US.

Table 4: World Olive Oil Consumption ('000 tons)

	1995-96	1996-97	1997-98	1998-99	1999-00	2000-01
Algeria	36.0	50.0	31.5	44.0	42.0	45.0
EU	1387.0	1566.5	1705.5	1709.0	1731.0	1776.5
Israel	7.5	7.5	6.5	9.5	12.5	13.0
Jordan	16.0	22.0	19.0	19.0	9.0	23.0
Morocco	25.0	50.0	55.0	55.0	55.0	47.0
Syria	78.0	85.0	95.0	88.0	90.0	110.0
Tunisia	34.5	70.0	52.0	49.0	60.0	60.0
Turkey	63.0	75.0	85.0	85.0	60.0	75.0
Australia	16.5	21.5	17.5	24.0	25.5	31.0
Brazil	23.0	21.5	27.5	23.5	32.0	35.0
Libya	5.0	10.0	7.0	16.0	11.0	12.0
USA	101.0	130.5	142.5	151.0	169.0	190.5
Canada	14.0	19.0	17.5	18.5	23.0	25.0
Japan	16.5	26.0	34.0	28.5	27.0	29.0
Other	24.5	84.0	84.5	93.0	75.0	108.5
Total	1892.5	2238.5	2380.0	2413.0	2422.0	2580.5

Source: http://www.internationaloliveoil.org/eng/Eco-OliveOilConsumption.html
Note: 2000-01 data are provisional

Based on some internal company data from the mid-1990s, Ayhan could see that per-capita consumption figures (Table 5) from selected countries showed that olive oil consumption was very small relative to vegetable oils both globally and in many of the major markets. However, given the increase in global olive oil consumption, Ayhan was sure that olive oil now accounted for a higher percentage of vegetable oil consumption, particularly in countries where segments of the population were health-conscious.

Table 5: Per-capita Annual Edible Oil Consumption

	Olive Oil (kg.)	Vegetable Oil (kg.)	% Olive Oil Share
Argentina	0.1	15.8	0.4
Australia	0.9	11.9	7.3
Brazil	0.1	13.0	1.1
Canada	0.5	17.4	2.9
Japan	0.1	12.5	1.1
USA	0.4	24.0	1.6
EU	3.9	19.5	19.8
World	0.3	9.5	3.6

Source: Internal company data, 1995

World Exports and Imports

As had been stated earlier, the Mediterranean countries accounted for the majority of global exports of olive oil (Table 6). Given the importance of olive exports to the economies of these countries, they, particularly the EU members, had been engaged in promotion programs in order to increase global olive oil import and consumption. In the 1998-99 season, Spain exported 275,000 tons, and Italy and Greece 180,000 tons each[*].

Table 6: World Olive Oil Exports ('000 tons)

	1995-96	1996-97	1997-98	1998-99	1999-00	2000-01
Argentina	4.5	6.0	7.5	6.0	6.0	4.0
EU	165.0	220.0	227.0	208.5	298.5	305.0
Morocco	11.5	35.0	7.5	15.5	0.0	0.0
Syria	11.0	6.0	3.0	4.0	2.5	10.0
Tunisia	26.5	115.0	117.0	175.0	112.0	108.0
Turkey	19.0	40.5	35.0	86.0	16.6	85.0
USA	9.0	8.0	4.5	6.0	5.5	6.0
Other	10.0	7.5	5.5	5.0	3.4	5.0
Total	256.5	438.0	407.0	506.0	444.5	523.0

Source: http://www.internationaloliveoil.org/eng/Eco-OliveOilExports.html
Note: 2000-01 data is provisional

---

[*] These numbers add up to more than the EU's export volume stated in Table 6 because all the EU figures in the case refer only to EU trade with non-EU countries whereas figures for individual countries reflect their total trade).

As can be seen from Table 7, there had been steady increases in world imports, due in part to the increased awareness of the health and other benefits of olive oil.

Table 7: World Olive Oil Imports ('000 tons)

	1995-96	1996-97	1997-98	1998-99	1999-00	2000-01
Argentina	0.5	6.5	7.0	3.5	2.0	7.5
EU	73.5	145.5	118.0	225.5	116.5	107.5
Australia	16.0	21.5	17.5	23.5	25.0	30.0
Brazil	23.0	21.5	27.5	23.5	32.0	35.0
USA	105.0	140.0	144.0	155.0	175.0	198.0
Canada	14.0	19.0	17.5	18.5	23.0	25.5
Japan	16.5	26.0	34.0	28.5	27.0	29.0
Switzerland	3.5	5.0	5.5	6.0	8.0	8.0
Other	40.5	49.5	50.0	67.0	59.5	77.0
Total	292.5	434.5	421.0	551.0	486.0	517.5

Source: http://www.internationaloliveoil.org/eng/Eco-OliveOilImports.html
Note: 2000-01 data is provisional

Company

History

Baser Food was a wholly owned subsidiary of Baser Holding, one of the leading industrial, commercial and financial groups in Turkey. Baser began in 1973 in chemicals and extended its operations into plastics, packaging, textiles, food, foreign trade and finance. The group's companies, such as Baser Chemicals, which operated a joint venture with Colgate Palmolive, have been successful in different sectors. Baser Food was a 100% family-owned company. Both Mehmet Baser and Altay Ayhan worked for several years for Colgate Palmolive in Turkey and were experienced brand managers in the fast-moving consumer goods sector.

Corporate Vision and Mission

Baser Food's vision was to produce the highest quality olive oil for customers all over the world. Hence, Ayhan's major focus was on sales and marketing activities for Baser's olive oil in both the domestic and international markets, and to assure a global brand presence. Both Mehmet Baser and Ayhan were committed to making the company's flagship olive oil brand (Cavallo d'Oro) a global one. However, given the high cost of global expansion, they were very careful in selecting export markets. Initially, they intended to focus on countries with per capita incomes over US$ 2000 and on certain low-income countries with large populations. In developing countries, it was felt that the higher socio-economic classes might be more willing to change cooking and eating habits and could also afford olive oil.

Product Lines and the Production

Baser Food specialized in the production of olive oil and was among the major olive oil producers in Turkey. Olive oil production, filling and packaging activities took place in the factory located in Mugla/Yatagan, on Turkey's Aegean coast. The factory employed the most recent technologies for the production of olive oil in accordance with the standards set by the International Olive Oil Council (IOOC) and regulations of the US Food and Drug Admisnistration. The processing, filling and packaging capacity of the plant in Mugla was around 3,000 tons per month[15]. The company was the only major Turkish olive oil producer that did not manufacture any products other than olive oil. In high yield years, the plant operated at approximately 80% of capacity and this fell to 40% during the alternate years, when olive oil production declined.

At the end of 2001, the company had an annual sales turnover of about US $25 million and employed approximately 50 people. Of its volume, $20 million was exported and the remainder was sold in Turkey both as a private label ($4 million) and under the company's brand, Cavallo d'Oro ($1 million). Private label brands included department store brands such as Migros and Metro in Turkey, and Quality, Tip and Aro in other European countries. Distributor brands such as Sclafani, Aurora and Roland were used in the US and Canada. Of the export volume, $12 million was unbranded, bulk exports, primarily to importers in Italy and Spain, where it was then repackaged and sold under the importers' brands. In many countries these exports were labeled as Italian or Spanish olive oil even though the contents were Turkish. US regulations required that such products had to be labeled as being imported from Turkey and state the source country (ies) of the olive oil although the label could indicate that the contents had been packed in Italy or Spain. Exports under the Cavallo d'Oro and other company brand names (MedOlive) accounted for $3 million of export volume and the balance was private label export such as the distributor brands mentioned earlier. Domestic sales growth had averaged a steady 10-15% over the last few years whereas exports had doubled over the past year. Margins varied from country to country and were approximately 15% for the company as a whole.

Brands

The key brand of the firm was Cavallo d'Oro. This brand was highly regarded in the many world markets where it had been introduced, due to favorable consumer perceptions about the quality of the oil, its attractive packaging and its strong image. The brand had been launched in the Turkish domestic market as well in retail chains such as Carrefour. (See Exhibit 1 for the brand positioning statement).

Exhibit 1: Cavallo d'Oro Strategy Statement

Brand:	Cavallo d'Oro
Primary Positioning:	Cavallo d'Oro branded olive oil contains only the best selected olives from the Ayvalik region of Western Turkey to give a delightfully aromatic taste to healthy meals. "The finest olive oil"
Objectives:	Brand awareness and trial in the short run To be a strong brand in the long run
Types:	Extra Virgin olive oil; Pure olive oil; Refined Olive Oil (light)
Competitors:	Spanish; Italian and Greek Brands
Source of Business:	Sunflower oil, corn oil, soyabean oil and margarine users and other olive oil brands in the market.
Target Market:	Health and taste conscious people
Physical Benefits:	Nutritional, good health, controlling cholesterol level, cell renovations, delays aging and heart disease. Helps improvement of muscles in children. Improves calcium in bones in older people
Emotional Benefits:	Feeling of heath and confidence
Reason to Buy:	Top quality olive oil from best selected olives of Western Turkey with right acidity and offering an enriched life.
Brand Character:	Natural, pure ,tasty, authentic
Pricing Strategy:	85 to 90% of market leader
Promotions:	Taste approval through sampling by taste panels, sachets and on-pack promotions
Sizes:	250ml–500ml –1lt glass 250ml–500ml –1lt –2lt plastic 3lt and 5lt tins

In certain foreign markets, such as Hungary and Israel, the company also used other brands such as MedOlive because the company used multiple distributors and each asked for a separate brand. So, whereas Cavallo d'Oro was the main brand as part of Baser's policy, the secondary brands were seen as well on store shelves in these markets. Baser felt that since many consumers in the US and elsewhere had strong favorable perceptions about Italian olive oil, it was to the company's advantage to use Italian rather than Turkish-sounding brand names.

International Operations

Baser Food was a member of the North American Olive Oil Association (NAOOA). The firm started to export Cavallo d'Oro at the end of 1999 and became the largest Turkish branded olive oil exporter in 2000. Thinking back over the past year's operations, Ayhan leaned back in his chair and felt very proud of the accomplishments of Baser Food. For the period November 1999 to September 2000, Ayhan estimated that his company had realized 37% of the total packaged olive oil exports of Turkey. And now in 2002, the company operated in about 20 international markets[16]. The main export market for Cavallo d'Oro was the United States where the product was offered for sale in major chain stores in 15 states. In addition, Baser Food also operated in other countries including Spain, Italy, Germany, Taiwan, Venezuela, Russia, Poland, Bulgaria, Georgia, Azerbaijan, South Korea, Malaysia, Canada, Romania, Saudi Arabia, and Ukraine.

In most foreign markets, Baser employed exclusive distributors who were not permitted to represent other companies' products. However, one of the two U.S. distributors also distributed Spanish olive oil as well as other canned food products such as fruits, tuna, and tomato paste. Two managers (one who majored in International Trade and the other with a degree in Economics/Business Administration) and two support staff assisted Ayhan at the Istanbul headquarters of Baser Food. Most market visits and distributor contacts overseas were handled directly by Ayhan. The assistants monitored and followed-up the company's plans and represented Baser Food at the many international food shows in which the company participated.

Since both Mehmet Baser and Ayhan traveled regularly to foreign markets and developed global strategic plans, they understood the need for patience when it came to international markets. Their experience with Colgate Palmolive, Polgat of Israel, and the sister company Baser Chemicals' operations in Ukraine had created an atmosphere in Baser Food that was strong in its international focus. The liaison offices in Russia and Kazakhstan were signs of the company's commitment to global business. Since Baser was an exporter, it faced little asset risk overseas but there were risks involved in the collection of accounts receivables. The use of a factoring payment system (i.e., selling receivables to a third party) and export credit insurance reduced these risks, but Ayhan recognized that some risk was unavoidable.

Future Objectives

Recently, the firm had begun to enter markets in Far East and the Pacific Rim including Japan, Australia, Taiwan and Malaysia since Mehmet Baser and Ayhan were very optimistic about the market opportunities in this part of the world. However, China with its 1.3 billion people only imported 2000 tons of olive oil annually (pure and extra virgin accounted for 40% each and pomace, because of its low price, the other 20%). This small volume of imports highlighted the task that lay ahead if a strategy of growth from non-traditional markets was to be pursued. At this point, the focus in these new markets was to gain distribution access and shelf-space, particularly in supermarkets that stocked and sold international foods.

Potential Markets

There were several foreign markets which Baser Food had entered, and others where olive oil consumption was expected to increase due to the promotional efforts of the IOOC[17]. While the domestic market was important, Ayhan had to weigh the risks and opportunities of focusing on Turkey versus attempting to expand in the markets Baser had already entered, or even enter new ones. He could certainly pursue multiple markets, but his resource constraints were forcing him to prioritize. He had gathered the following data on his key export markets.

<u>United States</u>

Ayhan attended the 2001 mid-year meeting of the NAOOA in San Diego, California. At this meeting, the association's chairman presented the following key data on the U.S. retail market (based on Nielsen and US Department of Commerce data):

- Nearly 50 new brands of olive oil had appeared in the US market in 2000
- Import volume for 2000 grew by 15% with extra virgin accounting for 45% of imports, up from 28% in 1991. At the retail level, extra virgin accounted for 37% of sales volume, up from 26% in 1996 and 47% by value, up from 35% in 1996.
- Olive oil accounted for 10% of all pourable oil retail sales by volume, and the category grew by over 16% in 2000. In terms of dollar sales, olive oil represented 32% of the value, making it the largest category by value. Annual sales were estimated at US $370 million.
- Household penetration was almost 30%.
- Most olive oil purchases were made in households with annual family incomes greater than $70,000, with a concentration on the East Coast. The New York metropolitan area accounted for over 33% of U.S. olive oil sales.

The growing trend in U.S. olive oil consumption could be seen from Tables 8 and 9. Household consumption had increased, partly due to the health benefits of the product, the growing interest in Mediterranean food (particularly Italian and Greek) and the incorporation of this cuisine into a healthy lifestyle. The success of Italian food chains meant that olive oil sales had been increasing in the food service sector as well, since many of these restaurants used olive oil in their cooking and often served it as an accompaniment to bread. ConAgra hoped to tap into this trend by launching Fleischmann's Premium Blend spread made with olive oil[18]. Also, the efforts of industry associations such as the NAOOA (www.naooa.org) and the California Olive Oil Council (COOC) (www.cooc.com) helped increase the awareness and usage of olive oil in the U.S. although the efforts of the COOC to promote U.S.-produced olive oils could hurt non-US producers such as Baser.

While the US market undoubtedly represented huge potential for Baser Food, the high costs and low margins concerned Ayhan. Because of the fierce competition, and relative lack of brand loyalty, chain store retailers were able to negotiate aggressively with manufacturers both in terms of prices and access to shelf-space. Ayhan estimated margins for Baser to be 10-15% and slotting fees to be between $25000 and $50000 for each SKU for the chain stores. Almost all of Baser Food's $500,000 annual marketing budget was spent on store-level promotion in order to gain retail support. Ayhan also estimated that $2 million would be required to implement a TV and radio campaign to build the brand. In 2000, Hormel Foods launched the Italian olive oil brand Carapelli in the US market with a $13 million TV and print campaign (compared with $8.5 million in total media expenditure for the entire category in 1999). Carapelli became the third largest brand in the US with annual sales of $31 million, with Unilever's Bertolli brand leading the market with $128 million in sales[19].

Table 8: U.S. Pourable Oils: Percent Volume Sales by Type

Type	1995	1996	1997	1998	1999	2000
Canola	22.9	23.2	23.0	26.1	25.7	25.4
Corn	20.4	20.7	19.6	18.5	18.2	17.5
Vegetable	47.0	46.9	47.0	44.5	45.2	44.4
Olive	7.7	7.0	8.0	8.4	8.3	9.6
Others	2.0	2.2	2.4	2.5	2.6	3.1
Total (Pounds MM)	1157	1184	1192	1182	1200	1211

Source: AC Nielsen (quoted in NAOOC chairman's report, Mid-year meeting, Jan. 2001)

The growth trend was also supported by AC Nielsen household panel data that showed a penetration of 29.8% for olive oil, up from 26.2% in 1997. At the retail level, olive oil sales had increased from $259 million in 1995 to $370 million in 2000. Canola oil continued to be popular because it was 2 to 3 times less expensive than olive oil. Also, some US companies imported canola oil and extra virgin olive oil that they then blended and packaged in the US. This blend retailed for a price lower than olive oil.

Table 9: U.S. Pourable Oils: Percent Value Sales by Type

Type	1995	1996	1997	1998	1999	2000
Canola	20.4	18.8	18.1	20.9	20.5	19.3
Corn	17.0	15.7	14.9	14.6	14.4	13.0
Vegetable	36.4	34.6	33.7	33.0	33.1	31.0
Olive	22.7	27.1	29.1	27.5	27.8	32.0
Others	3.6	3.8	4.0	4.0	4.2	4.6
Total ($ MM)	1037	1236	1221	1179	1158	1158

Source: AC Nielsen (quoted in NAOOC chairman's report, Mid-year meeting, Jan. 2001)

One trend in US imports (Table 10) was that virgin olive oil consumption, and therefore imports, was increasing, possibly due to its perceived health benefits and the industry's promotion efforts. (The figures in parentheses in the table represent the % share of virgin olive oil of total imports. For instance, 39% of imports from Italy in 1995 were of virgin olive oil).

Table 10: U.S. Olive Oil Imports by Country and Type ($ '000)

	1995	1996	1997	1998
Italy	248,929 (39)	341,937 (39)	313,140 (45)	243,350 (48)
Spain	46,265 (59)	63,996 (65)	53,782 (65)	53,349 (66)
Turkey	28,611 (23)	23,944 (23)	26,871 (40)	16,679 (31)
Portugal	2,076 (4)	2,936 (2)	2,805 (6)	3,320 (22)
Greece	9,500 (48)	12,584 (69)	13,098 (74)	9,981 (77)
Morocco	1,416 (28)	8,873 (65)	5,939 (52)	4,551 (84)
Tunisia	4,920 (81)	n.a.	2,876 (99)	3,511 (88)
Other	4,255	14,042	6,403	4,595
Total	345,972 (41)	468,312 (44)	424,914 (49)	339,336 (52)

Source: Compiled from Goksu, Caglar (2000). Olive Oil Export Market Research, IGEME

Australia

Australia was another country Ayhan was seriously considering as part of his expansion plans. There were several factors that made Australia an attractive potential market. These included:

- Its relatively high per capita income
- Political and economic stability
- Familiarity with Mediterranean cuisine as a result of immigrants from Italy, Greece and other countries in the region
- Australians' general concern with health and their diets – olive oil imports were growing at an average of 15% per year over the past several years.
- Although there was some domestic production, over 95% of olive oil consumed was imported, valued at close to US $100 million annually.
- Among the non-traditional olive oil consuming countries, its per capita consumption was high (Table 5)

As can be seen from Table 11, with the exception of a dip in 1997-98, there had been a steady increase in import volume. This suggested a growing acceptance of the product among Australian consumers. The olive oil market was less price competitive than the US and this enabled Baser Food to enjoy margins of 25-30%. Also, Ayhan believed that an initial investment of $100,000, in which local distributors would be willing to participate, would be sufficient to enter the market. Based on IOOC and Australian customs statistics for 1999-2000, Ayhan estimated 25% of these imports to be virgin/extra virgin, 74% pure and the remainder, pomace.

Table 11: Australia's Olive Oil Imports by Country (tons)

	1996/97	1997/98	1998/99	1999/00	2000/01
Spain	14,276	9,937	13,978	14,460	15,501
Italy	5,301	5,954	7,368	8,118	10,781
Greece	1,430	1,574	1,157	1,764	1,882
Turkey	143	156	671	87	540
Other	272	183	208	362	1195
Total	21,422	17,804	23,382	24,791	29,899

Source: http://www.internationaloliveoil.org/tm/australia/STATS06.html

Others

In addition to the U.S. and Australia, the IOOC had identified several other countries that they felt represented potentially viable markets. These were: Brazil, Canada, China, Japan, Mexico, Taiwan and Thailand. As a result of the IOOC's promotional efforts and the increasing popularity of the Mediterranean diet emphasized by the EU promotional campaigns, olive oil consumption had begun to spread into these non-traditional markets[20]. However, there was some instability because for the majority of the consumers in these markets, olive oil was still a non-essential product and the demand was therefore both more price and income elastic than in the traditional consuming countries such as Spain, Italy or Greece. One way of approaching these new markets would be for the major Turkish producers to create a joint fund, with some support from the Turkish government perhaps, to stimulate primary demand. However, Mehmet Baser felt that this was not likely in the near future and any demand stimulation would have to be done by Baser Food alone. This could prove to be very expensive.

Another opportunity for growth came from Turkey's membership in the Black Sea Economic Cooperation (BSEC) agreement and its customs union arrangement with the EU. As a result, Turkish exports enjoyed tariff-free movement within the BSEC and EU. Ayhan was considering the possibility of taking advantage of this by focusing on some of the member countries of these trading blocs (e.g., Russia, Bulgaria and Greece) as a way to increase Baser Food's global sales.

Ayhan had very limited information about these markets but knew that some behavioral change would be necessary in consumers' dietary habits in order for olive oil sales to increase significantly. This would clearly require heavy promotion to create awareness of the product and its health and other benefits before consumer acceptance could be achieved. For China, Ayhan estimated that it would cost US$ 1 million to properly launch Cavallo d'Oro in the Shanghai region alone. In many ways it was easier to grow from markets where the product was accepted and the category was already represented on supermarket shelves rather than to develop the entire category single-handedly. In other potential markets such as Eastern Europe, Baser played the role of the follower, allowing large companies from Italy and elsewhere to bear the high costs of gaining product acceptance and distribution. As a result, Baser spent just $200,000, shared with the distributor, to gain entry into Poland, for example.

On the other hand, some first-mover advantages were possible, despite the high initial entry costs, if Baser entered these countries before the competitors did. Mehmet Baser was also of the view that some of the emerging markets would be easier to penetrate because they had very few established competitors and the resource requirements needed to gain brand awareness and retail presence would be lower than in the more established olive oil consuming countries. Ayhan believed that the choice of market was critical for a small, emerging market multinational like Baser Food, particularly when the competition included companies such as Unilever Bestfoods and its powerful Bertolli brand.

References

[1] Kirmanli, Nilay (2000). Zeytin-Zeytinyagi Sektor Arastirmasi. (Olive – Olive Oil Sector Study). ITO. Yayinlari 22.12.2000.

[2] Sektor Dosyasi – Kati ve Sivi Yaglar (Sector Report - Fat and Oil). GIDA – Magazine Year: 6 November 2000; no.2000-11. Dunya Publications: Istanbul.

[3] http://www.igeme.org.tr/

[4] Kirmanli, Nilay (2000).

[5] Akcay Tuna, Sabahat (1997). Zeytin Agaci, Zeytin, Zeytinyagi (Olive Tree, Olive, Olive Oil). n.a.

[6] Interview with Altay Ayhan, April 15, 2002.

[7] Akcay Tuna, Sabahat (1997).

[8] Viola, Publio (1997). Olive Oil and Health – International Olive Oil Council: Spain. State Institute of Statistics – National Accounts.

[9] http://www.die.gov.tr/seed/nation/page12.html

[10] Tuglular, Taskin (2000). Bitkisel Yag Sektoru. GIDA Magazine Year 6, November 2000, No.2000-11. Dunya Publications: Istanbul. P.42.

[11] ibid

[12] Kirmanli, Nilay (2000).

[13] http://www.internationaloliveoil.org

[14] Goksu, Caglar (2000). Olive Oil Export Market Research, IGEME; Aegean Olive and Olive Oil Exporters Union, Working Report 2000-01.

[15] http://www.Baserfood.com

[16] Interview with Altay Ayhan, December 2001 and January 2002.

[17] http://www.internationaloliveoil.org

[18] Thompson, Stephanie (2001). Spreading Out Into Olive Oil. Advertising Age 72, Issue 34 (20 August), p. 39.

[19] ibid

[20] Quaranta, G. & V. Rotundo (2002). Economic and Commercial Prospects for Olive Oil in View of the Changes in the Common Market Organization (CMO) – Part one, OLIVÆ, No.91 (April): 20 – 24.

Case Study 11

RELTEK: Gluing Together a Growth Strategy*

It is a sunny California afternoon; Robert Lindberg, President and CEO of RELTEK, is seated in a deck chair in the grassy back yard of his corporate headquarters in Santa Rosa, California. It's an area of ranch homes, horse stables and vineyards ringed by oak covered hills. Tomorrow Lindberg is planning to meet with Tom Carter, president of Carter Venture Capital Group, in order to consider his personal commitment to grow RELTEK into a $10 million company. Lindberg has forwarded the company information to Carter, and is looking forward to their meeting to determine the future direction of RELTEK.

Company Background

RELTEK came into existence in 1996. For Lindberg, it was his seventh company. And this time the outlook was promising. RELTEK, a manufacturer of specialized adhesives and coatings for harsh environments, experienced rapid growth in sales and brand awareness. It had been a slow climb; a path marked with hard work and meager earnings. But the future looked bright. Yet there were some storm clouds. The economy was facing the prospect of recession and RELTEK needed an infusion of capital for equipment purchases.

Robert Lindberg had studied engineering and physics prior to deciding to pursue a Master's in Business Administration at Sonoma State University in 1980. On graduation, he went to work for Boston International Wire (BIW) as manager of engineering in its Santa Rosa division. The division was devoted to the development and manufacture of big connectors, i.e. electrical components essential in delivering electrical power to oil rigs, aircraft, ocean floor, space and other demanding environments and applications. As manager of engineering, Lindberg supervised a crew of seven engineers who served four divisional vice presidents. However, intense rivalries between the VPs often put Lindberg and his team at the center of a power struggle for resources.

In 1989, after a particularly frustrating experience, Lindberg recommended to the division president that the matrix organizational structure be disbanded and the engineers divided up and assigned to each of the VPs. His recommendation was accepted and his job became redundant. Instead of being promoted, Lindberg was given two months notice; the message was that he could stay on for two months and then leave.

Not one to sit around, he asked for and received a challenging assignment. As Lindberg recalls "It was a project that had been kicking around for a couple of years. No one had been able to solve it. The problem was 'cathodic disbondment'; I think they thought that no one could solve it. It had to do with a problem the Navy was experiencing with its submarines."

Prepared by Robert Girling and Elizabeth C. Thach of Sonoma State University and Fabienne Delibalta of Reims Management School (France) as the basis for class discussion rather than to illustrate either effective or ineffective handling of an administrative situation. Reprinted with permission from Robert Girling, Elizabeth C. Thach, and Fabienn Delibalta. Copyright 2004 by Robert Girling, Elizabeth C. Thach, and Fabienn Delibalta. All rights reserved.

A submarine has two hulls—an inner and outer hull. Cables connected to sensors must penetrate the inner hull. BIW manufactured the connectors and they were corroding at the point of penetration. The result was that every 12 to 18 months, the submarines had to be dry-docked, at an enormous cost, in order to replace the corroded connectors.

Lindberg took on the problem and within a month had a developed a product which BIW submitted to the Navy for testing (along with a half dozen other products by competitors). Halfway through the test, Lindberg's product was the only one that worked. At the end of the trials the product was accepted by the US Navy and given the name ***BOND-iT***.

As a result of this success, Lindberg continued working as a consultant to BIW until 1992, when BIW was reorganized and BIW's manufacture of BOND-iT was cancelled.

RELTEK is Founded

At that juncture Lindberg requested and received the rights to all technology he developed while working at BIW. Working out of his garage (a la Steve Jobs and David Packard) as an independent consultant, he set about developing applications for BOND-iT where customers needed a sealant that could withstand harsh environments. With each new product or application, Lindberg retained all rights to the technology.

In 1994, Lindberg won a contract funded by the U.S. Naval Labs and Met-ocean, an agency of the Canadian government, who were working jointly on a project to miniaturize huge buoys used for measuring ocean temperatures. They contacted Lindberg after reading a professional article he published describing a product he developed that would seal sensors and cables. In the article, Lindberg had named the product Reltec.

Then in 1995, he declared in a seminar that he would build a $10 million manufacturing business in five years. He set about to become a manufacturer of BOND-it and related sealing materials, such as Reltec, that could withstand harsh environments. On January 2, 1996, with just $10,000 in credit card debt he founded a company which he named Reltech -- later changing the name to RELTEK. Working under the guidance of a professional coach, he began placing phone-calls to every contact he had made in the preceding decade. "At that time, while I had developed the technology, I didn't have a product to sell. I had a conversation with each of my contacts about what I was intending to do. And I asked each person, 'How can I help you?"

After three months of daily phone calls without making a single sale, Lindberg received his first order for a tube of BOND-it at a price of $69. "I was ecstatic!" Within a week RELTEK produced and delivered its first products, cryptically called A-3 and B-1."

During the entire year, sales only reached $18,000. Lindberg's goal of $10 million in five years seemed as far away as the moon. But at the end of 1996 he received a contract from Hughes Aircraft for a product that would bond polyethylene plastics—a product where manufacturers claimed, "nothing can stick to it." Hughes was involved in bidding for a project to replace the SOSUS submarine monitoring system with a new cable employing state of the art sensors on the bottom of the ocean. Using RELTEK's design, Hughes won the contract and began sea trials in 2000.

Growth of the Firm

By this time Lindberg was becoming known as the "*glu-ru* of adhesives" through his personal contacts, writings and his web site. His business was slowly growing, and companies who required specialized adhesives and coatings sought him out to help them develop products to meet their needs.

With the revolution in telecommunication and fiber optics getting under way, General Dynamics, needed a product that could bond steel to polyethylene. A project engineer, working out of General Dynamic's New Jersey division, discovered how RELTEK had solved the problem of electric arcing in an underground high voltage fiber optic cable. He was working on a project to lay a high-voltage fiber optic cable on the bottom of the Atlantic Ocean and was in urgent need of a product that could seal the thousands of voltage boosting repeater stations that were needed to boost the electric signal. The highest quality and durability would be essential since any product breakdown would result in enormous expense of lifting and repairing the cable. The A-3 and B-1 combination was the only product that could withstand 15,000 pounds per square inch pressure and last 20 years.

The cable was made of polyethylene plastic, which resisted every previous bonding substance. General Dynamics needed to be able to splice the lengths of cable, attach the sensors and seal the cable. The only available technology -- developed by ATT -- molded sensors into the joints. The problem with this technology was that each joint took 2 hours of curing, adding enormous costs and delays to the project. Lindberg developed a product, SEA-6, that would seal the joints in minutes, not hours. Hughes successfully tested the SEA-6 product, and added it to the engineering specifications of the underwater cable project.

Marketing & Sales at RELTEK

From a marketing perspective, RELTEK positioned itself as a leading-edge technology firm, which designs, develops, and customizes high-quality and unique adhesives, sealants and coating products. RELTEK tripled its sales and the company generated annual sales of about $160,000. Projected sales for 2002 were $300,000 (for more financial data see Appendix 1, 2, 3 and 4).

Despite its positive growth pattern, marketing was an issue with which RELTEK was just beginning to deal. Following the initial blitz of marketing phone calls, there was never another follow-up effort. Knowledge of RELTEK's products was primarily by word of mouth. However, some big sales have come about through the company's web site, which received about 100 hits a day.

In general, RELTEK reached only a small element of its potential market. There was no advertising or outreach to trade associations, and the company did not sponsor seminars to promote the product. Marketing at RELTEK's was reactive -- coming in response to customer inquiries and web site queries. Technical literature to support the 20-plus products that the company manufactures was inadequate. Some products were being sold without data sheets, which list the specifications and applications of the product. Engineering and manufacturing processes were not being documented.

Most of the marketing was accomplished via direct sales to manufacturing customers. For example, SERCEL, one of RELTEK's largest customers, used the product in its manufacture of oil exploration cables for the ocean floor. According to an engineer at SERCEL, the company initially contracted Lindberg to analyze some sealing problems the company was experiencing with its underwater cables. The company had been using a primer manufactured by another company, and the result was that there was insufficient adhesion. Lindberg recommended substituting RELTEK primer, and SERCEL has been using the product successfully.

Recently, Ellsworth Adhesives, a $50 million company that carries a wide range of adhesives, approached Lindberg to explore the possibility of marketing RELTEK's products. Ellsworth Adhesives had a sales force of engineers that can reach many more customers than RELTEK. Ellsworth was interested in RELTEK because the company's products filled a market niche not covered by Ellsworth Adhesives. Lindberg was considering whether a marketing partnership with Ellsworth Adhesives would be a wise course to take or not.

RELTEK's Product Development Process

How did RELTEK develop new products? This was achieved primarily in response to customer requests. All main product lines came into being as a result of developing a product to meet a specific need of a customer. Lindberg usually contracted to develop the product charging an hourly rate for the research. For example, SERCEL was currently contracting with RELTEK to develop a one step potting, a primer and sealant, for use on their underwater cables that is impervious to water.

Another example was RELTEK's work with Borg Warner Automotive. Best known as producers of dishwashers the company is a conglomerate with many products. Their new product, B-46, was developed on contract to seal electric cables and components, which they sold as an original equipment manufacturer (OEM) to Ford and Chrysler.

A further example was C-6, a primer that is used by Raytheon in the manufacture of a large sensor cable system that could be deployed across the ocean to replace the SOSUS system for tracking submarines in the north Atlantic. Working with Alliant Tech Systems, which was acquired by Raytheon, RELTEK worked under contract to develop a product which incorporated a novel approach to seal the sensors from the extreme pressure and corrosiveness of ocean exposure, and which allowed Raytheon to win the contract for the largest cable project ever deployed.

The company was also involved in research on new products in its line of hot melt adhesives. One product could be used in the packaging of auto-body components for shipping by rail, which requires heat resistance as well as the ability to bond to polyethylene foam. Another product would bond recycled HP LaserJet cartridges for resale, replacing less reliable metal clips.

Yet another application was in protecting machinery used in offshore oil platforms. In this harsh environment the equipment is subject to continuous bombardment by salt spray and pounding storms. Related to this, RELTEK had developed analytical and empirical Accelerated Life Testing technology for underwater military and commercial products, as well as for nuclear products; and a new technology and process for manufacturing glass-to-titanium metal seals.

Through all of this, Lindberg developed a number of processes for which patents were pending. These include:
➢ Multiple bonding systems for difficult-to-bond and non-bonding plastics;

- Polymer to metal bonding systems to withstand caustic environments. (The U.S. Navy has adopted this system)
- Anti-fouling marine coating that did not leach poisons into the environment.
- Low-density polyethylene copolymer blends, capable of bonding both to metals and dissimilar polymers, plus sealing technology for down-hole cable splicing. (This product met military underwater application standards.)

Other product growth areas included a product for bonding with ultra high molecular weight (UHMW) polyethylene to be used by a RELTEK customer to develop a new lightweight snowboard.

RELTEK did not have ISO certification for its products, nor proper engineering documentation necessary to get certification. Lindberg viewed ISO as a bureaucratic procedure which would slow down product development at this stage in RELTEK's evolution.

RELTEK's Customers

RELTEK's customers were companies seeking products with extreme durability, resistance, and adhesion. RELTEK met this need by selling coatings, sealants and adhesives for use in a range of applications in construction and industrial uses. The product range was geared to the bonding of dissimilar materials and difficult to bond substrates as well as protection in harsh environments and from extreme conditions.

Among RELTEK's principal customers were Hewlett-Packard, which purchased hot melt adhesive, for use in cartridge recycling. Sales to HP were expected to grow from $6,000 in 2002 to $24,000 in the next fiscal year.

Other customers included SERCEL, the largest single customer of BOND-it A-3 -- purchasing $48,000 each year of the product. In addition, General Dynamics and Dow Corning were major users of BOND-iT and RELTEK primers.

The customers who used RELTEK's products frequently incorporate RELTEK's products into their own product. One could say that the company's market niche was industrial sealants, coatings and adhesives that met high performance specifications. As such RELTEK's customers were not price sensitive, but rather quality driven. The products they demanded must survive the harsh environments and meet demanding specifications in terms of durability and adhesion.

Wright Engineered Plastics, located in Santa Rosa, California, used BOND-iT to bond Teflon and acetyl products, which are known for their inability to adhere. As one employee at Wright described, "We first became aware of RELTEK by way of a cold-call. About a year later an engineer at Abbott Labs specified RELTEK's adhesive in a product we were manufacturing for them. The product has performed well and the service is very good. The product works well with tough to bond materials or in applications in which it's safer to use an adhesive rather than a screw."

The existing product mix offered RELTEK a range of opportunities to expand its customer base. Several promising lines, which may help the firm to meet its next level, were in development. In the rubber molding market it was developing a new powder coat epoxy that will be able to withstand higher temperatures than the primers currently used. A primary potential customer was a manufacturer of rubber washers molded to bolts. Another application was a primer for a new thermo-plastic rubber known as Santoprene, a product that was difficult to bond to or mold over substrates, and which could replace rubber in the automotive market.

Another potential customer base was the marine market, which was seeking environmentally friendly coatings for their products. RELTEK had strategic alliances with Sherman Williams Paint Company and with Magellan Companies Inc, with plans for a joint venture to develop a range of phytochemical based products. Phytochemicals, simply put, are extracts of essential oils such as grapefruit seed and chili pepper. These extracts, when present in coatings, prevent the growth of those mold, barnacles and other substances, which tend to attach to a marine surface. In the past, heavy metals, such as copper, were added to paints. However, the EPA recently banned the use of copper based paints. In addition, the State of California had given notice of its intent to ban any marine paint which pollutes the water. The use of phytochemicals was perhaps the only chemical system that coujld be environmentally friendly and one hundred percent effective.

Finally, another possible customer base was the large research laboratories in the US, such as Lawrence Livermore Laboratory and the Naval Research Labs. Some of the projects on which they were working require sealants for encapsulating low energy radiation waste products. RELTEK was working on development of a polymer coating that would contain radiation in low energy radiation waste products, such as lead bricks, which absorb high-energy alpha rays. If work were to be pursued on this project, then a costly separate protected laboratory room would be required.

International Sales and Contacts

In 2000, a distributor from the Republic of Korea purchased $5,000 of BOND-iT, but after two years had not made any additional purchases. RELTEK did not have a distributor in Asia or Europe. Consequently international sales had been minimal. Lindberg said "In order to sell my products in Europe, I'd have to go there and bang doors and make contacts. Alternatively, I could train an engineering sales staff. But I would have to train them personally, and, quite frankly, the investment of my time would be too costly in comparison with what I still have to do to service my customers in the US."

Meanwhile, Azko Nobel, the largest paint manufacturer in Europe, had requested the opportunity to develop an anti-foul paint using RELTEK's MAGREL 106 and 206 products. In addition, RELTEK had a cooperative agreement with a product-testing lab in India for screening and testing bio-foulants.

Plans for Growth

What would be required for the company to reach its next level? The main limitations were personnel, marketing, equipment and a building. With regard to personnel, Lindberg was the only qualified researcher and technical person. He had to divide his time between research and development, as well as the managerial functions and some marketing and sales activities. The company had qualified two manufacturers to outsource some of its products. One of these is Applied Poleramics Inc. of Benicia, California, which produced bulk sealants for RELTEK.

Until last year RELTEK was a one-person company. In the last 12 months it had added four part time staff members. Steve joined RELTEK after a successful career in the wine industry. He was also an artist as well as a ju-jitsu black belt despite being disabled by polio. Justin, 18 years old, was a lab technician, and according to Lindberg, a very talented individual. TJ was a jack-of-all-trades and pitches in where needed, while Tara was the company secretary. RELTEK was looking for a full time chemical or material engineer with lab experience and a full time sales representative.

With regard to equipment, a rheology machine, a durometer and a spectrum analyzer were needed to test for the properties of products and analyze their composition following chemical reactions. In addition, RELTEK's packaging equipment was unsatisfactory. This however was not an issue for outsourced products.

Present space was limited to about 200 square feet of office space and 400 square feet of garage space. RELTEK would require 5000 square feet for office and factory space for production to grow beyond the present level.

Obtaining Funding

Tom Carter closed the file he has been reading on RELTEK. He pondered what approach he might take with potential investor partners. "I find RELTEK to be a very imaginative company. Lindberg clearly is a talented inventor and capable of bringing a wide range of products to market. He has an uncanny ability to find customer's needs and meet them while getting his customers to pay for his R & D. But I'm just not sure whether this can become a $10 million company. Our meeting is tomorrow morning at 10 am and I have to develop a set of precise recommendations."

Appendix 1: Sales ($)

Year	1996	1997	1998	1999	2000	2001	2002
Sales	18 000	57 000	57 000	48 000	85 000	160 183	220 135

Appendix 2: Income Statement Summary ($)

INCOME STATEMENT	2001	2002
SALES	**160183**	**220135**
COGS (excluding depreciation and amortization)	29050	66229
GROSS PROFIT	**131133**	**153906**
Selling, general & administrative expenses	75621	116425
EBITDA	**55512**	**37481**
Depreciation & Amortization	7239	4381
EBIT or Operating Income	**48273**	**33100**
INTEREST EXPENSES	3562	684
Other income (deductions)_net	-15027	-15748
EARNINGS BEFORE TAXES	**29684**	**16668**
TAXES	11874	6667
NET INCOME	**17810**	**10001**

Appendix 3: Balance Sheet

BALANCE SHEET ($)	2001	2002
CASH and EQUIVALENT	4155	9821
ACCOUNTS RECEIVABLE	19662	26051
INVENTORIES	9060	5644
Other current assets	3960	4274
TOTAL CURRENT ASSETS	36837	45790
Net PLANT and EQUIPMENT	15333	10952
INTANGIBLE ASSETS after amortization	5384	5384
Other ASSETS after amortization	728600	728600
TOTAL FIXED ASSETS	749317	744936
TOTAL ASSETS	**786154**	**790726**
ACCOUNTS PAYABLE	1486	1127
Other Current Liab.	791	1637
TOTAL CURRENT LIABILITIES	2277	2764
LONG TERM DEBT payable in more than 1 year	10084	1756
EQUITY CAPITAL	773793	786206
TOTAL LIABILITIES and EQUITY	**786154**	**790726**

Appendix 4: Statement of Cash-Flow ($)

STATEMENT of CASH-FLOW	2001	2002
NET INCOME	17810	10001
non cash adjustment		
DEPRECIATION and AMORTIZATION	7239	4381
adjustments due to change in working capital		
(increase)/ decrease in ACCOUNTS RECEIVABLE	-3541	-6389
(increase)/decrease in INVENTORIES	978	3416
Increase/(decrease) in ACCOUNTS PAYABLE	-87403	-359
Increase/(decrease) in other current liabilities	354	846
NET CASH from OPERATING ACTIVITIES	-89612	-2486
LONG TERM INVESTING ACTIVITIES	-2096	-3442
Sales of short term investments	0	0
Increase/(decrease) in notes payable	0	0
Increase /(decrease) in long term loans outstanding	-8771	-8328
Payment of DIVIDENDS	0	0
CASH from FINANCIAL ACTIVITIES	-8771	-8328
NET CHANGE in CASH	-75430	126

Case Study 12

Critter Campus

Toni and Jill, sisters in their late 20s, sat on Toni's porch watching their dogs romp around the yard and play fetch with tennis balls on a sunny spring morning in April of 2002. They lived about five blocks apart so this puppy play time was a regular occurrence.

"Do you realize how much I spent boarding my dog over the weekend?" Toni asked Jill.

"I know it's not cheap. How much was the damage?" Jill asked, with a knowing smile and a tennis ball toss.

"About $50 for two nights. At least he had a bath when he came home." Toni said ruefully. Another tennis ball went flying.

"Wow," Jill said as she looked at Toni, with three Border Collies drooling over the tennis ball Jill held in her hand. Then she added, "What do you think it would take to run a boarding kennel? Seriously." Away went the tennis ball.

Toni looked at Jill and, with a small smile, said, "I don't know, but I bet I can find out. We might be able to run our own kennel. I know there is a professional boarding kennel association because I checked out kennels before I left my dog in one. I bet they have information. I'll check out their web site." Toni tossed the tennis ball again.

Jill and Toni continued to talk about the possibility, and the more they talked, the more excited they got. But both knew that excitement wasn't enough. Did they have what it took to own and operate a successful boarding kennel?

INTRODUCTION

Jill and Toni grew up on a farm in central Iowa. Both had extensive experience caring for cats, dogs, horses, cows, pigs, rabbits, birds (parakeets and chickens), and sheep. Toni worked for the state government as a consultant manager, dealing with contract negotiations and budgeting on a regular basis. She also held a Master's of Business Administration degree from a state university. But one of her passions had always been animals. She began training and showing horses in 1982 and received many awards including several Grand Champion titles and High Point Horse awards. Recently, she had started training dogs for obedience and search and rescue. Currently, she was the Assistant Coordinator of the STAR 1 Search and Technical Rescue central Iowa K9 team, responsible for publicity, curriculum development, and personnel issues. She was also training her dog for wilderness, forensics and cadaver searches.

Jill currently worked at a home improvement store and had extensive experience in the retail industry. She was responsible for training new employees and scheduling. But, like her sister, Jill's hobbies revolved around animals. She had been training dogs in obedience for eight years, competed in many shows and events, and pursued many different teaching methods. Her training expertise had produced many championship titles. Jill currently instructed classes for the local kennel club and was also a member of STAR 1 Search and Technical Rescue. Like Toni, she was currently training her two dogs for wilderness and water cadaver searches. Together, the two of them had extensive contacts in the pet industry (although not specifically in boarding kennels) because of their involvement in STAR 1 and kennel clubs. Neither sister was married or had significant others dependent on them.

While both Toni and Jill were successful in their current positions, neither felt particularly wedded to their jobs. They enjoyed doing things together, and they often talked about going into business together. They figured that their combination of retail experience and business education was good preparation for owning their own business. So far, however, they had just talked about doing it. This time—well, this time, there was an energy to their conversation as each realized they had an idea that appealed to both of them. The next day, Toni started gathering information about the pet and boarding kennel industries.

THE PET INDUSTRY

The pet industry (all retail and services related to cats, dogs, horses, reptiles and birds) was a major segment of the U.S. economy. In 1999, American pet owners spent over $26 billion on their small companions, and in 2000, this figure surpassed $27 billion. Recent growth in all segments of the pet industry provided an opportunity for both existing players and new entrants that had been increasingly active since the beginning of the 1990s. Changing demographics, new lifestyle trends, and a shift in American attitudes toward pets led to an increase in consumer expenditures during the past five years. The maturing pet industry had been transformed into a dynamic, highly competitive environment due to several factors: a growing number of players; consolidation among manufacturers, retailers, and service providers; globalization of the American economy; and the explosive growth of e-commerce through online catalogs.

According to the 2001-2002 National Pet Owners Survey conducted by the American Pet Products Manufacturers Association (APPMA), which was the nation's leading pet industry trade association, pet ownership was on the rise. More than 63 million U.S. households owned pets. This finding, representing approximately 62 percent of all U.S. households, was an increase of nearly two percent over the results from the previous study conducted in 1998, and six percent over the trade group's initial results published in 1988.

Other interesting findings in the APPMA study included:

At least one-third of all homes in the U.S. owned a dog or cat.

An estimate of the total number of pets indicated that Americans owned 68 million dogs, 73 million cats, 19 million birds, 19 million small animals, nine million reptiles, 159 million freshwater fish and six million saltwater fish.

Almost half (47 percent) of U.S. households owned more than one type of pet.

Nearly five percent of pet owners said they would purchase a casket upon the death of their pet.

Except for reptiles and fish, more than 60 percent of pet owners in all other categories said they bought gifts for their pets.

Compared to all U.S. households, pet owners were younger, married and had higher incomes.

The APPMA study also found that three out of 10 dogs visited a pet groomer in the previous six months, up slightly from 1998. Forty-two percent of small dogs were groomed. The number of large dogs being groomed increased to 25%, up from 15% in 1998, making small dogs more likely to be professionally groomed compared to medium and large dogs.

The growing number of pets in the United States led to the pet industry being one of the fastest growing markets. The APPMA National Pet Owners Survey also found that pet owning households (households that owned at least one cat, dog, horse, reptile, or bird) would spend an estimated $460 each on their pets in the coming year.

Table 1	Total U.S. Pet Industry Expenditures
Year	Billions Dollars
2003	$31 est.
2002	$29.5 est
2001	$28.5 est
1998	$23
1996	$21
1994	$17

*Converted from 1991 to 2001 dollars using the CPI

More specific statistics from the Humane Society of the United States outlined the actual breakdown of costs related to owning a dog, in Table 2. According to the American Veterinary Medical Association U.S. Pet Ownership and Demographics Sourcebook (1997), pet-owning households were more likely than all U.S. households to be young couples, working older couples, middle parents, older parents or roommates; the household types are defined in Table 3. These five pet-owning households represented 48.1% of all U.S. households but represented 58.2% of pet-owning households. The largest portion of pet owning households was among older parents (19.8%). A total of 44.5% of pet owning households had household income of $40,000 or more. In addition, pet owning households were 4.8 times more likely to be homeowners than

Table 2	Dog Ownership Costs
Initial training	$65-$130
Each year thereafter for training	$65-$259
Annual feeding	$201-$518
Annual toys, grooming supplies	$207
Grooming per visit	$65

Annual flea and tick care	$104
Daily boarding	$27-$39

*Converted from 1991 to 2001 dollars using the CPI

Table 3   Types of Pet Households in the U.S.

Young couples	Multiple members, household head less than 45 years old, no children
Working older couples	Multiple members, household head 45 or more years old, household head employed, no children.
Middle parents	Multiple members, household head less than 45 years old, youngest child 6 or more years old
Older parents	Multiple members, household head 45 or more years old, children of any age present
Roommates	Multiple members, unmarried head of household living with nonrelative.

renters. Three out of four pet owning households lived in a house, with 39% of pet owning households living in communities of less than 500,000.

The American Veterinary Medical Association also published formulas for estimating the number of pets in households, using national percentages and national number of pets:

Dogs:

Number of dogs = 0.534 x total number of households

Number of dogs = 1.69 x number of dog-owning households

Cats:

Number of cats = 0.598 x total number of households

Number of cats = 2.19 x number of cat-owning households

Birds:

Number of birds = 0.126 x total number of households

Number of birds = 2.74 x number of bird-owning households

161

THE BOARDING KENNEL BUSINESS

The boarding kennel industry was in a state of transition. Traditionally, boarding services had been provided by veterinarians. However, the past few years had seen the emergence of commercial kennels in select markets; commercial kennels were owned independently of veterinary clinics either as solely-owned enterprises or as franchises. There were several factors that indicated this growth in commercial boarding kennels would continue:

Pets were increasingly thought of as a 'member of the family.'

People were increasingly mobile, whether for work or pleasure and relied on others to provide pet services. Increasingly, people were relying on kennels rather than acquaintances to care for pets, because friends and family were also mobile.

People were becoming increasingly sensitive not only to the physical conditions of boarding kennels, but also to the manner in which pets were treated while at a boarding kennel.

In 2000, there were approximately 10,000 boarding kennels across the nation that together had the capacity for approximately 640,000 dogs and 173,000 cats (see Exhibit 1). Further information, in Exhibit 2, provided historical information on the average charges for boarding and grooming. However, the boarding business was noted to have a cyclical usage pattern. Traditionally, boarding services were in very high demand during the Christmas holiday season, spring break, summer vacation season, weekends, and most other major holidays. Other times of the year the boarding business was relatively slow.

The American Boarding Kennel Association (ABKA) was the international trade association for the owners and operators of commercial boarding kennels. The ABKA administered the Voluntary Facilities Accreditation (VFA) Program, a professional program that required participating boarding kennels to demonstrate adherence to a comprehensive set of operational standards. These standards included over 200 detailed requirements for boarding kennels and had been developed over many years by the ABKA. The standards reflected the views of kennel operators, veterinarians, pet owners, and humane organizations and thus represented the "state of the art" in animal care and management. Kennels that successfully met VFA standards received an ABKA stamp of approval, which kennels could use in promoting their facilities. However, kennels were also allowed to register with the ABKA without participating in the VFA program; kennels choosing this option did not carry the ABKA stamp of approval. In addition to the ABKA, there were professional organizations that offered specific business development, management, and marketing training for people in the boarding kennel industry.

Toni also found detailed information on operating expenses and income for boarding kennels, broken down by size of the kennel. According to this information, in Exhibits 3, 4, and 5, the larger the kennel, the higher were the net profits. The greatest percentage of earnings was related to boarding services, but grooming services significantly contributed to the profits of small, medium, and large kennels, as did training services for small and large kennels.

A few weeks later Toni and Jill were again watching their dogs play in the back yard. As the dogs romped and chased tennis balls, Toni shared with Jill the information she had learned about the pet and boarding kennel industries.

By Robin Habeger and Kay M. Palan of Iowa State University as the basis for class discussion rather than to illustrate either effective or ineffective handling of an administrative situation. Reprinted with permission from the *Case Research Journal*. Copyright 2003 by Robin Habeger and Kay M. Palan and the North American Case Research Association. All rights reserved.

Toni concluded, "I think running a boarding kennel is possible. We grew up on a farm taking care of all sorts of animals, are used to working odd hours and have experience in retail. I really think we could do it. And the research I've done so far suggests there's a growing need for high quality kennels."

"Well, this information is fine and dandy on a general level. But is there a need for a kennel right here where we live, and if there is, what would it take for a kennel to be profitable?" Jill asked.

"We'll have to check into local market needs and competition," Toni said. "From the data I've gathered, successful kennels are larger and offer several different services. I think a kennel would do well, especially if we added in some extra services and boarded more than just dogs or even offered obedience classes. We could also do retail, like selling toss toys!" Another tennis ball went flying across the yard.

"We could also board cats! I know several people who have cats they need someone to watch while they go on vacations," Jill said as she dodged the dogs returning with the ball. "It could be our own little K9 University with classes."

"Yeah, we could have our own critter campus. What a great name! Critter Campus…it says we board more than dogs!" Toni gleefully tossed the ball, then turned to Jill. "Critter Campus, the ivy league location for your pet to stay, play, and learn!"

LOCAL MARKET AND COMPETITION

Toni and Jill began to collect more information about the pet and boarding kennel industries in the Des Moines area in central Iowa. Both were familiar with the area, having lived and worked there for most of their lives, and they wanted to stay in the area.

They first looked at population demographics. Over 91 percent of adults age 25 and older in the Des Moines MSA (metropolitan statistical area, >500,000 people for the population included) held a high school diploma. Nearly one in three of those had earned at least a 4-year college degree. The Des Moines area ranked ninth out of 150 housing markets for affordability and percent of income required to meet mortgage payments on a home. The average cost for a single-family detached home was $94,200, $20,500 less than the national average of $114,700.

Nearly 76 percent of homes in Des Moines were owned by their occupants. Residential and non-residential building permit valuations in the Des Moines area in 1998 totaled $426 million. Major industries included financial services, insurance, government, manufacturing, trade and service.

The area was projected to have a population growth rate of .49% from 1998-2025, according to Woods and Poole Economics, Inc., an independent firm that specialized in long-term county economic and demographic projections; a breakdown of these projections for the near future were calculated, as shown in Table 4.

In addition, population growth in the Des Moines area was projected to be to the west and south of the city; consumer expenditures for pet-related purchases were expected to be consistent with these growth trends. Exhibit 6a and 6b show consumer expenditures for pet related supplies and services in 2001 vs. projected 2006 expenditures.

163

Table 4	Population and Household Projections: Des Moines MSA (in thousands)				
	2000	2001	2002	2005	2010
Population	998.28	1003.39	1008.49	1023.56	1047.93
# Households	390.73	393.54	396.37	404.56	416.83
Income per capita (current $)	21,185	28,892	30,034	33,788	41,801

According to statistics compiled by Scarborough for the local radio stations, the typical pet (either a dog or cat) owner in the Des Moines area was a female working full-time in an administrative support or executive, administrative, or managerial position. This pet owner had at least a high school or higher education, was between the ages of 35-54 and earned over $35,000 per year. They owned their homes and had two or fewer children under the age of 17 residing in the household. See Exhibit 7 for more segmented data.

Next, Toni and Jill researched existing competitors in the Des Moines area, including boarding kennels and training facilities. There were sixteen boarding kennels operating in the extended Des Moines area, however, Toni and Jill considered only four to be serious competitors based on their facilities and services. The remaining twelve kennels were not facilities they would leave their own dogs in so they discounted them as major competitors. None of the four kennels they chose as competitors offered specific facilities for police/working dogs or open play, and many employed the use of interior-only runs made of chain link. Moreover, none of the kennels offered on-site training and only one boarded other animals besides cats and dogs.

Puppy Palace

The first kennel identified as a serious competitor was Puppy Palace, a 20,000 sq. ft. facility located southeast of the Des Moines metropolitan area. The kennel was large, with a maximum capacity of 150 dogs and 45 cats. Staff, consisting of five veterinarians and a support staff of 40 full-time and part-time employees, was on the premises 24-hours a day. In addition to the dog and cat runs, the facility had eight exam rooms. The front lobby was tiled and contained a very small retail space (3x6 wall-mounted). No training classes were offered. The usual office hours of the kennel were Monday – Friday, 9am-6pm; Saturday, 9am-12 noon; and Sunday, 5pm-6pm (checkouts only).

Reservations could be made at any time, but Puppy Palace booked reservations two months in advance for the holiday season. During vacation seasons, runs typically filled a week in advance.

Dorm rooms and vacation suites were available for lodging dogs; the charge for dorm rooms was $20 per day, while the charge for vacation suites was $30 per day. The vacation suites had separate themes such as a hunting lodge, Caribbean, jungle, sports, etc. Amenities of the vacation suites and dorm rooms are provided in Table 5.

Pet owners could provide their own food for boarding pets, or the kennel provided Science Diet and Iams food. Three walks per day were included in the boarding package, as was a courtesy wellness exam. After a stay of two days, dogs received a free bath. Additional services included dog playtime.

Table 5   Dog Accommodations: Puppy Palace

Dorm Rooms (18 or 24 sq ft.) Quantity: 80-100	Vacation Suites (40 sq ft.) Quantity: 9
Privacy divider (opaque wall up to ~4 ft.) Bed Heated floor Chain link doors and walls up to ~10ft	Window TV Bed One-on-one playtime Treat at playtime Bubble bath

Cat condos were located away from the dogs; the charge was $11 per day. Each condo offered a resting shelf and an east window along with a fleece bed. Staff visited each cat three times a day and attended to the litter box, food, and water. The cat playroom provided extra space to explore the aquarium and climbing tree; it also featured a view of the Cat Hospital lobby. Feline playroom visitors were required to be tested negative for feline leukemia.

Doggy Doodles

Doggy Doodles, a second serious competitor, was located on three acres of wooded property in a residential district in central Des Moines. Doggy Doodles was licensed by the State of Iowa. The animal runs were located in a converted home at the rear of the lot. The facility was heated and air conditioned. Office hours were Monday-Friday, 9am-12 noon and 3pm-6pm; Saturday, 9am-12 noon; and Sunday, 5pm-7pm; however, the property was monitored by the owners 24 hours a day. In addition to dog and cat runs, the facility offered on-site grooming and doggy day care.

Each large dog got its own indoor/outdoor run. The price varied by size of run: small runs were $12 per day, medium runs were $13 per day, and large runs were $14 per day. Each dog was exercised outside four times a day. Complementary food and treats were provided, although if preferred, owners could provide their own food. Doggy Doodles offered day care, however, there was no community playtime.

Table 6   Large vs. Small Runs: Doggy Doodles

Large Runs	Small Runs
Indoor/outdoor capabilities Plywood floors and walls Painted chain link doors Outdoor runs have cement floors, chain	Wire cages Wooden cages with wire insets (2x3)

link walls with no privacy fence and are
covered by fiberglass roofing

Cat cages were located upstairs in the same building with the dog runs. The price was $11.50 per day. Complementary food and treats were provided, although owners could provide their own food, if preferred.

Dog Days

Dog Days was located in a predominantly industrial area in south central Des Moines, in a yellow warehouse next to construction storage. This business had recently been taken over by new management. The facility consisted of five large runs, constructed of painted cement block with chain link gates; these runs were in a partitioned area away from the remaining runs, which were constructed with chain link fence unsecured to the floor. Floors were painted. Soundproofing seemed to be nonexistent because it was a very noisy facility, creating difficulty in carrying on a conversation. Doggy day care was provided on Tuesdays and Thursdays at a rate of $10 per day or $5 for ½ day. The day care play area was located immediately outside the large runs. Grooming was also available on site. The office hours of the facility were Monday – Friday, 7:30am – 11:30am and 1pm – 6pm; Saturday, 7:30am – 10:30am; and Sunday, 4pm - 6pm. Dog Days was registered with the ABKA, but had not gone through the certification process.

Dog Days offered a VIP option for dog-related services. It included the pre-pay of 20 nights at a 20% discount. For this fee, dogs were taken on a walk at least four times a   day, five or six if there was time. The only outside fenced-in area included two 3 x 10 foot runs located just inside the front entrance on the driveway. All other walks were located next to the facility in an open unfenced field.

Table 7	Dog Run Prices: Dog Days	
Run Size and Quantity	Price for 1 dog	Price for 2 dogs
30 runs, 4x4	$15/day	$22.50/day
20 runs, 6x6	$17/day	$26.50/day
5 runs, 15x10	$25/day	$40/day

Prices for dogs varied considerably, depending on the size of the run and number of dogs being boarded. Cats were boarded upstairs from the dog runs in small rooms Unlike other kennels, there was a differential charge depending on how many cats owners boarded; one cat was $9 per day, but two cats was $15 per day.

Superior Kennel

The last major competitor Toni and Jill identified was Superior Kennel, located in a western suburb of Des Moines. All runs were constructed out of four-foot tall painted cement brick walls with chain link gates and chain link used as a roof. Most runs were 3 ½ x 5 feet with a few large ones being 5 x 9 feet. The large ones could also be modified into smaller runs using removable doors, meaning that a cement brick wall split most of the larger runs. The floors of the runs were slanted to allow for waste to flow into floor grates. Grooming was offered on-site. Office hours were Monday – Friday, 10am-6pm; Saturday, 7:30am – 10:30am; and Sunday, 4pm-6pm. Dogs were allowed outside twice a day for a twenty-minute solitary playtime. This playtime was in a large fenced-in grassy area located at the rear of the lot. Dogs under 50 pounds were boarded for $11 per day, while dogs over 50 pounds were boarded for $12 per day.

Cats were boarded in five cat cages located in an interior room. The price to board cats was $9 per day.

Toni and Jill summarized the information about the four major kennel competitors, provided in Exhibit 8.

With respect to training facilities, Toni and Jill identified only one location in Des Moines that the general public knew to go to for training. It was the local obedience training club. As Toni and Jill asked around about the quality of instruction it became clear than many people were not satisfied with the level of instruction received for the price paid. They also learned that several individuals in the area offered private training lessons, but at prices prohibitive to most pet owners.

"Compared to all this information, what we want to do—having a high quality facility with external dog runs, having room for open play, boarding all kinds of pets, providing training and grooming—would give us a definite competitive advantage. But where should we locate?" Jill asked as the sisters walked in the park with the dogs.

"Well, the city council person I have been working with suggested a location next to the airport since they are putting in a brand new highway interchange to ease traffic. It's right on a main road in town and just 5 minutes from the airport to catch those vacationers who need to drop off their pet." Toni said excitedly, "We would be located in a commercial district so our neighbors wouldn't be too disturbed by the barking. Plus, it's in the southwest part of the metropolitan area, where growth is projected."

"That sounds like a great location! We would be able to move into those new apartments nearby. How many runs should we have in our kennel? How big should the building be?" Jill said as she tossed a Frisbee.

"How many runs and how big the building is going to be depend on finances," Toni said as she pulled the Frisbee away from one of the dogs.

FINANCIAL SITUATION

After completing a few site visits, Toni and Jill got together to review all of the data one more time. Based on all they knew, it was clear to them that a boarding kennel that offered the general pet owner comprehensive high-quality boarding and training services at reasonable prices would have a competitive advantage and do well in the Des Moines area. The only remaining issue looming large on their minds was whether or not they could financially afford to start their own business.

"How much will this cost?" Jill asked. Where would we find the money? I don't have much in savings because I'm still paying off my student loans."

By Robin Habeger and Kay M. Palan of Iowa State University as the basis for class discussion rather than to illustrate either effective or ineffective handling of an administrative situation. Reprinted with permission from the *Case Research Journal.* Copyright 2003 by Robin Habeger and Kay M. Palan and the North American Case Research Association. All rights reserved.

"I don't have a whole lot saved up either," Toni said. "I suppose the costs would depend on the size of the kennel, what kinds of runs we want, the image we want to project, whether or not we need to build a new facility or can we lease an existing one....."

"I would gladly quit my job if I could do this full time and live decently," Jill added.

"We would probably need money for a down payment, and we'd need money for operating costs to sustain the business long enough until it makes money on its own. I'd love to quit my job as well and do this fulltime, but I don't think we could afford that right away." Toni stated.

Toni was quiet for a few seconds. "Let me make a few calls concerning funding, I have a few business contacts through my job, and there's supposed to be an organization in Des Moines that helps new businesses find investors."

Toni used her network of business acquaintances to explore funding resources and found that through the city economic development office some funding opportunities were available that would enable Critter Campus to receive some funding to help with down payments. Toni also investigated the costs of building boarding kennels, and contacted a real estate broker regarding geographic locations and existing facilities. Buying any of the existing facilities would require significant renovation in order to have the quality facility Toni and Jill had in mind; moreover, none of the existing facilities was for sale. Building a brand new facility with high quality features would cost about $100 per square foot, in addition to the price of a lot, which could easily be $200,000-$300,000 more for an urban kennel and between $100,000 and $200,000 for a suburban kennel. If existing urban facilities could be purchased or leased, completing the needed modifications to the building and installing high quality dog runs would cost approximately $3000 to $5000 per run.

Her investigation identified a major financial obstacle—most financial institutions required a 30% owner investment for projects like this and also required a guarantor for the mortgage. If Toni and Jill could come up with the down payment, they could fund the remaining 70% of the project with a Small Business Administration 504 Loan (7% over 20 years). It was possible that various other economic development incentives could be applied for to help meet the initial 30%.

Another possibility for the down payment was to seek monetary "gifts" from potential investors; that is, the type of loan Toni and Jill was considering required that any monies received be "gifts" versus loans or investments. While talking with a real estate broker concerning locations, Toni was put into contact with someone who loved animals and was known to make business investments.

CONCLUSION

"He would really help us out with the down payment?" Jill asked excitedly when Toni called to tell her about the investor.

"Yes! I can't believe it! He was very interested and wants to sit down and talk about projections and what services we are going to offer. Now all we have to do is figure out how many runs, how much land, the cost of the building, what services we are going to offer, and

what we need for operating costs! I am going to need some help with this so come on over!"
Toni said as she fired up her computer.

Exhibit 1   1998 Boarding Kennel Industry Statistics

Estimated Number of U. S. Boarding Facilities – 10,000			
Size of Kennel (dog runs)			
Small (under 50)	2500		
Medium (50-99)	5000		
Large (100-300)	2500		
	% of kennels offering this service	Avg. Income from this service	Estimated total income
Dog Boarding	100	$112,525	$1,125,250,000
Cat Boarding	85	$14,950	$124,015,000
Grooming	90	$40,100	$240,600,000
Retail Sales	33	$7,000	$23,100,000
Training	23	$5,513	$12,679,900
Cemetery/Cremation	5	$4,350	$2,175,000
Other	40	$6,500	$26,000,000
Average Gross Income			$190,578
Estimated Total Gross Income in 1996			$1,553,819,900
Total number of dog runs available		640,000	
Total number of cat enclosures available		173,000	
Total number of full-time employees		32,000	
Total number of part-time employees		31,000	

Source: American Boarding Kennel Association's Survey, 1998.

Exhibit 2   Boarding Industry Statistics (2001) – Average for all Boarding Kennels

Average Boarding Prices (in dollars)						
	1990	1992	1994	1996	1998	2000
Cocker	8.09	8.86	9.63	9.91	11.21	14.03
Doberman	9.19	9.83	10.61	10.77	12.23	14.77
Great Dane	10.15	11.18	11.35	11.60	12.97	15.49
Cats	5.57	6.38	6.80	6.85	7.71	9.00
Exotics	4.50	4.70	5.65	5.75	6.30	7.00

Boarding (in dollars)		
Average daily charge per dog	2000	1998
Cocker	14.03	11.21
Doberman	14.77	12.23
Great Dane	15.49	12.97
Average daily charge per dog run	14.76	12.13
Average annual income per dog run	3,366.70	2,022.59
Average dog occupancy	63.36%	51.65%
Average days stayed per dog	5.30	5.70
Average daily charge for cats	9.00	7.71
Average annual income per cat enclosure	950.00	795.49
Average cat occupancy	35.12%	26.93%
Average days stayed per cat	6.63	6.69

Grooming Prices (in dollars)					
	1992	1994	1996	1998	2000
Miniature Poodle	22.80	22.98	25.79	27.21	28.90
Cocker	36.30	26.82	28.98	30.17	30.20
Schnauzer	22.95	23.30	25.85	26.91	27.65
Airedale	31.20	31.77	34.52	43.62	44.00
German Shepherd	24.40	23.10	37.56	29.26	30.88
Collie	31.65	33.90	36.41	39.81	39.86
Old English (comb out)	41.40	46.12	47.35	49.38	50.66
Old English (clip down)	40.35	43.92	44.52	48.76	55.44
Lhassa	23.30	22.32	25.88	27.38	29.38
Dachshund	14.85	16.10	16.44	18.39	18.88

Great Dane	23.60	23.65	27.40	28.17	29.15
Cats	22.34	20.88	24.76	26.07	28.06
Hourly Charge for Combing	16.60	17.95	18.16	23.08	21.53
Extra Charge for Dips	5.10	5.86	5.75	7.41	7.20
Toenail Clip	5.00	4.94	5.28	6.21	6.5

Exhibit 3   Small Kennels, 1-49 Runs

Direct Costs		
	% of Gross	% of Income Generated
Pet food	4.62%	1.39%
Groomer commissions	6.17%	25.3%
Cost of resale goods	1.49%	27%
Total Direct Costs	12%	
Gross Operating Profit	88%	

Operating Expenses	% of Gross	Income	
Payroll	37.27%	Average gross income	$131,465
Employee benefits	4.61%	Average number of dog enclosures	30
Auto/truck	4.88%	Average income per dog enclosure	$2,399
Travel & entertainment	2.98%	Avg number of cat enclosures	14.8
Kennel insurance	1.7%	Average income per cat enclosure	$615
Repairs & maintenance	2.7%	Urban kennels	16%
Office supplies	1.8%	Suburban kennels	32%
Utilities	3.8%	Rural kennels	52%
Telephone	1.8%	Indoor/outdoor	76%
Yellow page ads	2.5%	All indoor	23%
Other advertising	2.0%	Both	1%
Office & administration	2.6%	Avg # fulltime employees	2.5
Professional services	1.8%	Avg # part time employees	2.8
Veterinary expense	2.0%	Avg # years kennel in business	10.8
Licenses	.02%	Avg # years owner in industry	12.25
Other	.06%	# dogs groomed per week	31
Total Operating Expenses	72.18%	# cats groomed per week	5
Net Proceeds Available	15.82%	# small mammals groomed per wk	0
Net Proceeds (for mortgage/rent & owner profit)	$20,797		

	% of Kennels Offering This Service	2000 Avg Income	% of Gross
Dog boarding	100%	$71,991	54.76%
Exercise programs	30%	$37,900	28.83%

Community daycare	23%	$20,000	15.21%
Cat boarding	80%	$9,105	6.92%
Grooming	79%	$32,022	24.3%
Retail sales	49%	$6,129	4.66%
Training	40%	$10,262	6.62%
Pick-up & delivery	25%	$670	.51%
Exotics boarding	14%	$573	.44%
Shipping	10%	$100	.08%
Pet sitting	2%	$2,900	2.21%
Veterinary services	4%	$950	.72%
Cemetery	1%	$1,500	1.14%
Cremation	1%	$1,500	1.14%

Exhibit 4   Medium Kennels, 50-99 Runs

Direct Costs			
		% of Gross	% of Income Generated
Pet food		4.46%	5.99%
Groomer commissions		10.25%	62.9%
Cost of resale goods		2.04%	40%
Total Direct Costs		16.75%	
Gross Operating Profit		83.25%	

Operating Expenses	% of Gross	Income	
Payroll	33.21%	Average gross income	$254,874
Employee benefits	4.19%	Average number of dog enclosures	69
Auto/truck	1.73%	Average income per dog enclosure	$2,747
Travel & entertainment	.52%	Avg number of cat enclosures	17
Kennel insurance	1.55%	Average income per cat enclosure	$886
Repairs & maintenance	2.75%	Urban kennels	17%
Office supplies	1.32%	Suburban kennels	33%
Utilities	3%	Rural kennels	50%
Telephone	1.28%	Indoor/outdoor	80%
Yellow page ads	2.34%	All indoor	19%
Other advertising	1.47%	Both	1%
Office & administration	1.4%	Avg # fulltime employees	4
Professional services	1.2%	Avg # part time employees	5.4
Veterinary expense	.89%	Avg # years kennel in business	21
Licenses	.23%	Avg # years owner in industry	16
Other	1.07%	# dogs groomed per week	33
Total Operating Expenses	58.14%	# cats groomed per week	2.6
Net Proceeds Available	25.11%	# small mammals groomed per wk	1
Net Proceeds (for mortgage/rent & owner profit)	$63,998		

	% of Kennels Offering This Service	2000 Avg Income	% of Gross
Dog boarding	100%	$189,583	74.38%
Exercise programs	47%	$19,723	7.74%
Community daycare	17%	$13,527	5.31%
Cat boarding	88%	$15,063	5.91%
Grooming	78%	$41,506	16.23%
Retail sales	64%	$4,983	1.96%
Training	44%	$1,450	.57%
Pick-up & delivery	28%	$2,757	1.08%
Exotics boarding	19%	$2,192	.86%
Shipping	5%	$10,000	3.92%
Pet sitting	2%	$1,000	.39%
Veterinary services	5%	$2,500	.98%
Cemetery	3%	$15,000	5.88%
Cremation	3%	$10,000	3.92%

Exhibit 5   Large Kennels, over 100 Runs

Direct Costs			
	% of Gross	% of Income Generated	
Pet food	4.11%	5.8%	
Groomer commissions	11.86%	50.41%	
Cost of resale goods	1.29%	63.03%	
Total Direct Costs	15.12%		
Gross Operating Profit	84.88%		

Operating Expenses	% of Gross	Income	
Payroll	33.73%	Average gross income	520,544
Employee benefits	1.92%	Average number of dog enclosures	122
Auto/truck	1.08%	Average income per dog enclosure	$3,011
Travel & entertainment	.41%	Avg number of cat enclosures	33
Kennel insurance	1.07%	Average income per cat enclosure	$838
Repairs & maintenance	3.65%	Urban kennels	12.5%
Office supplies	1.30%	Suburban kennels	50%
Utilities	2.69%	Rural kennels	34.5%
Telephone	.89%	Indoor/outdoor	75%
Yellow page ads	2.22%	All indoor	22%
Other advertising	1.23%	Both	3%
Office & administration	.71%	Avg # fulltime employees	8
Professional services	.73%	Avg # part time employees	7
Veterinary expense	.49%	Avg # years kennel in business	29
Licenses	1.24%	Avg # years owner in industry	25
Other	.29%	# dogs groomed per week	126
Total Operating Expenses	53.65%	# cats groomed per week	6
Net Proceeds Available	29.09%	# small mammals groomed per wk	0
Net Proceeds (for mortgage/rent & owner profit)	$151,426		

	% of Kennels Offering This Service	2000 Avg Income	% of Gross
Dog boarding	100%	$367,395	70.58%
Exercise programs	32%	$37,156	7.14%
Community daycare	16%	$69,000	13.26%
Cat boarding	98%	$27,668	5.32%
Grooming	75%	$122,469	23.53%
Retail sales	52%	$10,691	2.05%
Training	31%	$42,715	8.02%
Pick-up & delivery	21%	$3,883	.75%
Exotics boarding	31.5%	$3,783	.72%

Shipping	15%	$3,500	.67%
Pet sitting	1%	$1,500	.28%
Veterinary services	10%	$21,000	4.03%
Cemetery	1%	$15,000	2.88%
Cremation	1%	$8,000	1.53%

Exhibit 6a   2001 Expenditures on Pet-Related Supplies and Services

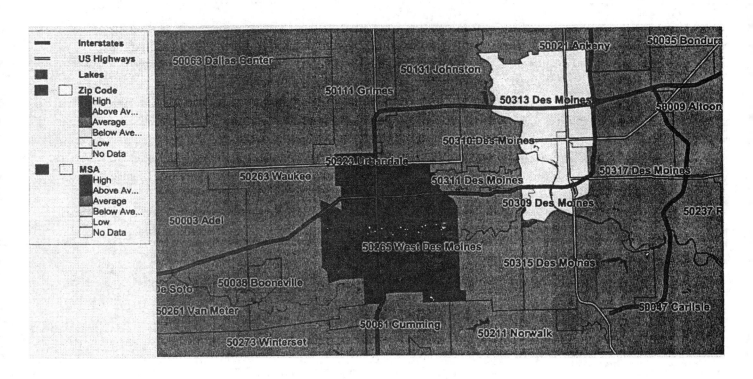

Exhibit 6b   2006 Projected Expenditures on Pet-Related Supplies and Services

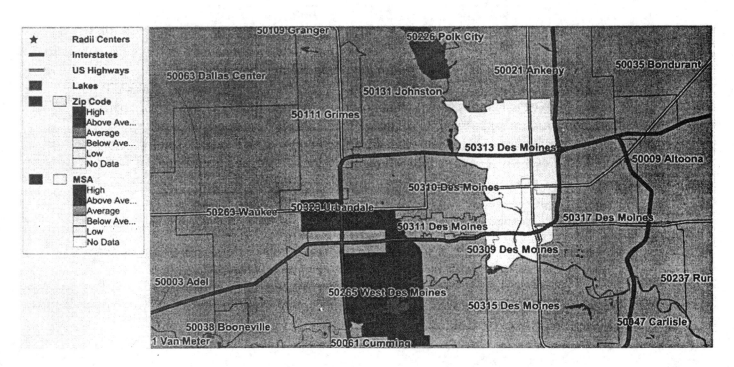

Exhibit 7   Pet Owner Statistics in the Des Moines Metropolitan Area

	Total Market = 396,260		Pet Owners = 45,515[1]	
	Base Persons	Base % Comp	Base Persons	Base % Comp
Gender				
Male	188,885	47.7	17,975	39.5
Female	207,375	52.3	27,540	60.5
Employment Status				
Employed full time	223,115	56.3	27,910	61.3
Employed part time	60,180	15.2	6,550	14.4
Not employed				
Homemaker	27,920	7	3,735	8.2
Student	12,035	3	2,105	4.8
Retired	56,035	14.1	3,735	8.2
Disabled	7,445	1.9	595	1.3
Temporarily laid-off	2,005	0.5	280	0.6
Not employed-looking for work	6,620	1.7	605	1.3
Other	905	0.2	0	0
Occupation				
Administrative assistant	62,845	15.9	9,245	20.3
Executive, administrative & management	49,735	12.6	7,320	16.1
Farming, forestry & fishing	3,145	0.8	300	0.7
Laborer/cleaner	11,010	2.8	1,220	2.7
Machine operators, assemblers, inspectors	6,470	1.6	1,450	3.2
Precision production, craft & repair	28,375	7.2	2,840	6.2
Professional specialty	45,540	11.5	2,585	5.7
Sales	26,295	6.6	1,810	4
Service	25,580	6.5	3,685	8.1
Technicians & related support	17,415	4.4	3,390	7.4
Transportation & material moving	6,885	1.7	615	1.4
Education				
Less than 12th grade	20,400	5.1	2,465	5.4
High school graduate	112,430	28.4	15,715	34.5
Some college	163,265	41.2	18,295	40.2

177

By Robin Habeger and Kay M. Palan of Iowa State University as the basis for class discussion rather than to illustrate either effective or ineffective handling of an administrative situation. Reprinted with permission from the *Case Research Journal*. Copyright 2003 by Robin Habeger and Kay M. Palan and the North American Case Research Association. All rights reserved.

	College degree or more	100,165	25.3	9,040	19.9

Exhibit 7, Continued

	Total Market = 396,260		Pet Owners = 45,515[1]	
	Base Persons	Base % Comp	Base Persons	Base % Comp
Demographic Breakout				
Persons 18-24	58,980	14.9	8,075	17.7
Persons 25-34	74,645	18.8	8,240	18.1
Persons 35-44	84,455	21.8	10,940	24
Persons 45-54	72,650	18.3	11,835	26
Persons 55-64	43,795	11.1	3,305	7.3
Persons 65+	61,735	15.6	3,120	6.9
Household Income				
Less than $25,000	71,755	18.1	6,125	13.5
$25,000-$34,000	60,700	15.3	4,760	10.5
$35,000-$49,999	92,715	23.4	10,890	23.9
$50,000-$74,999	78,130	19.7	9,950	21.9
$75,000 or more	92,960	23.5	13,790	30.3
Home Ownership				
Own	287,810	72.6	34,575	76
Rent	100,725	25.4	10,085	22.2
Other	7,725	1.9	855	1.9
Number of Children Under 17 in Household				
None	239,880	60.5	15,575	34.2
One	64,195	16.2	13,160	28.9
Two	60,230	15.2	10,945	24
Three or more	31,955	8.1	5,835	12.8

Source: Taken from research conducted by Scarborough for Des Moines area radio stations in 2002.

[1]Represents number of surveyed pet households, which is approximately 35% of the total number of pet households in the Des Moines area.

Exhibit 8   Competitor Summary

Name	Location	Services Offered[1]	Total Dog Runs	Daily Boarding Prices	Day Care	Cats	ABKA[2]	Features
Puppy Palace	SE Des Moines	B,G,DC,V	9 suites 80-100 runs	5 x 8 = $30 3 x 6 = $20	None	3 2ft cubes $11/day	VFA	Family lives on site
Doggy Doodles	Central Des Moines	B,G,DC	16 large 40 small cages	Inside/outside small = $12 med = $13 large = $14	No play time	Upstairs $11.50/day	----	
Dog Days	West central Des Moines	B,DC	5 large 20 medium 20 small	4 x 4 = $15 6 x 6 = $17 15 x 10 = $25	$10 per day	$9/day	R	
Superior Kennels	Western Suburb of Des Moines	B,G	50-75	<50lbs=$11 >50lbs=$12 3 1/2 x 5 5 1/2 x 9	None	5 indoor cages $9/day	----	Full fenced in lot split in two for daily exercise

[1] B = Boarding, G = Grooming, DC = Day Care, V = Vet Care

179

By Robin Habeger and Kay M. Palan of Iowa State University as the basis for class discussion rather than to illustrate either effective or ineffective handling of an administrative situation. Reprinted with permission from the *Case Research Journal*. Copyright 2003 by Robin Habeger and Kay M. Palan and the North American Case Research Association. All rights reserved.

² American Boarding Kennel Association certification. VFA = successfully completed certification process, R=registered only, not certified

By Robin Habeger and Kay M. Palan of Iowa State University as the basis for class discussion rather than to illustrate either effective or ineffective handling of an administrative situation. Reprinted with permission from the *Case Research Journal*. Copyright 2003 by Robin Habeger and Kay M. Palan and the North American Case Research Association. All rights reserved.

CASE STUDY 13

Industrial Data Systems Corporation

It had been some time since Bill and Hulda Coskey had been able to spend a long weekend at their lakefront home. The recent months had been tumultuous, demanding every waking hour as they scrutinized the details of the prospective acquisition by their company, Industrial Data Systems, of Petrocon Engineering, Inc. of Beaumont, Texas. Finally, the deal was done in principle, and Bill and Hulda could retreat for a brief respite and possibly catch a few of those prized, East Texas bass. As they sat on the porch that evening, they began discussing the pending acquisition, and what lay ahead. As the discussion continued, the issues that emerged became rather disquieting. The negotiations surrounding the acquisition had addressed the "big picture" issues, and established the framework for the settlement. Now, as Bill and Hulda talked, the challenges of making it work began to emerge. As was often her role, Hulda asked far more questions than Bill was prepared to answer (not because he didn't want to; he hadn't thought of them yet!). Finally, exasperated by the issues before them, Hulda blurted out, "Well, Bill, what do we do next?"

Overview of Industrial Data Systems

Industrial Data Systems Corporation (IDS) Houston, Texas, was the parent company of four subsidiaries: Industrial Data Systems, Inc. (IDSI), IDS Engineering, Inc. (IED), Thermaire, Inc. dba Thermal Corp (Thermal), and Constant Power Manufacturing, Inc. (CPM). However, as of the fourth quarter, 2002, IDSI operations were being phased out while CPM provided continuing in-the-field support for existing IDSI customers.

In addition, IDS had just announced its intention to merge with Petrocon Engineering, Inc., Beaumont, Texas, with IDS as the acquiring partner. Petrocon was a significantly larger engineering company. They had primary office facilities in Lake Charles, Louisiana and Beaumont, Texas, locations that were geographically beneficial for the pursuit of oil-related business. In 2002 Petrocon revenues totaled $68 million whereas IDS's revenues were $17 million.

IDS had achieved significant growth milestones in the last year. In fiscal year (FY)2002, operating profits grew 124% on a 39% growth in revenue base. Net income increased 218%. (Refer to Exhibit 1, Consolidated Income Statements 2000-2002). [1]

These changes were attributable to changes in the product mix revenue for the various subsidiaries. The most aggressive change was with the engineering segment. In 2001 the engineering segment represented 48.8% of the revenue for IDS. In 2002 it

By Joseph K. Kavanaugh Nancy Green and Dennis Schnell of Sam Houston State University and Carol Cumber of South Dakota State University. Copyright by Joseph K. Kavanaugh. All Rights Reserved.

[1] The financial statements for all IDS subsidiaries are consolidated. The information presented in the following tables was derived from the consolidated balance sheets and income statements provided in the Industrial Data Systems Corporation 2002 Form 10-KSB for FY ended December 31, 2002.

increased to 63.3% of the revenue base, a 80% increase in annual revenue. The air-handling segment revenues increased 8.6%, Manufacturing , the remaining segment (which includes all other operations), decreased 9.5% from 2001 to 2002.

Table One
Financial Summary

	2001	2002	Net Change	% Change
Revenues	$12,238,449	$16,976,023	$4,737,574	38.7%
Operating Profit	$232,518	$521,491	$288,973	124.3%
% of Revenue	1.9%	3.1%		1.2%
Gross Profit	$2,848,440	$3,949,269	$1,100,829	38.6%
Selling, General & Admin. Expenses	$2,615,922	$3,427,778	$811,856	31%
S, G, & A % of Revenue	21.4%	20.2%	1.2%	5.6%
Net Income	($323,315)	$380,878	$704,193	217.8%

Table 2 FY2000 Revenues by Segment

Revenue	2001 % of Total	2002 % of Total	Increase/(Decrease) % change
Engineering	$5,978,180 48.8%	$10,739,874 63.3%	$4,761,694 79.6%
Air Handling	$3,151,295 25.8%	$3,421,184 20.2%	$269,889 8.6%
Manufacturing	$3,108,974 25.4%	$2,814,965 16.6%	($294,009) -9.5%
Total Revenue	$12,238,449	$16,976,023	$4,737,574 38.7%

The basic and diluted earnings per common share increased from ($.02) in 2001 to $.03 in 2002. The company's common stock, $.001 par value per share, had been quoted on the American Stock Exchange since June 16, 1998, under the symbol "IDS." The stock movement had been volatile ranging from a high of $5.125 in the first quarter of 2002 to $1.00 as a high for the fourth quarter 2002. As of December 2002, 189 stockholders of record held the company's common stock. The largest shareholder of IDS stock was Alliance 2000 Ltd. This partnership held 9,500,000 shares. Mr. William A. Coskey and Mrs. Hulda L. Coskey served as General Partners for Alliance 2000, Ltd. (For additional information, refer to Table 3, Consolidated Balance Sheets, 2000-2002 at the end of the case).

Structure and Capabilities of IDS

IDS Operating Segments

Industrial Data Systems Corporation

Industrial Data Systems Corporation (IDS) had ten employees that provided administrative support for the various subsidiaries. IDS provided most of the accounting, payroll and investor relations functions. The administrative staff was located in an office space adjacent to the engineering segment's primary facility. In 2003, IDS implemented a new job cost and resource allocation software system to better manage projects, control costs, and accurately bid projects for all of its divisions.

IDSI

In the early years of the company (1985-1993) IDSI competed with small industrial computer makers such as Advantek, Contec and Industrial Computer Source. In the later 1990s, the most serious competition came from the large computer manufacturers such as Compaq Computer Corporation, Dell and IBM. These large competitors set the pricing and drove margins for the market but their products were considered a lesser commercial-grade product. IDSI manufactured a high quality industrial grade product that could withstand the harsh environment of the oil field. Quality-driven customers who recognized the difference in the two grades of product and were willing to pay approximately two times the price of the commercial price-setters had dwindled to a few. Until the mid-nineties, IDSI was able to compete very well with the larger competitors and reasonably well with the competitors that were comparable in size. Specialization of the equipment required and the need in the market for contract-based equipment due to specific project requirements had allowed IDSI to work within a niche market. Their size and flexibility in the areas of engineering and manufacturing for specialized components was of great benefit to them, but the market had changed.

Mostly, IDSI was concerned with the companies that produced similar industrial grade equipment. They had competitors that had longer operating histories and financial, technical, manufacturing, distribution and related advantages that posed a threat to IDSI's market share.

As of 4Q2002, IDSI withdrew from the market and ceased actively marketing their computers, but continued to serve existing accounts through the CPM division.

IDS Engineering (IED)

IDS Engineering (IED) was the largest segment within the corporation. IED was incorporated in the state of Texas on October 15, 1997. This segment provided 63% of IDS FY 2000 revenue. It provided engineering consulting services to the pipeline and process divisions of major integrated oil and gas companies. Its focus continued to be providing engineering services primarily to the energy-producing industry.

Operationally, IED was well organized and managed. Its workspace was well designed with good workflow although the office environment itself was rather bland with low-quality furniture and fixtures, not atypical of many engineering firms. Scheduling was handled with a magnetic board where all employees could see projects for the next six-month period. Importantly, there was strong communication between project managers, design, and field personnel.

IED had twenty-one blanket service contracts in place. The company provides their services on a time and materials basis. They also had eight fixed fee contracts in place to provide turnkey services to major oil companies at their process facilities. These services included the development, management and turnkey execution of projects for primarily upstream oil equipment and processes. The downstream portion of the oil and gas industry represented the transportation and refined product segment processes. The upstream portion of the oil business represented the exploration, drilling and refining processes.

In Houston, the staff of 150 employees included licensed professional engineers, designers, and administrative personnel occupying over 70,000 sq. ft. of office space and manufacturing facilities. This Houston business office supported the administrative and accounting functions for all of the IED projects and current company operations. Operations were quite lean; the workspace was tight with limited room for expansion, and key personnel performed many diverse functions. Clearly, the firm's resources were placed into its operating divisions rather than operating overhead.

In February 2001, IED established a business office in Tulsa, Oklahoma. This office was strategically placed in order to pursue similar projects in the oil processing industry in Oklahoma and Midwestern states. There were 40 employees that operated out of the Tulsa facility. The overhead costs for this office were considerably higher than for the Houston office due to general startup expenditures. The Tulsa location also produced considerably fewer billable hours than the Houston office.

IED set up a division called Advanced Controls in 2002. It fabricated and packaged complete control systems for pipeline-related and industrial applications. Its focus was on providing expertise in the design and implementation of automated control systems for processing facilities. Its capabilities included feasibility studies, engineering, design, estimating, configuration, construction, and the commissioning, programming and startup trouble shooting for process applications.

For the future, IED expenditures for research and development were limited, but were directed toward two important projects for IED: 1) Expansion of the capability of its standard meter skid product, and 2) Design of an uninterruptible power supply product. Both were expected to contribute to revenues in 2004 and beyond as IES fought to maintain product satisfaction with its customers.

IED competed in a market place where most of the competitors (Jacobs Engineering, Mustang Engineering, Fluor-Daniel) were substantially larger. This created some problems for them in that they did not have the financial resources and number of personnel that some of their larger competitors had. To counter this competitor strength, IED instituted a program of cross-functional job performance between operating units (IED, COM, and Thermal). This enabled them to capitalize on scarce engineering talent without duplicating personnel.

Their competition was also able to be very aggressive because they could provide services at a higher volume while actually lowering their margins. In their market and for some customers, price was king. One way that IED competed was by providing quality service and products and by providing them in niche areas within the market. However, in the niche areas, there were also a few smaller firms that were able to provide comparable service. Efficiency and quality service to customers continued to help IED survive in this sector. At the end of 2002, IED had a limited six-month backlog of engineering work.

Thermal

Thermal was an air handling equipment and commercial heating ventilation and cooling (HVAC) systems provider acquired by IDS in 1997. They were a well-established company, having been in business since 1945. They were acquired primarily to add diversity to the company and to increase company assets. Certain requirements needed to be met in order to go public and Thermal provided the diversity and assets needed to help IDS meet these requirements. With this acquisition, IDS was able to comply with the requirements set forth to trade on the American Stock Exchange in June 1998. IDS was previously traded on the NASDAQ Electronic Bulletin Board under the symbol "IDDS." Thermal owned its facility located in northwest Houston. Thermal was purchased for $212,563 in cash and 193,719 shares of common stock on February 14, 1999. Last fiscal year the company posted 20% of the corporation's total revenues. Thermal provided its own accounting and operations management at its site.

Thermal operated in a highly competitive market. The competition was both small, quality-driven companies and large, volume-driven companies. Principal competitive factors were superior delivery dates (four to six weeks), flexibility in terms of providing custom-engineered equipment, quality, customer service and price. All of these factors were generally what other companies sought to provide so it was essential that Thermal operate its business better than the competition. In the past they had been able to differentiate themselves in these areas by creating a customized, high quality product, so continued focus would be a necessity.

CPM

CPM was a Texas corporation formed in June, 1989 and acquired by IDS March 1998 for $200,000 cash and 300, 000 shares common stock. CPM manufactured industrial and commercial grade uninterruptible electrical power systems and battery chargers. They provided their products to refineries, petrochemical plants, utilities, offshore platforms and other facilities that may benefit from these specialized power systems components. They also provided field services support for installation and maintenance of their products. CPM was responsible for approximately 17% of IDS FY 2002 revenues. IDS performed all of the administrative and accounting functions for CPM. The company was housed in the same office space as IED.CPM was also in a highly competitive market. There were a few larger companies that had the bulk of the market share and a few smaller companies that shared the smaller portion of the market equally. CPM believed that they would be able to enhance their position in the market by the introduction of a new product line of microprocessor controlled battery chargers. This product was relatively new in the market place and having it should help COM increase its customer base and improve market position and revenues. During the fourth quarter of 2002, the responsibility for continuing field support of previous IDSI customers was assigned to CPM.

Mission

The mission statement posted on the IDS web page (www.idscorporation.com) reads: "It is our mission to continuously expand our position as an industry leader by performing superior and cost-effective services for our <u>clients</u>, ensuring safe, secure and rewarding employment for our staff and increasing value for our shareholders."

The IDS Employee Handbook stated the firm's mission as "to provide superior service and products to our clients/customers while maintaining the highest standards of integrity and professionalism."

Sales and Marketing

The company's sales approach depended on the subsidiary from which the sales are derived. Generally, sales were pursued through in-house sales efforts, direct sales to customers, sales representation or catalog sales. Sales representatives were teamed with inside sales managers who assigned the sales territories. Management believed that this was the best way to go to market and that this method provided better product penetration in the market, and the customer with better service overall. The sales philosophy was to build long-term relationships with customers and to provide a high level of expertise and service before and after the sale. The sales force was expected to cross-sell the various products and services offered from each subsidiary, giving the sales force greater opportunity to meet a full spectrum of customer need.

The company believed that providing in-house marketing for their products (as opposed to contracting outside) allowed more freedom and flexibility, thereby providing a better approach to the market. Methods of marketing included general and trade advertising, participation in trade shows, telemarketing, and on-line Internet communication. The company was in the process of updating each of the subsidiaries' websites for completion in mid-2003. Management supported continuing and accelerated use of the Internet as a marketing tool. They expected each subsidary to be using this valuable resource, taking advantage of it as e-business evolved within the industry.

Human Resources

Compensation for the sales force was an incentive-based system. Sales force commissions were based on either a percentage of revenues from products sold, or gross profitability from their sales. All employees received a basic benefits package; management and professional employees participated in a stock option incentive program.

In recent years management had changed its staffing philosophy, significantly reducing contract and temporary staff, reducing layoffs, and moving toward more permanent staff. Employees were encouraged to seek advancement and further their skill development through cross-training internally, or the pursuit of additional education. Senior management was well qualified and accessible, visible and encouraging to employees, and recognized employees for project accomplishments

Research and Development

Only two of IDS' subsidiaries were involved in research and development through the year. Total R&D expenditures in 2002 were approximately $32,000, down from $79,000 in 2001. The two companies involved were IED and CPM. IED was expanding capability of an established product and working on a standardized specification package for project-related execution. CPM was evaluating the design of an uninterruptible power supply source. In mid-2002, work on CPM's proprietary battery monitor was put on hold pending additional developmental funds becoming available.

Customers

The majority of IDS' customer base consisted of Fortune 500 companies within each of its business segments. Virtually all of their customers were in energy-related sectors: Exploration, production, refining, distribution, chemicals, and oilfield services. Approximately 60% of the company's revenues were derived from their ten largest customers. Management believed that this trend would continue. There were no long-term contracts in place so continued superior service to existing customers would help ensure continuing business. While IED was currently managing a large project in Russia, the firm lacked the broad global presence of some of their larger competitors, and had limited capability to develop global operations.

Asset Management

The company's cash flow from operations had been affected primarily by the timing of its collections of receivables. The company typically sold its products and services on short-term credit terms and tried to minimize risk by doing credit checks and self-collection. The company had year-end accounts receivable of $2,540,835 and $3,555,933 for 2001 and 2002 respectively. The number of days' sales outstanding in accounts receivable as of year-end in 2001 and in 2002 was 76. Bad debt expenses had been insignificant at approximately .01% for each of the periods. Their 2002 current ratio was 2.33 (2.50 was industry standard), indicating that their existing liquidity position was not as strong as creditors might prefer.

Investing activities for both 2001 and 2002 consisted primarily of capital expenditures. The total cash involved was $208,923 in 2001 and $467,753 in 2002. While IDS financials were well-managed, their financial resources were limited in comparison to their major competitors such as Fluor-Daniel and Mustang Engineering. IDS did not engage in long-term budget planning or forecast future cash flows. At the end of 2002, IDS had a $1,000,000 line of credit with $850,000 available to finance working capital.

The Petrocon merger will increase IDS assets from $7,322,867 to combined assets of both companies of $39,923,109. This will greatly increase the borrowing power of the firm, but the acquisition will also increase substantially the debt carried by IDS; long-term debt will rise from $386,303 to $5,016,594. In FY2001, IDS stock traded in a range of $.75 - $10.75; in FY 2002, the range was $.438 - $5.125.

2003 Plan

IED sought to continue increasing revenue by development and marketing of their full service concept. This was an Engineering, Procurement and Construction (EPC) full service concept, which dictated that IED expand into new areas to meet customer needs. In the past they had focused primarily on the engineering portion of the projects, an estimated 15 percent of any project's total installed cost. The trend was for customers to evolve toward a fixed price contract versus a time and materials contract. The fixed rate contract allowed for potentially higher profit margins. IED would have to add staff in order to expand in engineering, and strengthen project proposals and quotation generation. Continued emphasis would be placed on Advanced Controls' product line in order to help gain market share for IED.

Thermal would focus on establishing and supporting its sales force and working efficiently within their niche market. The sales manager would make site visits to current customer contracting firms and to end users of their products. Traditionally, the staff had contacted customers by phone only.

In management's view CPM had not made enough progress in the development of a good sales representative network. They had also not marketed themselves well and these were areas that were expected to improve in 2003. Management planned to add in-house personnel with the intent of improving the sales force and marketing efforts in the forthcoming year.

Agreement to Merge with Petrocon Engineering, Inc.

In mid-2002, IIDS announced that they had reached an agreement to merge with Petrocon Engineering, Inc. At the time of the announcement, IDS had approximately 190 employees and Petrocon had approximately 800 employees. The proposed merger included the following components.

1) Exchange stock for stock; IDS would issue 9.8 million shares common stock to Petrocon shareholders for 100% Petrocon stock, representing 43% of the 22.8 million IDS shares outstanding.

2) Mike Burrow, CEO of Petrocon, would be named CEO of IDS. Bill Coskey, founder and CEO of IDS, would become President of the combined companies.

3) There was little or no overlap in client base or services provided which would make this a good co-operative agreement for the two companies. Historically IDS Engineering had served the upstream portion of their industry business and Petrocon had served the downstream segment. The merger would give them complete coverage to fully serve the energy producing, refining and petrochemical segments of the oil industry.

4) The agreement provided increased geographical coverage primarily in US energy markets and allowed for potential expansion domestically and internationally if that opportunity arose.

5) Exchanged forgiveness of debt; Alliance 2000, Ltd. (IDS major stockholder) would grant IDS an option to redeem 4,000,000 shares common stock in mid-2005.

6) A significant Petrocon creditor agreed to convert $9 million Petrocon debt into 2.5 million shares IDS Series A Convertible Preferred Stock (convertible into 1,050,000 shares common stock), cash and a promissory note.

Rationale for Petrocon Merger

As it examined its competitive environment, IDS concluded that, as a small business, it was a well-positioned niche player serving primarily the domestic energy market. While it had engaged in some ventures outside of the U.S., it lacked depth in the delivery of engineering services to the global oilfield. However, the firm was growing and saw emerging opportunities that it wished to pursue but could not address given its current capabilities and resources.

The firm held significant strategic assets for servicing its primary clients, the major global petroleum companies such as ExxonMobil, Shell, BP Amoco, Total, etc., but that it was missing significant elements that were critical for it to compete effectively with major engineering firms such as Mustang Engineering and Fluor-Daniel. IDS needed to make a decision to either remain a small business serving its specific niche markets or to take its business to the next level and become a major engineering-services competitor in the global oilfield. To achieve the latter goal IDS would need to identify a partner who already had some global presence and whose product and service lines would be complementary to IDS' portfolio. They needed another engineering company who could fill out their existing product lines and bring additional service capabilities that would make them a comprehensive engineering services firm focused on the global oilfield. The acquisition of Petrocon Engineering, although it was a larger firm, would fulfill this strategic objective admirably.

Structure & Capabilities of Petrocon

Petrocon Engineering, Inc., was a multi-discipline, professional engineering, process controls, information technology, and construction management firm with offices in Houston and Beaumont, Texas, and Lake Charles and Baton Rouge, Louisiana. They provided a full range of services in the following industrial segments: Petroleum refining, chemical, petrochemical, exploration and production, co-generation, manufacturing, process controls, advanced automation and information technology sectors.

With headquarters offices in Beaumont, Petrocon Engineering was a holding company for subsidiary operations organized into five operating units. These were: Petrocon Engineering, Inc., RPM Engineering, Inc., Petrocon Systems, Inc., Petrocon Construction Resources, Inc., and Triangle Engineers and Constructors, Inc. Petrocon asserted in its marketing materials that

> "through (its) innovative project execution methods, and the diverse
> resources available through (its) subsidiaries, Petrocon is a single source
> for customers interested in engineering, procurement, and construction
> management services for projects worldwide. Our services range from
> feasibility studies and conceptual and detailed engineering through total
> responsibility for turnkey projects and project financing. Established in
> 1973 and reincorporated in 1988 as a new entity, Petrocon has become one
> of the leading and fastest growing engineering firms in the United States."
> (Petrocon web site)

The core business, Petrocon Engineering, was a general engineering services firm with worldwide response capability. Petrocon's primary markets were the petroleum, oil and gas, petrochemical, and refining operations located on the Texas and Louisiana Gulf Coast.

Petrocon's subsidiaries provided valuable integrated service offerings that complemented its core engineering business. Petrocon Construction Resources focused on inspection and QA/QC services as well as process plant operations. RPM Engineering was a full-service multi-discipline engineering company that served the Louisiana market from its Baton Rouge offices. Petrocon Systems was described as

> "a full service Systems/Controls/Advanced Controls/IT engineering,
> integration, advanced automation and information technologies services
> company, while Triangle Engineers and Constructors, Inc. provides
> engineering, design and construction services to (the) refining, chemical
> and petrochemical industries. A major portion of the business of this
> subsidiary is to provide personnel in the client's facility to work under the
> direction of the clients."

The Future

IDS had been a well-run and well-respected company that had benefited from a strong market, good economy and self-perpetuating positive growth. Bill and Hulda Coskey, and soon Mike Burrows of Petrocon, had some issues that they needed to address in order for the company to achieve optimal performance.

Although both IDS and Petrocon had been very successful in each of their respective fields, together they would form a company with different business dynamics. The two companies would merge but continue to operate as separate entities in the short term. Both companies had experienced growth through evolution, acquisitions and mergers. They had experienced integration with other companies, but not to the extent that this merger presented. Issues that confronted them included integrating the work force and key personnel, consistency of internal administrative practices, potential for differences of opinion within the managerial ranks, and perhaps organizational power issues arising from the fact that the smaller firm was acquiring the larger firm.

Failure to address these problems could result in 1) inefficiency of operations, 2) internal strife possibly leading to reduced revenues, 3) profit pressure, and 4) the inability to continue to grow and operate at the predetermined rate.

In addition, what might be the long term plans for the company? Will IDS/Petrocon complete the merger of the two companies then merge again with someone else? What was the time line for the company's growth strategy? Where does management see IDS/Petrocon in 1 year, 3 years and in 5 years? Given these questions how would the company address the multitude of changes that presented themselves with the rapidly expanding business?

As Bill talked with Hulda on the porch that evening, his thinking became increasingly clear. The scope of the tasks ahead appeared almost overwhelming, yet the essential questions seemed simple and clear. In order to fulfill the potential of the pending merger, how should the company be structured, what infrastructure development needed to take place to realize available synergies, and where should the company go from here?

Table 3
Industrial Data Systems Corporation And Subsidiaries

Consolidated Balance Sheet

Assets	2000	2001	2002
Current Assets:			
Cash and cash equivalents	$ 1,225,821	663,972 $	242,592
Marketable securities, at market value - available for sale	676,647	300,000	--
Municipal bond, at cost	--	--	400,000
Accounts receivable - trade, less allowance for doubtful accounts of approximately $17,000 in 2002, $,6,500 in 2001, $40,000 in 2000	2,913,128	2,540,835	3,555,933
Inventory	917,097	771,808	865,341
Notes receivable from stockholder	162,000	150,000	--
Cost and estimated earnings in excess of billings on uncompleted contracts	--	--	330,000
Federal income tax receivable	--	53,000	--
Deferred income taxes	8,000	--	--
Prepaid and other	228,115	329,441	190,369
Total current assets	6,130,808	4,809,056	5,584,235
Property and Equipment, net	1,050,568	1,070,218	1,404,017
Goodwill	745,760	34,650	18,450
Deposits and Other Assets	1,500	--	45,563
Total Assets	$ 7,928,636	5,913,924 $	7,052,265
Liabilities and Stockholder's Equity			
Current Liabilities:			
Notes payable	$ 620,383	342,010 $	433,729
Current maturities - long-term debt and capital lease payable	52,530	39,259	45,356
Accounts payable	1,557,985	779,017	1,333,003
Deferred income taxes	--	45,000	37,000
Income taxes payable	157,000	--	160,013
Accrued expenses and other current liabilities	695,619	297,454	387,680
Total current liabilities	3,083,517	1,502,740	2,396,781
Long-term debt, net of current portion	422,483	384,658	365,368
Capital lease payable, net of current portion	--	--	120,212
Deferred Income Taxes	14,000	52,000	11,000
Commitments and Contingencies (notes 5, 7 8, and 15)			
Total liabilities	3,520,000	1,939,398	2,893,361
Stockholder's Equity:			
Common stock, $.001 par value; 75,000,000 shares authorized; 12,964,918 shares issued and outstanding in 2002 & 2001; 13,073,718 shares issued and outstanding in 2000.	13,074	12,965	12,965
Note receivable from stockholder	--	--	(196,500)

Additional paid-in capital	2766163	2,640,154	2,640,154
Retained earnings	1,644,722	1,321,407	1,702,285
	4,423,959		
Treasury stock, 15,323 shares, at cost			
	(15,323)		
Total stockholder's equity	4,408,636	3,974,526	4,158,904
Total liabilities and stockholder's equity	$ 7,928,636	5,913,924 $	7,052,265
	$		

Accompanying notes to these consolidated financial statements are available in
Annual Reports.